TOMORROW'S LASTING JOY

HISTORICAL CHRISTIAN ROMANCE

NAOMI RAWLINGS

TEXAS PROMISE BOOK 5

DESCRIPTION

His pa named him Cain because his birth was a curse. Now he's the only one who can save the town...

Anna Mae Harding has always dreamed of being a wife and mother, but she never expected that finding a man to marry would be so difficult. She might have had an easier time if she hadn't fallen in love with the wrong man years ago. But no matter how much she tries to forget her childhood friend, no one else she's met has ever measured up.

When Cain Whitelaw's job as a Texas Ranger leads him back to his hometown—and to Anna Mae—neither of them can deny the feelings swirling between them. The trouble is, Cain's the last man who will ever settle down and start a family. He had too rough of an upbringing for that, and his job means he doesn't stay in one place for more than a month.

But when an old enemy reemerges and puts Anna Mae and the town of Twin Rivers in danger, Cain must confront his past and decide just how much he's willing to risk for the people he loves.

Want to be notified when my next book releases? Sign up for my author newsletter.
(Subscribers also receive a free novel.)

1

Chihuahuan Desert, Mexico; July 1886

She was going to die. Anna Mae stared down at the giant wound on her ankle and tried to suck in a breath of air, but breathing only seemed to make her lungs constrict.

Calm down. You have to calm down. You won't be able to get yourself out of this situation if you panic.

She inched herself a little higher, letting the rocky wall of the outcropping where she was hiding support her back, and stared out at the mountains surrounding her.

Bald, rocky peaks jutted up toward a brilliantly blue sky, while the pinks, yellows, and grays of the mountains almost made the rocks look like a gentle, streaked sunset. It would normally be a pretty view, the kind she could look at for hours, taking in the majesty around her.

But seeing how she hadn't come across a single person since she'd taken the turnoff onto the narrow mountain trail yesterday morning, the view before her only made a sad desperation spring up in her chest.

She was almost out of water, but she couldn't walk on her ankle to search for a creek. And if she left the little outcropping where she was hiding, there was a good chance the wrong men would find her.

Which meant her odds of surviving another night in the desert were nonexistent.

She gritted her teeth against the fiery wave of heat in her ankle, then leaned her head back against the warm sandstone wall.

She should probably count it a success that she'd survived as long as she had. After all, the men who'd kidnapped her outside of Fort Ashton five days ago could have killed her right away. But instead, they'd tried to cart her clear down to Mexico City, which had given her a chance to steal a horse and rifle three days into the journey and escape them.

In fact, if a woman was going to be kidnapped, everything about her situation had seemed downright successful—right up until a rattlesnake had bitten her yesterday afternoon.

She crumpled her skirt in her hands, pulling it up a bit farther as she looked down at the dirty, burning cut. After she was bitten, she'd hobbled to the little outcropping that formed a shallow cave above the mountain trail and lain down, tucked securely out of view from anyone who might search for her. And she'd sent the horse away, since she'd had nowhere to hide it, and trying to keep it was more likely to lead the desperadoes who'd kidnapped her right to where she was hiding.

Then she'd taken a knife to the bite, hoping to cut out the venom before her ankle swelled overmuch.

But now she wasn't sure taking a knife to her skin had ended up better than leaving the rattler venom inside her. A thin rim of white was growing around the edge of the wound, surrounded by puffy, pink skin that felt tender to the touch. Inside the cut burned as though it was on fire, and the whole thing had swelled up just as big as it would have without trying to cut out the venom.

Dear God... She slid down the sandstone wall until she lay on the single blanket she had—the one she'd taken off the horse before sending him away. *Dear Father, please...*

But the rest of the words wouldn't come.

What should she pray for? Rain?

Judging by the cloudless sky, there'd be no rain today, and she didn't have enough water to last until tomorrow, when there was a slim chance rain might form over the mountains in the afternoon.

She couldn't pray for rescue either, not in such a remote stretch of desert.

When she'd escaped her abductors, getting far away from the large trail that ran from Chihuahua to San Antonio had seemed like a smart choice. After all, it was sure to be the first place her kidnappers would look for her.

But it was also the first place her brother, Daniel, the sheriff of Twin Rivers, would look. And now that she'd been away from Twin Rivers for five days, he and his friends were sure to be searching.

But it was almost as though this stretch of desert, with its wild and craggy mountains, had been forgotten by every living person.

She pulled up her skirt a bit more, then stared down at the red lines streaking from her wound up her leg, inching ever closer to her heart. If only she had something to clean the wound with, but she couldn't afford to even dribble a few drops of water on it, not when she needed every last bit of water for herself.

Sweat beaded on her forehead, and she slid her tongue over her cracked lips in an attempt to moisten them, only to find her tongue itself was too dry for that. Her stomach was starting to feel ill, too, and her head had been pounding for several hours—sure signs that the heat was making her sick.

She rolled onto her side, wincing at the burst of pain in her leg but managing to shift just enough to look up at the scorching sun from beneath the shaded outcropping of rock.

Should she ask God to spare her life for another day?

Or was it pointless even to try?

∼

"What do you mean she escaped?" Ranger Cain Whitelaw grabbed the youth by the shoulders and dragged him close enough that the boy's shaky breath fanned against his chin.

The sun beat down on them, its unrelenting rays brutal in the July heat. But Cain didn't give the summer heat a thought as his hard gaze bore into the brown gaze of the boy who wasn't quite old enough to be a man.

He needed to calm down. This was just another missing person. Just another body needing to be found in the desert.

If he'd done it once, he'd done it a hundred times. His mission was simple. Track down the missing woman, recover her body, and bring it back to her family.

Except it didn't feel nearly that simple, because it wasn't just any missing woman. It was Anna Mae Harding.

A curse nearly rose up in his chest, but he tamped it down. This was exactly why his father had taught him not to get too close to people. Not to care. To shake the dust of his hometown off his boots and never return.

Because caring made a man weak, and a Ranger couldn't afford to be weak.

So Cain tried not to let himself care about the boy's answer, tried to pretend that the search for Anna Mae was no different than searching for any other woman who'd been abducted. Tried to pretend that he didn't know how it felt to run his hands through the soft, silky strands of her hair or press his lips to hers.

Confound it! He was never going to find her if he kept letting himself get distracted.

It didn't help that her brother was with him. As sheriff of Twin Rivers, Daniel Harding had put together the posse to search for Anna Mae, and ever since Cain had joined him, he'd wanted to know every last detail about how Cain planned to find his sister.

Even now, Daniel was edging steadily closer to where Cain stood with the boy, likely trying to hear every word of their conversation.

Not that Cain could blame him. If someone else was running the search for Anna Mae, he'd behave the same way.

It also didn't help that three of the other seven men in the posse were Cain's childhood friends. In fact, it seemed every last man in the posse cared far more about what happened to Anna Mae than was advisable given the situation.

The best way to find a hostage was to stay unemotional and logical. That was true for every lawman, whether a Ranger or a Marshal or a sheriff.

But there was nothing detached or professional about their mission. Every time they searched a canyon and found nothing, or shook out their bedrolls to get some shut-eye, Cain felt the disappointment of seven other men piling on top of his own.

It was almost too much for a man to handle.

"Answer me!" Cain snapped at the boy, who'd spent far too long staring at him and far too little time giving him answers. "How did she escape?"

Something in his gaze must have told the boy he was serious, because the youth licked his lips and started yammering. "W-we woke up one night and she was gone." He jabbed a thumb over his shoulder to where three older men sat tied up on the dry desert ground. "Just ask them. We didn't do anything to her."

Cain looked at the men. His posse had ambushed them in a narrow canyon a quarter hour ago.

"I wouldn't call kidnapping her not doing anything." Cain's hands involuntarily tightened around the boy's shoulders, and he glared into the youth's dark eyes.

Two splotches of color appeared on the boy's cheeks. "I meant, we didn't hurt her any. *El jefe*'s orders. We were just taking her to him."

"That's still a crime in Texas and Mexico." Did the boy really think not hurting Anna Mae somehow made it all right for the men to abduct her?

His jaw clenched.

"Tell me about the horse." He jutted his chin toward the old beast that the desperadoes claimed Anna Mae had stolen from them when she escaped two nights ago. "Where did you find it?"

"'Bout a half mile back." The boy nodded toward where the trail disappeared around a mountain. "That's why we've been searching."

Cain followed his gaze. He didn't like this. Not one bit. Oh, he could believe the part about Anna Mae escaping her abductors. If anyone was bound to give a gang of kidnappers trouble, it was Anna Mae Harding.

The woman might be beautiful, but she had a tongue sharp enough to peel the skin off a rattler. She wouldn't have made a compliant hostage for a single minute.

But having the horse show up on the trail without Anna Mae could only mean trouble.

Another woman might have been careless tying the horse while stopping for water and allowed the beast to get away. But not Anna Mae.

Daniel had finally inched himself close enough to hear

everything being said, and the dark look in the sheriff's eyes told Cain that his friend was thinking the same thing about the horse appearing without Anna Mae.

Had she run into another group of bandits? Or maybe more of Velez's men had found her, but the horse had gotten away?

Or was she lying dead somewhere, waiting for him to stumble upon her sun-bleached body?

Cain gulped in a breath of air, trying to shove away the image filling his mind.

"Bryce," he called to Daniel's deputy, who was standing guard with the rest of the posse. "Take him back to the others and tie him up."

The lanky lawman strode forward and grabbed the boy, then jerked him toward the others.

"We need to keep searching," Daniel said the moment the deputy led the boy away. "She's got to be out there somewhere."

"After five days, she's likely not alive." Cain kept his voice firm, his gaze steady, trying to shove aside that they were discussing the woman with wavy, dark hair and vibrant eyes who used to share her lunch with him at school because his ma never bothered to make sure he was fed.

The woman who'd invited him to Easter dinner this spring as though he somehow belonged in a room full of smiling, happy people. The woman who'd come to his tent the last time he'd ridden into Mexico and told him she was worried about him.

As though his life mattered enough to worry over.

Cain swallowed, doing everything he could not to let loose a string of curses, then scanned his sorry-looking posse and the four outlaws they'd somehow managed to capture.

When he'd ridden into Mexico last time, he'd been on official Ranger business and had thirty Rangers with him, plus the posse Daniel had rounded up from the border town of Twin Rivers, Texas.

Yet he wasn't on Ranger business now. If anything, the director and assistant director back in Austin would be furious with him. It wasn't every day a Ranger captain left his post, which was currently Alpine, a town about two days north of Twin Rivers. But when he'd gotten a telegram that Anna Mae had gone missing, he'd simply had to leave his lieutenant in charge and ride straight to Twin Rivers.

Evidently his previous assignment wasn't quite as finished as he'd thought in June, when he and his men had packed up camp and left.

Daniel and his posse had already been searching for Anna Mae south of the border, but none of them had spent the past thirteen years tracking down criminals like he had. They'd searched the main roads and obvious places where desperadoes might hide.

"My sister's still alive," Daniel quipped. As though there was no other option for how they might find Anna Mae. "The desperadoes said they had her three days ago, and she escaped that night. Anna Mae can survive two days and two nights in the desert on her own."

"I agree," another voice said.

Cain looked over to see that Harrison Rutherford had sauntered up behind them.

Being a Ranger, Cain didn't often claim he had friends. But if there was one man in all the world he could still call a friend, it was the dark-headed lawyer who'd insisted on accompanying him into Mexico with the rest of their childhood friends, Sam, Wes, and Daniel.

Harrison repositioned his dark hat on his head, better shielding his face from the sun. "If anyone can survive this long in the desert, it's Anna Mae."

"If she has water," Cain shot back, his throat suddenly thick. Because if she didn't have water...

He shook his head. "The lot of you will need to take these

desperadoes back to Twin Rivers. No plea deals this time. That young one was arrested before."

"I remember." Daniel sent the boy a dark look.

"The men said Velez was behind this?" Harrison asked. "I thought this business with Velez was over."

"Reckon it ain't as over as we thought." Cain raised his eyes to the mountains surrounding him, scanning them for any sign that more of Velez's men might have found them and were planning an attack.

For half of last year and the beginning of this year, Cain had spent nine months stationed in Twin Rivers with his men, trying to root out cattle rustlers that had moved into West Texas and driven thousands of cattle over the border. But no one had realized just how powerful the man behind the rustling was.

Or rather, there was more than one man behind the cattle rustling. Harrison's father, Bartholomew Rutherford, had been powerful too. He'd owned a trading company that transported goods that crossed the border from Twin Rivers to San Antonio. When Bart Rutherford had joined forces with Javier Velez and launched a massive cattle rustling operation, Rutherford had seen it as a way to make easy money. Velez had seen it as a way to steal Rutherford's shipping contracts before ultimately poisoning the man.

"We'd better get moving." Daniel glanced up at the sun, likely judging how many hours they had left until darkness fell. "We'll split the group. I'll have Bryce, Sam, and Martin take the outlaws back to Twin Rivers while Harrison, Wes, you, and—"

"No." Cain glanced over his shoulder at the outlaws. "I'm not going to send four seasoned criminals back with only three men. Everyone goes back—except me."

Daniel's lips pressed into a flat line. "If you think I'm going to tuck my tail between my legs and stop searching for my sister—"

"You're not going to tuck anything anywhere. What you're

going to do is take these here men back to Twin Rivers. Leastways, that's what you'll do if you don't want the rest of us to end up dead. You understand?"

"Don't see how we'll end up dead." Daniel's eyes bored into him. "They'll be three of us plus you left here."

"And how many men are in the other group of desperadoes looking for Anna Mae? At least four. And who knows this section of desert better? Them or us? And who's to say the other desperadoes didn't ride to *La Colina* or Chihuahua or wherever Velez is running things to get more men?" Cain gave his head a shake. "No. The lot of you are going back to Twin Rivers. We've got men in need of a jail cell."

"But we don't have my sister," Daniel growled.

"Her body. We don't have her body." Cain jabbed a finger into Daniel's shoulder, his gaze flat and hard. "Don't go getting your hopes up about things that aren't likely to be."

Daniel's jaw turned to granite. "I refuse to believe she's dead."

"Fool man." Cain dropped his hand, then dragged a breath of hot desert air into his lungs. "Alive or dead, none of that changes the fact that I'm the best tracker you know. If more outlaws come looking and it's just me, I can disappear. It's a heap easier to hide one man in these mountains than four."

"I don't like it," Daniel growled.

"Neither do I," Harrison agreed.

Cain took a step closer to Daniel, bringing them nose to nose. "Do you want my help or not?"

Daniel met his gaze evenly, his face haggard from too many sleepless nights and endless days spent under the hot desert sun looking for his sister. "I want to do what's best for Anna Mae. Leaving only one man to search for her isn't it, and you're not going to convince me otherwise."

"And just how much experience do you have finding abducted women?"

A muscle pulsed at the side of Daniel's jaw, and his hands clenched into fists.

"I get at least three cases like this a year," Cain drawled. "Sometimes as many as five."

"How successful are you at recovering the women?" Harrison asked.

Cain sighed, then reached up and dabbed at a streak of sweat trailing down his cheek with the bandana knotted about his neck. "I'm always successful at recovering them—or rather, their bodies. And then I track down the men who killed them and bring them to justice."

Daniel pressed his lips together, his gaze sharp enough to cut through the boulder that the desperadoes were sitting beside. "Fine. I'll leave you here alone like you ask, but you better bring my sister back, and I expect to see her alive."

He spun on his heel and stalked off, his hands still clenched into fists and the rocky ground crunching beneath his boots.

Cain rubbed the side of his jaw, thinking he should probably count himself lucky Daniel hadn't swung one of those fists at him."She's his only sister, Cain." Harrison drew in a breath beside him, his shoulders slumping. "Go easy on him."

"I can't. There's nothing easy about any of this. And the last thing I'm going to do is stand here and lie to him about the likelihood of seeing his sister alive."

"You really think she's dead, don't you?" Harrison lowered his voice, even though there wasn't anyone close enough to overhear them.

Cain frowned. "I've been a Ranger too long to imagine any other outcome five days into an abduction, but I promise you I'll do what I can. Now please, get the desperadoes out of here before nightfall. This stretch of desert has far too many mountains and canyons that would make for a good ambush. I don't want a one of us here after dark."

Harrison heaved out a breath, his deep-brown eyes scanning the jagged peaks surrounding them. "I don't see things like you do, I suppose. Neither does Daniel, and he's a lawman who was raised in a lawman's home. The rest of us, we look out over the desert and mountains, and we just... We don't see where the bandits might be. We don't know which route they're most likely to take. We don't..."

Cain settled a hand on the back of Harrison's shoulder. "Few men do. But I promise you here and now, I'll do everything in my power to bring Anna Mae back to her brother."

Harrison sighed. "Do you think there's still some chance, any chance she might be alive?"

Cain wanted to shout the word *no* and release a string of blistering curses. But there'd been hope in Harrison's voice when he'd asked the question, just as there'd been in Daniel's. And it was flickering in Harrison's eyes, too, much the same as it had in Daniel's.

It also made him dread what was going to happen when he rode into Twin Rivers with Anna Mae's body in a few more days.

2

Cain scanned the mountains, each jagged peak cast in the warm pink and orange hues of dawn. Each crevice and crag a place where Anna Mae's body might be lying.

Last night after the men had left, searching had seemed almost futile. Not because he didn't think he could find Anna Mae but because he wasn't in the mood to stumble across a dead body.

But he'd searched anyway, and just before dusk, his search yielded a single set of horse tracks, which he'd followed through the twisting mountain valleys until the light grew too dim for him to press on.

The tracks weren't dug all that deep into the dirt, telling him that whoever had been riding the beast didn't weigh much, and a child or woman wouldn't likely be this far into the desert by herself—unless it was Anna Mae trying to stay hidden from her kidnappers.

Dear God, give me strength. He cast his gaze heavenward. *Daniel, too, and his wife Charlotte, and Anna Mae's parents when they get the news.*

Most people who looked at him wouldn't think he was a praying man.

They'd be wrong.

A person didn't see the kinds of things he'd seen and not learn to pray. And the sick feeling in his stomach told him he was going to need to do a whole lot more praying before the day was over.

Dear God, is there any way you could spare her? Is it at all possible I might find her alive?

He looked back at the heavens, but nothing stirred around him except the hot wind.

Look at him, being just as ridiculous as Daniel and Harrison. How many times had he searched the desert for dead bodies?

But never before had he searched for a woman who had a secret smile that she appeared to show only him.

Never had he searched for a woman who baked treats for his entire unit just so she'd have an excuse to come down to the Ranger camp and see him.

A memory rose in his mind. Her wavy black hair cascading about her shoulders, the swishing of her skirt about her ankles as she bustled around the kitchen. The smell of dough and sugar and jam that had filled the room. He'd told her she needed a husband to keep her in hand. Her eyes had flashed in response.

And then she'd asked if he was offering to be that man.

His entire body had gone still, and his lungs had refused to work.

"Me? Are you mad? I'm a Ranger. I can't marry you."

She kept her head down as she folded one of the doughy squares in half over the spoonful of jam in the center, forming a triangle. "Other Rangers are married."

There was something about the way she said it, about the sudden quietness in her voice and the slowing of her movements that made him pause. "You're serious."

She kept right on working, folding the doughy little squares over until they formed jam-filled triangles.

"Anna Mae?"

"You asked me before if I had feelings for someone in your camp. What if..." She sighed, then swiped a strand of hair from her cheek, causing flour to smear across her skin. "What if you're the man I have feelings for? What then?"

Every muscle in his body suddenly refused to move. He sucked in a breath, but it felt as though the air shattered inside his lungs, causing jagged pieces of glass to catch inside his chest. "You can't have feelings for me. I was gone for over a decade."

"Why would that change anything?" She finally looked up at him, but he almost wished she hadn't.

It suddenly seemed like they stood too close, like he could almost feel her breath brush against his chin, like if he stayed there and looked deep enough into her eyes, he could read every single emotion inside her.

"Every time we talk, it turns into an argument," he croaked, unable to make himself step away from her.

She rolled her eyes.

"I've never even courted you."

"And yet I've loved you for years... ever since you were a boy who needed a friend."

"No! He jumped back from her. "You don't love me. You never have and you never will. There is nothing between us. Nothing at all. There never can be."

"I understand."

"Good." He heaved out a breath, then stilled as another thought struck him and dread filled his stomach. "Why haven't you married?"

"I told you a few weeks ago, no one's caught my fancy." She picked up a spatula and started placing the doughy triangles on a baking sheet with brisk, efficient movements.

"Then how can you say you've loved me for years?"

"All right, let me rephrase. Once upon a time I met this boy who needed a friend. A real friend, not some other boys his age that let him tag along, but someone who actually saw him for what he was, someone who wouldn't let his prickliness push them away." She didn't spare him so much as a glance as she spoke, just kept moving the triangles.

"After a while, it became clear that this boy needed a family, too, a real one that loved him and cared about him rather than a single mother who used him to her own advantage. So I became his friend. I packed him lunches I snuck to him every day at school, and when I figured out he liked to fish at the river at all hours of the day and night, I joined him.

"But then his mother died, and he moved in with a real family, with a man and woman who didn't have children of their own but treated him with love and kindness. He didn't need me to pack him lunches anymore, and he stopped running off to the river at odd times. But one day his true father came back for him, and so he rode off into the wide Texas sunset, never mind the family and friends he left behind in Twin Rivers."

Anna Mae slid the last turnover onto the tray, then braced her hands on the table and looked up at him. "But his friend from his youth never met anyone who compared to him, not in all the years he was gone, and so she didn't get married. When he finally came back to town, she hoped..."

Her words had died off then, and he hadn't asked for another explanation. But even now, he could still hear the raspy quality in her voice, still see the tears reflecting in her eyes as she'd taken all the ugly, painful parts of his childhood and made him seem redeemable, lovable.

Just like she'd made him feel lovable when she invited him to Easter dinner.

Cain's hands tightened around his horse's reins, and he raked in a breath of air.

Of all the women he knew across the entire state of Texas, why did it have to be Anna Mae that Velez had gone after? Why did it have to be her body he now searched for?

Please, God, anyone but her. If there's some way, any way, that she could still be alive, please lead me to her. Please keep her safe.

And now he was back to sounding just as ridiculous as Daniel and Harrison, hoping for the impossible after her horse had been found yesterday afternoon.

He needed to start thinking about this logically instead of...

The thought died as he stared at the trail ahead. There were footprints beside the horse tracks, indicating the horse had stopped and the rider had dismounted. It looked as though the rider might have even sat atop one of the rocks near the trail. Maybe for lunch.

One thing was clear from looking at the tracks. There hadn't been a struggle, and no one else had been there. Just one set of footprints headed toward a large rock, and another set of horse prints continued the opposite direction on the trail, but not digging quite as deep into the earth, indicating the horse had been riderless.

Where could Anna Mae have gone?

Cain swung off his horse, then stepped closer to the rock. The imprints in the desert dust atop the rock showed someone had sat there. But why sit there and then not get back on the horse?

Rattling sounded from beneath the rock, and Cain jumped back just as the head of a rattler emerged, its tongue flicking out.

More rattling filled the air.

Not just one snake, then, but a nest of them. Cain studied the flat-topped rock that rose to a perfect height for a person to sit on. It stuck out like a small, slim outcropping above the mountainside, creating a perfect nook for rattlers to make their home beneath it.

Cain's hand slid to his pistol, but then he let it go. The noise from a gunshot would ricochet through the valley, and he couldn't afford to draw any attention to himself. He could always throw his knife and cut off the snake's head, but then he'd have to reach down beside the rock to pick up the knife, and he couldn't risk getting bit by one of the other snakes.

Was that what had happened to Anna Mae? Had she been bit by a rattler?

Two or three days ago?

The small flicker of hope inside his chest turned to ash. If he'd been holding out any hope of finding her alive, it died in that instant as he stared beneath the rock at the dark hole concealing the rattlers.

Even so, he forced himself to scan the earth around the rock. He still had a body to recover, and he wasn't going to let himself become emotional about it.

Not when he'd recovered bodies more times than he could count. Not when he'd been warned never to let himself care about a woman, and he'd gone and gotten his heart tangled up anyway.

There. Uneven footprints led up the side of the mountain.

Walking would only have killed her sooner, each step pumping the poison in her blood closer to her heart.

Cain swallowed. Whatever he found at the end of the footprints, he deserved to see, if for no reason other than to remind him that he should have never let himself care about Anna Mae in the first place.

He walked back to Maverick and grabbed him by the reins, making sure to skirt far around the rattler's nest as they started up the mountain.

The loose rocks didn't make for easy walking, and Maverick scrambled more than once to get his footing.

How far had Anna Mae gone? He scanned the peak rising

above him and narrowed his eyes, trying to make out where the tracks led.

There, a small outcropping was wedged into the mountain maybe fifty yards from him. The footprints slowly wound upward to where the outcropping sat near the peak.

He urged Maverick forward, his heart pounding against his chest as cold sweat coated his body.

Please, God, give me strength.

"Anna Mae," he called softly. "Anna Mae, are you there?"

No answer.

He'd known there wouldn't be. Why was he letting himself even hope?

Dear Father...

But he didn't have any words to pray, only a heavy sensation in his chest and an immovable lump in his throat.

He tethered Maverick to a shrub jutting up from the mountain, then crept closer to the outcropping.

He saw the dark red of her skirt first and her foot poking out from beneath it. Then he moved close enough for the rocky wall to reveal her dark mass of hair and her sun-scorched face.

Her sun-scorched, trembling face.

"You're alive."

She didn't respond, didn't even look his direction as he knelt beside her.

Her entire body was shaking—he wasn't sure how he'd missed the quiver in her foot moments earlier—but her eyes were glassy, her red face streaked with dirt.

"You need to drink."

He reached for the canteen lying beside her, only to find it empty. He grabbed the one slung over his shoulder, gathered her against his chest, and held the metal opening to her lips.

Water trickled out the side of her mouth.

"Come on, Anna Mae, swallow." He set the canteen down,

held her up a bit higher, and massaged her throat until she swallowed the liquid in her cheeks.

He let out a little breath of relief, then repeated his actions a second time, and a third and a fourth, until he'd given her a quarter of the water from the canteen.

She was still shaking. From dehydration? From the rattler venom?

Her skin was hot to the touch, almost as though she had a fever. But that wasn't right. A rattler bite didn't give people fevers. That was more the symptom of an infection.

"I'm going to lay you back down now and look for where the rattler got you," he rasped.

He didn't know why he bothered explaining himself to her, not when she couldn't understand a word he was saying. He set her down on the thin blanket she'd been lying on, then crawled down to her feet.

Her hands were free from the swelling that accompanied rattler bites, and while it was possible for her to be bitten anywhere, considering where the snake nest had been, it made the most sense to start looking at her feet.

Her first foot was booted, which he'd seen when approaching the outcropping, but the second foot was tucked somewhere beneath the fabric of her dusty skirt. He seated himself by the hem and slowly lifted the material.

The sour aroma of sepsis nearly knocked him backward. "Anna Mae, what happened to you?"

His gaze settled on an open, festering wound on her ankle, and everything became clear.

The infected hole in her leg wasn't a rattler bite, though it had likely started as a bite before she'd tried to cut out the poison.

The red streaks running up her leg could mean she either hadn't gotten all of the venom or the infection from her wound was moving through her body. He had no way of knowing which, but either way, the wound had to be treated.

He dropped her skirt and scrambled out of the opening. Only as he was striding toward Maverick did he realize he'd forgotten to check for Velez's men before leaving the protection of the rocky outcropping. Fortunately, no one was about, but Maverick would be visible from the trail below, meaning he'd need to find a better hiding spot for his horse as soon as he tended to Anna Mae.

Was she going to live?

Dear God, please don't let her die.

He couldn't think God had allowed her to survive this long only to die after he found her, but he'd seen people pass away from less.

Cain rummaged in his saddlebag for the small medical kit he'd learned to carry with him during his first months as a Ranger. It held a familiar array of needle and thread, tweezers, bandages, laudanum, whiskey for cleaning wounds, and white powder to use as a poultice after a wound got infected.

He hurried back to the outcropping, crouched inside, and drew out the bottle of laudanum. "You're going to want a swig of this."

He raised her head enough to dribble some of the medicine into her mouth, then coaxed her to swallow it. After that, he tucked the blue bottle back into its pocket inside the kit, then crawled back down to her ankles.

He sat there for a few minutes, staring at the ghastly wound until he was sure the laudanum had begun to work, then he took a firm hold of her ankle. "I'm sorry, sweetheart," he whispered to her still-trembling body.

He drew in a deep breath and poured a thin stream of liquid onto the sore.

Her body jerked against his hold, and a low moan rolled off her lips. Then she went limp, likely passed out from the pain.

It was just as well. He'd rather not see her suffer.

He went back to work, trying his best to clean the wound. Once he was sure he'd coated every inch of it with whiskey, he retrieved the powder and bandages from his kit and wrapped the infected skin.

Then he crawled back up to her head, lay down on the ground beside her, and gathered her against his chest.

He'd found plenty of women in the desert over the years, some alive and some dead, but never before had he wanted to lie down on the earth and simply hold one of them.

"You're gonna be the death of me," he muttered into her hair.

Then he curled his body around hers and drew her snug against his chest, almost as if holding her tighter would save her life.

∽

"Water." Anna Mae turned her head to the side, her mouth burning. "I need water."

She reached blindly for her canteen in the darkness, but rather than touching dry desert rock or the leather that covered the metal of the canteen, her fingers bumped something smooth and warm.

A rattler. Her eyes flew open and she jerked her hand back, then screamed. Or rather, she tried to scream, but her throat was too dry for more than a small croak to escape her lips.

She rolled to the side, anything to get her away from the snake, but that only caused pain to sear her ankle.

"Anna Mae. What's going on?"

"A rattler." Her voice emerged loud enough to be heard this time. "There's a rattler. It's going to bite me."

Silence followed, then a shuffling sound.

She scrambled to the back of the crevice, where the coolness of the dark rock behind her soaked through the fabric of her shirt.

"There's no rattler," the voice said a moment later.

No, there was no rattler. Instead, there was a man beneath the outcropping with a rough, laid-back drawl she'd recognize anywhere.

She squinted at the moving shadow rimmed by the faint orange and pink of dawn lighting the sky behind him. "Cain?"

Even in the darkness, just enough light filtered through the mountain peaks beyond to reflect off the golden color of his long hair.

"I see you're feeling better, darlin'."

"Why...?" She looked around. Was she hallucinating? Had she become so dehydrated that she was imagining things that weren't so?

But the cool rock of the outcropping felt real beneath her palms, and the rangy, dry sound of Cain's voice was just as she remembered it.

And he was talking about her feeling better, as though he knew how ill she'd been when she closed her eyes against the hot summer sun, dribbled the few remaining drops of water from the canteen onto her parched tongue, and went to sleep.

"How are you here?" she whispered.

Even shadowed by the cave, she could see him shrug. "Followed your trail. Found the rattler nest. Tracked you here."

Her throat suddenly felt too thick to work. "I thought... when the rattler bit me, and then I ran out of water, I thought..."

"Seems like God had other plans."

Her eyes burned as though she wanted to cry, but no tears came, probably because she'd had so little water.

Which reminded her of just how dry her tongue felt.

She scooted closer to him. "Do you have water?"

He held out the shadowed circle of a canteen. "I'll need to

get more later today, but I've got enough to get us through the morning."

She took the bottle and unscrewed the top, the metal cool to her touch. She raised the canteen to her mouth and let the water soothe her cracked lips and swollen tongue for a moment before she swallowed once, then twice, then so many times she lost track.

"Easy there." Cain tugged the canteen away from her. "Don't want to get yourself sick."

He took a sip himself before screwing the top back on and then reaching out to cup her cheek with his palm. It felt soft and cool against her skin.

"You still have a fever, but you're not burning up anymore."

"I had a fever?"

"From the infection in your leg."

She looked down at her leg, though it was too dark to see anything. "My bite must have gotten infected."

"You didn't realize that?"

Had she known? "I just remember being thirsty and my leg hurting too badly to find water."

"And thinking you were going to die."

She looked up at him. "Yes, that too."

He shifted closer to her, his back braced against the wall near where the rocky outcropping opened to the mountain, the only place the crevice was tall enough for a person to sit up fully.

"Come here." He spread his legs and opened his arms, beckoning her to sit on the patch of ground directly in front of him. She crawled to him, not quite able to resist the appeal of his arms as she rested her back against his chest and he tucked her head under his chin.

The familiar scents she'd come to associate with Cain wrapped around her. Leather, sun, wind, and beneath it all, a masculine sort of fragrance she could only describe as Cain.

"Why are you even here?" she whispered. "I thought you'd left Twin Rivers for good."

He shrugged lazily, the movement causing his chest muscles to shift beneath where her head rested. "When I learned you were missing, I couldn't stay away."

"Didn't the Rangers need you in… wherever it is you were?"

"Not as much as you did. A few more hours, and I'm not sure you would have made it."

No, she likely wouldn't have.

She looked out over the desert as the sun crested the mountain to the east. In a matter of seconds, the dark purples and blues of night scattered, suddenly replaced by a dusty pink that stretched its fingers over the craggy piles of boulders and walls of rock.

Cain didn't speak as he held her there, only moved his arms to settle them more securely around her, his hold neither too tight nor too loose, just enough to make her feel like she belonged where she sat…

Even though she knew full well she'd never belong in Cain's arms.

3

"What do you think, boy?" Cain patted the side of his stallion's neck, then walked the beast deeper into the narrow canyon. "Looks like the perfect spot to make camp."

The horse snorted.

As much as he didn't want to move Anna Mae, now that she was awake and her fever was going down, he didn't have much choice. They needed to be closer to water, and they needed a hiding place that allowed him to keep Maverick with him. Given the fact that Anna Mae wouldn't be able to walk on her own for another couple weeks, it was going to take far too long for them to get out of Mexico. But if someone happened upon the larger cave where he'd been hiding Maverick and stole him, that would delay them even more.

Part of him still couldn't believe she'd woken up. For three days her body had burned with fever. For three days she'd been delirious and trembling as he coaxed nothing but water and tiny bits of water-soaked hardtack down her throat. For three days he'd held her close and begged God to let her live, only to feel like the life was slowly draining out from her.

And now she was awake. Sure, she was sleeping at that exact moment, but he could rouse her if he needed too.

He could still feel the way her body had curled into his that morning as she'd drifted to sleep in his arms. It was almost enough to make him wonder what it might feel like to hold her every night as she fell asleep.

Where were those thoughts coming from? He was a Ranger, not a clerk who went home at the same time every day and ate dinner with his family. He'd go mad if he had to be sequestered in an office for hours at a time, with glimpses through a window his only taste of the outdoors.

No, it was better to be where he was, stranded in Mexico and surrounded by God's creation than cooped up in some office the way his lawyer friend Harrison Rutherford spent his...

Voices.

Cain stilled, every muscle growing tense.

Had someone entered the canyon?

He looked one direction, then the other, but he saw no movement against the backdrop of towering yellow rock surrounding him.

The voices floated through the unstirring air, too distant and indistinguishable for him to know what they were saying. But they were coming from the direction of the creek.

He tethered Maverick to a nearby rock, then unholstered his pistol and crept toward the canyon's opening. The voices slowly grew more distinguishable until he was able to make out words.

"How much longer are we going to keep looking?" someone asked.

"Until we find her." The next voice was deeper, gruffer.

"What if all we find is her body?" The first voice again. It sounded younger than the other one.

Cain reached the narrow opening between the towering

walls of sandstone, then pulled off his hat and tied his hair back, making his head smaller and less noticeable before he peeked around the edge of the rocky wall.

Seven men on horses were meandering along the creek. More than he'd be able to take by himself, even with surprise on his side, and Maverick's tracks led straight from the creek to the canyon. Had he known he'd need to hide, he would have swept the tracks away and rolled a few boulders in front of the canyon's opening.

But now those tracks were imprinted on the rocky earth for all to see. Though he had to admit, it didn't seem like the men were too interested in tracking anything. A couple men bothered to look around the valley, but most of them were either looking at each other or the trail ahead. And the ones who were trying to scan the valley were moving their heads too quickly to notice small details...

Like the fact that horse tracks led away from the stream to what looked like a solid wall of rock.

"Gabriella," one of the men called.

Cain jolted. *Gabriella?* Had he heard that right?

"We know you're here. May as well come out."

Was that who they were looking for? Gabriella? Harrison's sister-in-law?

Had she been abducted too?

It seemed impossible. Who would have abducted her with Velez's men focused on tracking down Anna Mae?

The desperadoes Cain had captured earlier that week gave no hint that Velez had many resources.

Unless... unless they thought Anna Mae was Gabriella.

Unless they'd kidnapped the wrong woman to begin with.

But the desperadoes he'd captured with the posse never said...

Wait, had he even used Anna Mae's name, or had he just asked where the woman was? He tried to think back, but he couldn't remember. He'd only been with the men a half hour or so before he'd struck out on his own.

Fort Ashton was a walled trading post and hotel that sat just on the edge of Twin Rivers. it had been built by Harrison's father, Bart Rutherford as a base of operations for his massive trading company. Now his friend Harrison owned it, and lived there with his wife Alejandra and sister-in-law Gabriella.

Who also happened to be Javier Velez's nieces.

In fact, if not for Alejandra's help spying on her uncle and his son, the Velez family might still be running roughshod over West Texas.

Anna Mae had been leaving the side entrance of Fort Ashton when she'd been abducted. What if the wrong woman with long dark hair and dark eyes had emerged from the door, and the men had grabbed her?

It made sense. Anna Mae might have been only a quarter Mexican, but the dark features she'd inherited from her mother meant she looked more Mexican than he did, even though he had more Mexican blood than her.

But if the outlaws thought they'd kidnapped Gabriella, then that meant Velez hadn't been trying to kidnap Anna Mae to seek revenge against Daniel.

Were they trying to kidnap Gabriella to get revenge on Harrison instead? Or did they want her for some other reason?

Cain rubbed his jaw. He needed more information. When he'd been stationed in Twin Rivers, he'd put together a network of informants who could help supply him with news of the rustlers' movements. But he'd thought his work in Twin Rivers was over and done, so he hadn't bothered to keep in touch with any of the villagers who had been helpful before.

Yet it made sense that the men would want to abduct Gabriella rather than Anna Mae. Before he and Daniel had uncovered who was behind the rustling operation, Velez had planned to marry both Alejandra and Gabriella off to form advantageous business alliances.

Now that Alejandra and Harrison were married, Alejandra couldn't be used as bargaining chip in the Velez family business schemes. But Gabriella could still be used as a pawn in her uncle and cousin's machinations—never mind the girl was only sixteen.

"We're going to find you, Gabriella," the first man called again.

"It's been a week since she escaped," another man answered. "No one can survive in the desert that long without water."

"What's to say she didn't find water? A woman who's wily enough to sneak off with a horse and a rifle is smart enough to look for water. She might even be hiding somewhere around here."

The group of men ambled along the small stream, still more interested in the water and scraggly cottonwoods growing beside it than searching the surrounding mountains.

Then the man at the front of the group pulled his horse to a stop and swung off. Though he wasn't tall, he carried himself with a sense of confidence. "Looks like a good enough spot for lunch."

Great. Cain glanced over his shoulder at Maverick. Chances were the horse was far enough away that he could nicker or snort without drawing attention, but that didn't mean Cain wanted to be stuck in the canyon for an hour or better while Anna Mae was alone and unprotected two mountains away.

"What'll we tell Velez if we don't find her?" the young-sounding man asked.

"We tell Velez we found her, but she was dead," another man answered as he bent to refill his canteen in the water.

"You do that, and he'll shoot you dead where you stand,

seeing as you were the one who let her get away." This from the leader, who'd pulled a pouch of food out of his saddlebag.

"It wasn't me who did it." The man in the river raised his hands. Even from a distance, Cain could hear the fear in his voice. "It was Juan who tied her up that night."

"Surprised she didn't bolt sooner." Another man pulled off his boots and stepped into the creek, the gravelly sound of his voice marking him as older than the others. "She was a smart one."

"We keep looking until we find her," the leader said.

"Do we have to go back if we don't? *El jefe* is sure to shoot one of us if we show up empty-handed."

"I agree with Martinez. If we don't find her, I'm heading south."

"And what makes you think he won't track you down and shoot you for deserting him?"

Cain tried to follow who was speaking, but the words were coming faster and faster, and he was too far away to catch all of them.

"*El jefe* doesn't have enough men to track anyone down, not since the attack on *La Colina.*"

There it was. The name of the house Javier Velez once owned that had burned to ashes when he and his men had raided it in April.

"Do we even know if Gabriella's still in Mexico?" the older man asked. "We're doing all this searching, but what if she made it back to that town? Are we supposed to grab her again?"

"If we need to," the leader said. "Miguel and Martinez, you two ride to Twin Rivers when we finish here."

"Shouldn't that have been checked before now?" one of the men mumbled.

The leader pulled the pistol from his holster and pointed it at one of the men in the creek. "You run your mouth like that again, and I'll be the one to shoot you dead, not Velez. You understand?"

Cain poked his tongue into the side of his cheek. The man in the creek was right. Any leader worth his salt would have someone watching Twin Rivers to make sure "Gabriella" didn't return.

But just what would the men find when they reached Twin Rivers? That Gabriella was still at Fort Ashton? That they'd abducted the wrong person?

Did that mean the men would try to abduct Gabriella while he and Anna Mae were still in Mexico?

Cain stepped quietly away from the entrance and leaned his head back against the cool sandstone wall.

If only he had way to get word to Daniel. Sending the rest of the men back to Twin Rivers had seemed like the best choice a week ago. But he hadn't expected to find Anna Mae alive and injured.

Dear God, please warn them somehow. Please help Daniel and Harrison to figure out that Gabriella is in danger.

Praying was all he could do at this point.

But he'd learned long ago that no matter how quick a man could draw his gun or how fast a man's horse could race across the desert, in the end, God was the only one who stood between life and death.

And if God said a person's time was up, there was nothing any man on the whole wide earth could do to stop it.

4

Anna Mae woke with a start, her chest heaving and sweat soaking her palms. Was there another rattler, or had she dreamed it again?

She licked her cracked lips and searched the floor of the shallow cave.

Nothing resembled a snake.

She drew in a breath and tried to still her trembling hands. How many times would she wake in a panic, convinced another rattler was about to bite her?

A quick glance around the cave told her Cain was gone, and the height of the sun in the sky said it was long past noon.

He'd said something that morning about going to get water, but she'd slipped off to sleep before he'd given her any details.

Now she was completely alone in the cave, unable to move more than a few feet.

A tear rolled down her cheek, and she swiped it away. She couldn't say why she was quite so bothered by the idea of being alone. Maybe because she'd been convinced the place where she was lying would become her grave.

But now Cain had found her, and if anyone could get her safely back to Twin Rivers, it was him.

She rolled onto her side and stared out at the mountain peaks, so beautiful with their jagged crests. How long had she been gone from Twin Rivers? Cain hadn't said earlier. She knew she'd been in the desert for five days before Cain had found her, two with her captors and three on her own, but how long had her fever lasted?

She swiped at another tear on her cheek. Her friends in Twin Rivers probably all thought she was dead, right along with Daniel and Charlotte.

Mr. Cunningham too.

Here she'd been taking baked goods to the general store every day for him to sell, earning money so she could save enough to open her own restaurant. But if Mr. Cunningham didn't think she'd be returning to Twin Rivers, he might have hired one of the other women in town to bake for him.

And where would that leave her?

She pressed her eyes shut. Without money to save so she could start her own restaurant, or even a way to pay her rent—that was where.

And what about Charlotte's baby? Had it been born yet? She'd wanted to be there when her best friend, who also happened to be her sister-in-law, brought the tiny infant into the world.

What color would its hair be? Would the child be thin and scrawny or big and robust, with a healthy layer of fat? A boy or a girl?

Another tear leaked down her cheek. Growing up, she and Charlotte had always talked about becoming mothers together and letting their children grow up playing the way the two of them had.

Her hand crept down to rest upon her flat, empty stomach. Paul Fordham had been paying her special attention over the past few months. Maybe he would ask for her hand by the end of the summer.

Because as much as she loved to cook and wanted her own restaurant, she wanted a family more.

Lo, children are an heritage of the LORD: *and the fruit of the womb is his reward.... Happy is the man that hath his quiver full of them.* The verse from Psalm 127 popped into her mind, much as it did whenever she thought of having a child of her own.

That verse alone showed there wasn't anything wrong with wanting children. But she needed a husband first, and that was proving a bit harder to find, though she didn't know why. Proverbs 18:22 said, *Whoso findeth a wife findeth a good thing, and obtaineth favour of the* LORD.

But no one seemed to think marrying her was a "good thing," except for maybe Paul Fordham.

Oh, she'd had offers of marriage aplenty over the years, but never from men who actually bothered to court her or become her friend. They took one look at her face, decided they wanted someone to cook and keep house, and asked her to marry them with about as much forethought as one put into whether to serve biscuits or rolls for dinner.

She wasn't an expert on marriage, but she knew better than to commit her life to a man who couldn't bother to take her on so much as a picnic before proposing.

Was there something about her that made her decidedly unwife-like? Something that pushed men away? Because all of her friends had found husbands within the last year, and half of them were having babies.

Anna Mae sniffled again, her eyes flickering open as a wave of pain swept through her leg. *Please, God, if you ever decide to let me be a mother, I promise to be a good one. A good wife too. If you could just give me a man who...*

A vision of a man popped into her head—and not Paul.

No, this man had long blond hair and a lazy smile and clear hazel eyes that she could stare into for hours.

The trouble was, she'd already told him last April that she loved him. And he'd told her to marry someone else, then turned around and walked away from her.

Anna Mae shook her head, squeezing her eyes so tightly that the image of Cain disappeared. God might have sent him to rescue her and bring her back to Twin Rivers, but she was not going to let herself get attached to him again. She couldn't.

Because there was no question about what he'd do the moment they arrived back in Texas. He'd drop her off at her brother's office and ride straight out of town to where his Rangers were stationed.

Which was why she was better off setting her sights on Paul Fordham.

He was kind and polite.

And dependable.

Not the kind of man who would ride off into the sunset with nary a glance over his shoulder.

But there was nothing about Paul that made her want to be constantly near him or brought his image to mind when she drifted off to sleep.

Because she was still in love with Cain?

No. She couldn't be. She was doing everything in her power to forget him.

She drew in a breath and stared out at the mountain valley. *Dear God, thank you for allowing Cain to save me, but please help me not get too attached to him again. Please bring someone into my life that I can love... and who will love me back.*

Because that was the crux of the matter, wasn't it? She couldn't convince a man like Cain Whitelaw to stay by her side any more than she could convince the desert dust not to scatter with the next gust of wind.

∽

MARSHAL JONAS REDDING scrawled his name at the bottom of yet another report, then shifted against the hard wooden chair behind his desk.

Why did the Marshals Service require so many blasted reports? It seemed he'd been holding a pen for hours. Didn't the attorney general in Washington know his men were better spent in the field, hunting down criminals rather than playing clerk?

A knock sounded at the door, and Jonas lifted his head, looking across the small office he shared with two other agents, both of whom were in the field at the moment.

The small lightbulb hanging from the basement ceiling barely gave off enough light for him to make out the shadow in the doorway, but it was hard to mistake Neville Darrowich's scrawny form.

"Look who's finally back in his office." Neville stepped inside, offering a smile that was so thin Jonas didn't even attempt to smile back. "Congratulations on your cases."

"Thanks."

"It's not every day a man solves five murders."

"It's not every day a man has to fill out five all-fired reports, either." Jonas scrawled his name across the bottom of another one of the reports, then slid the page to the side. "You'd think the directors would let a man celebrate solving five cases, not drown him in paperwork."

"Ulrich and Moore are sure to be impressed." Neville offered another one of his thin smiles.

"Of course they are. It will look good on the report they send to the attorney general at the end of each month."

It was probably why the greasy-haired little Marshal had moseyed down to the basement.

This month, Jonas would be solving more cases than

Neville, and both the director and assistant director were sure to notice—right along with the bureaucrat in Washington who read the reports from all the different field offices scattered around the country.

Jonas scrawled his name across the bottom of the next report and set it atop the growing stack of papers. "How'd the embezzlement case you were working on turn out?"

Neville took a couple steps into the office. "I solved it. Along with two others."

"I wouldn't expect any less."

Practically speaking, the small man with the smarmy smile made the worst Marshal in US history. Jonas wasn't sure Neville even knew how to hold a gun, let alone fire one. But the man had a head for numbers that could ferret out the smallest discrepancies in any ledger. He ran through embezzlement and fraud investigations at lightning speed, solving more cases than any other Marshal in the state, and all while never leaving his office.

Jonas, on the other hand, had taken months to solve the murder cases represented in the reports sitting on his desk. And sometimes, if he was tracking a gang wanted for bank or train robberies, he might solve only one or two cases over an entire year.

That's how it was for every other Marshal working out of the Austin office. And it was precisely why the directors upstairs loved Neville. The number of cases he solved meant the Austin field office was a favorite of the attorney general all the way across the country in Washington DC.

"Is there something more you need from me?" Jonas asked as he scrawled his name on the bottom of the last report. He wouldn't claim to have filled it all out correctly, but hopefully by the time Assistant Director Moore got around to reading it, he'd be out in the field and not in Austin to hear a lecture. "Otherwise, I need to file these with the clerk."

Neville slid into the chair opposite Jonas's desk, apparently not in any hurry to leave. "I was just coming to see if there was any information about Velez you thought I might find useful."

"Velez?" The name emerged from his mouth as little more than a sneer. He couldn't help it. Javier Velez had single-handedly turned the border near Twin Rivers into chaos, starting a territory and trade war that had resulted in the deaths of almost two dozen men, five of which made up the murders Jonas had just solved. "Why do you need information about him?"

"For the tariff evasion case. He's being extradited here in September, and Moore wants me to get evidence ready to turn over to the prosecution."

"You're handling the Velez case?" Jonas sat back, the air rushing from his lungs in one giant breath. "But I thought—"

"That you would get it?" Neville pasted another patronizing smile on his face, and Jonas could almost swear it was a secret type of sneer. "Why would you think that? Tariff evasion is a game of numbers, comparing ledgers and shipping manifests for hours upon hours."

"We can pin Velez for more than tariff evasion. There should—"

"Not according to Moore. The assistant director wants it simple and done. Tariff evasion and nothing more." Neville shrugged his scrawny shoulders, then his lips turned down into a scowl. "It's always best to keep cases like this simple, but your Ranger friend did the exact opposite when he rode into Mexico, didn't he? Caused all kinds of problems."

Jonas planted his hands on the desk and leaned forward. "My 'Ranger friend' was trying to stop Texans from losing more cattle. Or have you forgotten just how large and far-reaching Velez's criminal network was?"

As far as Jonas was concerned, Cain Whitelaw should be

commended. The man had brought down a powerful criminal using only the few dozen men assigned to him.

When Cain had been sent down to Twin Rivers the previous year with his Ranger unit, no one had expected that the man behind the rustling would turn out to be Javier Velez, the former governor of the State of Chihuahua who still wielded a tremendous amount of power and influence. Once Cain traced the rustling back to Velez, he'd gathered his men, plus a posse of volunteers from Twin Rivers, and swooped into Mexico, raiding Velez's estate when the man least expected it.

The trouble was, both the Texas attorney general and the US attorney general were furious Cain had ridden into Mexico with so many men. The bureaucrats all claimed that Cain's actions could strain diplomatic ties with Mexico and possibly even spark further altercations along the border.

It didn't seem to matter that Cain had little choice if he wanted to stop the rustling, or that lawmen in Texas often crossed the border in pursuit of outlaws.

Jonas pressed his lips together. If he had been in Cain's position, he would have ridden into Mexico too. Justice couldn't be ignored simply because a criminal was powerful and wealthy.

In fact, his own cases would never have been solved without Cain's actions. He hadn't realized the cases had been connected to the rustling when he'd opened his investigations, but it turned out all three men whose disappearances he'd known of had been murdered, plus two others he hadn't known about. Each of them had been killed because they'd gotten too close to one of the rustlers' secret cattle trails at one time or another. So even though the murders had occurred at different times and different places, they had still been connected to the rustlers.

Jonas blew out a breath and looked across his desk at Neville. "How long ago did Moore give you the Velez case?"

"Two days ago." The man covered his face with a yawn, but

there was something about it Jonas didn't trust. Neville's beady little eyes were watching him far too closely for the man to be tired. "So, do you have any records that might be helpful? I wanted to ask before I sorted through the files in the records room."

"Let me help with the case." Jonas wasn't exactly sure how long he'd be able to tolerate working with Neville, but he didn't want to leave the entire case up to him either. "Like I said before, we should be able to pin more on Velez than just tariff evasion."

Neville gave him a slow blink. "Don't you have other cases to work?"

"Just the Giffard one, and it's cold."

"Has it been marked cold?"

He barely stopped himself from rolling his eyes. Only Neville and the directors cared about how a report had been filed. "No, but..."

Neville stood. "Then I suggest you work on that. I was stopping by for records, not advice on how to conduct my investigation."

"Wait." Jonas stood and came around the side of the desk. "I think Velez might be behind the murder of a Texas businessman. Jedidiah Smoak went down to Mexico to meet with him about a shipping contract but decided not to sign anything. Two days after he returned home to Del Rio, he was killed leaving his office after work. We can probably nail Velez for that too."

Neville blinked at him with flat, bored eyes. "The assistant director was clear. Velez is only to face tariff charges while he's here. No one wants this to turn into a bigger diplomatic mess than it already is."

"You talking about how Whitelaw went back into Mexico?" a voice said from the doorway.

Jonas looked up to find Barry Winslow leaning against the

doorframe with a cup of coffee and a limp-looking pastry in his hand. "Cain went back into Mexico?"

Barry raised an eyebrow. "You haven't heard?"

"Heard what? I've been in court for the past week." And it had apparently left him oblivious to all the goings-on at the office.

"Yes, he went back into Mexico, and it's going to complicate everything even further." Neville sniffed. "I, for one, don't want another war with Mexico."

"This isn't going to lead to a war with Mexico." At least Jonas hoped it wouldn't.

Barry took a sip of coffee. "Rumor is Hogg's fuming."

Hogg would be Jim Hogg, the attorney general of Texas, who ultimately oversaw the Rangers. Jonas pressed his eyes shut and rubbed at his temple, where a headache was starting to form. Wasn't that just like the bureaucrats in Austin? More concerned about ruffling feathers in a faraway place than supporting the lawman who was risking his life to see justice served.

And in Cain's case, if Velez was involved again... "Wait, why did Cain go back into Mexico?"

"Didn't I say?" Barry took a bite of the sorry-looking croissant in his hand. "The sheriff down in Twin Rivers had his sister kidnapped and taken across the border last week."

Jonas stilled. "Anna Mae?"

"Is that her name?" A curious look flashed across Barry's face.

"It doesn't matter," Neville said. "If she was taken into Mexico, she's as good as dead. Now if you'll excuse me, my time is better spent in the records room, not gossiping." He turned and strode out of the office, his pointy little nose stuck into the air so high that the man just might drown if it rained.

"What's gotten into him?" Barry came farther into the room and leaned against the desk.

"Pretty sure that's usual behavior."

Barry looked out the door, where Neville was turning the corner in the hallway. "I don't know why the directors like him so much."

Could Barry really not figure it out? "It's the number of embezzlement cases he closes. It makes the field office look good to Washington." Jonas sighed and shook his head. "So was Velez the one behind Anna Mae's abduction? Is he trying to get revenge on the sheriff somehow?"

It was the most logical explanation. Who else would want to kidnap the sheriff's sister?

"Can't say." Barry's face turned grim. "All I know is word reached Austin about two days ago, and no one is happy about it. They're saying Whitelaw abandoned his post."

Jonas's jaw clamped shut. Abandoned his post? By searching for a kidnapped woman? Rangers took an oath to protect and uphold the law, same as Marshals. Ignoring the kidnapping and not trying to track down Anna Mae's abductors seemed like it would have been a much bigger abandonment of Cain's duties than leaving wherever he was currently stationed.

"Apparently, the sheriff from Twin Rivers sent a messenger to Alpine for Whitelaw," Barry added. "It's only a two-day ride between the two places. Could even be done in a day and a half, if a man was in enough of a hurry."

"Let me try to understand." Jonas rubbed the back of his neck. "After a woman was abducted from US soil, Cain realized there was still some cleaning up that needed to be done with his previous assignment and went back to Mexico to see to it. And now the Texas attorney general is upset?"

Barry dunked the end of his already soggy croissant into his coffee. "That's politicians for you. Always finding some reason to complain about a lawman doing his job."

"I'd have gone into Mexico after her too," Jonas muttered.

"I think we all would have. That's why something about the situation just doesn't seem right."

Jonas blew out a breath. No, nothing about the situation seemed right. He'd watched politicians and directors of different agencies squabble before, but he never remembered anyone in the Rangers or Marshals getting upset about a Ranger trying to save a woman's life.

5

Warm, there was something warm beside her. Anna Mae scooted closer, seeking out the soft feel of...

"You're awake."

Her eyes jolted open, and she looked up to find Cain sitting beside her, his leg pressed against her side.

That had been the warmth she'd sought? Cain? Her face heated, and she pushed herself up, ignoring the pain in her leg as she propped her back against the stone wall.

"How are you feel—?"

"You're sketching." Anna Mae looked down at the sketchbook and pencil in Cain's lap, then out at the mountains, with their craggy peaks and shadowed valleys. "It looks just like the landscape."

Except there was something almost better about Cain's sketch. Even though it was only black and white, the image on the paper somehow made the mountains seem warm and welcoming, like the kind of place a person would intentionally visit—rather than a place to be stranded.

"Do you know how long you slept?" Cain set the sketchbook aside and reached out to touch her forehead.

"Uh, I woke once while you were gone."

"Once? That's it?" His brows drew down in concern. "Are you crying?"

"I... no, of course not. I'm just..." She reached up to touch her cheek, only to find it damp.

Wait. Was she crying?

A tear chose that moment to slip from her eye and race down her face.

"Maybe I am crying." She sniffled. "But I don't know why. You're here. I'm safe. I shouldn't be crying."

Hang it all, another tear slid down her cheek.

"Never said there was no reason for it."

"Oh..." Well, it sure felt like there was no reason to cry now that Cain was here. So why did his statement make her want to cry even more?

Another tear crested, then another and another. "I'm sorry." She swiped at her cheeks again. "I don't know why... That is, you're here. And I know you'll find a way to get me back to Twin Rivers. I shouldn't..."

She hiccupped, and she swore it was the most mortifying sound that had ever emerged from her mouth.

"It's normal, Anna Mae." He reached out and brushed a tear away with his thumb.

"Crying? No. I've never been a watering pot."

"You almost died, and we're stuck in the desert miles away from home. A grown man would be crying too."

"You're not crying."

His hand dropped from her face, and the side of his mouth tipped up into a lopsided smile. "I'm talking about when a person almost dies. Even after they're saved, all they want to do is cry. Their body trembles. A lot of times they feel cold. It happens to men and women and children alike. Even my Rangers cry and feel cold if they almost die. There's a doc in Austin who thinks there's a medical reason for it."

She swiped at another tear leaking down her cheek. "I suppose you've rescued enough people to know."

"Just don't turn into a mess of tears once I get you home, or I'll be forced to pretend I don't know you. Now come here." He opened his arm for her, then wrapped it around her shoulder and dragged her closer until her head rested against his chest.

This man. He smelled of sunshine and wind and something masculine that she couldn't quite name, and he was going to be the death of her if he kept holding her every chance he had.

His hand stroked up and down her arm, an absent gesture that he seemed to not even be aware of as they sat there staring out at the colorful palette of the mountains.

"What next?" she finally asked. "How long do we stay here?"

"Until you stop trembling."

Was she trembling? She looked down only to find her hands had gone back to shaking, and they felt cold despite the afternoon heat, just like Cain had described. It was almost as if her body had been overtaken by someone else.

"I meant in this cave. How long do we stay? I figured I was about two days from Twin Rivers when the rattler bit me. Do you think the same? Can we leave tonight?"

He looked down at her, his eyebrows raised. "You want me to take you on a two-day trip across the desert when you're still a touch feverish and can't walk? No."

"You have Maverick. It's not like I have to walk all that way. Besides, if we come to a town, maybe we can buy another horse."

"And leave a trail for the desperadoes tracking us to follow? No towns. No conversations with other travelers. No busy trails or well-traveled roads. Getting out of Mexico isn't going to be easy, and I'll need you at your full strength for it. Can't risk having your fever come roaring back, and I'm certainly not starting off while your wound is still infected."

Anna Mae looked down at her throbbing leg, which felt too

sore for her to move an inch, let alone try to walk on. "It might be weeks before my leg is better. We can't stay here for that long."

The very idea made panic claw into her chest. This cave was too small. There was no water. And there was nowhere for her to even try standing or practice walking without being seen by anyone who could be on the trail below.

"I agree. That's why I found a canyon to move us to, one by a stream and big enough for Maverick to hide with us. That's where we'll wait things out."

"But Daniel and Charlotte..."

"Want you back in Twin Rivers safe," he growled. "And there's no fast way to do that."

She pressed her eyes shut. "I just want to be home."

A fierce ache rose in her chest. But where was home? The first place that came to mind was the small house behind the sheriff's office where she'd grown up. But her parents had sold that last year so they could move to Houston, where her pa was now attending seminary.

They had invited her to go with them, but after spending her entire life living in the wild, open desert, she couldn't imagine being content in a crowded, humid city.

So she'd set about finding a room to let and had gotten serious about selling her baked goods and meat pies in the general store. Charlotte and Daniel hadn't had room for her in their small house, especially with a baby on the way. But Wes had plenty of space, and he'd offered to rent her one of his guest rooms as soon as he heard she was looking for a place to stay.

So far, her pastries and breads were bringing her more money than she'd expected, and Wes and Keely had been nothing but kind. But still, nothing about the A Bar W felt like home.

That's because home was...

What?

Her own house, a husband, a small yard where she could grow a few plants, never mind that she'd need to water them almost constantly to get them to thrive in the desert.

And children. She wanted a whole passel of them. Six, seven, maybe eight? Was there such a thing as too many?

Oh, how was it she had turned twenty-two, and she didn't have a single thing she'd dreamed of as a child?

Her eyes filled with another bout of tears, and this time they had nothing to do with almost dying.

"Did you eat while I was gone?"

"What?" She blinked at Cain.

"The first thing you need to do is get your strength back and keep your infection at bay. Did you eat the hardtack and pemican I left you?"

"You left me food?"

Cain muttered something under his breath, then reached over and plucked a pouch from the head of the blanket where she'd been lying. "How long were you awake for earlier?"

The question pulled a yawn from her. "Only a few minutes, but even with all that napping, I still feel tired. Maybe I'll sleep more after I eat."

"And here I thought you wanted me to take you back to Twin Rivers tonight."

She grimaced. "I just want to be home."

"Do you want me to soak the hardtack in water or coffee?"

The idea of coffee made her stomach sour.

"Water, please." The hardtack would taste like flavorless mush, but at least she wouldn't need to worry about casting it back up. "Then can I lie down?"

He crawled away from her and grabbed the stack of tin dishes that had evidently been sitting beside the food she hadn't noticed.

"I need to change the dressing on your wound first. I was

hoping to move to the canyon today, but if you're this tired, we'll wait until tomorrow." He busied himself adding water from the canteen to a small tin bowl, then dropping a couple pieces of hardtack in it.

"Do you think you're awake enough to tell me about the men who kidnapped you while you eat?" He handed her the bowl and a piece of pemican. "Did they think you were Gabriella?"

Her eyes shot to his. "How did you know?"

"Ran across a group of men while I was out. They're still searching for you."

She dropped her head back against the wall and raised her gaze to the ceiling. The notion they were still searching for her, and close enough that Cain had crossed paths with them, made her want to curl up in the very back of the outcropping and cry all over again. What would happen if the outlaws found them?

They'd kill Cain on the spot, and she'd never be able to escape with her wounded leg.

"The four men we apprehended when we found the horse you stole should be back in Twin Rivers by now, locked up tight. But I expect the other group will keep looking for a while. No one wants to go back to Velez and admit they can't find you."

"It's Velez's son running things. Not the one Harrison killed, but the older son. He was in Mexico City when you raided *La Colina*."

Cain sat back on his haunches, his hazel eyes sharp as they studied her. Then he gave a small shake of his head. "You learn anything else that might be useful?"

"Only that the son Eduardo is having trouble running things with his father in prison. Too much was either lost in the house fire or confiscated as evidence for the trial. And the police in Chihuahua are searching for him."

"Do you know where the men were taking you?"

"To Mexico City. It's where Gabriella's fiancé is, and the Velezes still want the marriage to go forward. There's something about a business contract, one Eduardo doesn't feel he can afford to lose after everything they lost at *La Colina*."

"So there's little support for the Velez family in Chihuahua, but Velez still has influence elsewhere in Mexico." Cain ran a hand over his jaw. "That's interesting."

She took a bite of the pemican, letting the flavors of dried fruit and meat fill her mouth before answering. "It seems that way, yes. Eduardo is trying to build back some of what was lost."

"I should have killed Velez when I had the chance."

"Why didn't you?" It was something she'd wondered before. Considering the number of cattle Javier Velez had stolen from the Texas side of the border, and the fact the Ranger headquarters in Austin had needed to send an entire unit of Rangers commanded by Cain to bring them down, it seemed Cain would have been justified in shooting him.

"He was unarmed, trying to extricate himself from the horse that fell on him. I may have shot men dead before, but never an unarmed man who isn't firing at me. I'm not a murderer." His voice had turned deep and rough, and he didn't look at her, staring at the hardtack instead.

He fiddled with something in the dish before handing it to her. "Here, you best eat this while I get what I need to clean your wound."

She raised the canteen to her lips, then broke a bite of the half-mushy, half-hard cracker off with her fork and put it in her mouth.

It tasted just as bland and chalky as she remembered.

She made it through half the hardtack and a third of the pemican before Cain returned with a little leather case. It looked almost like a man's shaving or shoe-shining kit, but when he undid the buckles that held it closed, it looked more like something a doctor might carry.

She set down the bowl, then took a few more bites of the pemican before setting that down too. "I'm too full to finish."

He ran his eyes over her, studying her until she had the urge to fidget. But was it any wonder he stared at her? She must look a fright after so many days in the desert.

She reached up and touched her hair, only to wince as her hands landed on a nest of tangles and snarls. Her face was sure to be dirty too. She knew that much just by looking at the dust and baked dirt streaking her arms.

"I'll wake you to eat once more before sundown," he finally said. "What you ate just now isn't enough nourishment if it's going to be your only meal of the day."

She settled a hand atop her extended stomach. "I feel like I'm going to burst."

"Only because you haven't been eating enough. How much did your kidnappers feed you?"

She sucked in a breath, then looked away from him. That was something she'd rather not remember.

"Answer me, Anna Mae." He settled himself by her feet and untied the leather thongs holding his case closed. "I can't get you better if I don't understand your condition."

She sighed. "Let's just say I wasn't too keen on eating anything they gave me."

"Fool woman. That's probably half of why you're so weak. You know better than to go without food in the desert."

It was true. Everyone always talked about drinking water in the desert, but there was something about food too. If one drank all water but ate no food, it was almost as bad as drinking no water at all. "It wasn't like I ate nothing. Just as little as I could manage. If you ever get captured, will you eat food at your captor's hands?"

He laughed, but the sound had a bitter edge. "Darlin,' the

chances of me being taken alive are about as high as the Rio Grande freezing over. But if I were to get caught, my captors wouldn't bother giving me food."

No. They'd beat him, probably until he couldn't see. They might even take a knife to him. It was one of the dangers that went along with being a lawman in such a lawless place, especially a Ranger who'd made a name for himself for being good at his job. Any criminal who got their hands on Cain Whitelaw wouldn't be fast about his death.

She swallowed the sudden lump in her throat and stared absently at the rocky wall across from her. "My captors weren't kind to me either. They might not have hit me, but their jokes were..."

She closed her eyes, trying not to think of the things they'd said, the names they'd called her, the things they'd threatened to do to her if her betrothed—who was actually Gabriella's betrothed—decided not to marry her after all. "Let's just say, I didn't want to eat anything they gave me. Every time I took a bite, they... There are other things a woman can put in her mouth, not food, and I..."

"I'm going to kill them," Cain growled. "Each and every one."

Her gaze fell to her lap, where her hands had twisted themselves in her skirt. "They were just words. It could have been worse."

"Words that made you not want to eat, even though you knew you'd need your strength if you escaped."

"I stole a rifle along with the horse. I didn't envision I'd have trouble finding food on the trail."

"Fine. I'll break their jaws instead. See to it they can't talk for a few weeks. That'll teach them to disrespect a woman."

She pressed her lips together to stop herself from smiling. "All right, maybe that. But only if it won't get you in trouble with headquarters."

He offered her another lopsided smile. "Always looking out for me, aren't you?" He touched the hem of her skirt. "Pull this back. I need to look at your wound."

Her face heated. The rattler had bitten her just above the ankle boot she'd been wearing, but never before had a man seen so much of her leg. And after what they'd just been talking about, the thought of Cain seeing even a glimpse of her skin made her feel as though her fever was coming back in force.

"Anna Mae. Your skirt." Cain pulled bandages and a bottle from his case. "Or do you want me to move it?"

There was nothing romantic or suggestive about his demeanor. On the contrary, his actions were quick and confident, his voice brisk and businesslike.

He was doing no more than a doctor would do in the same situation.

She shifted so that her sore leg was fully extended, then bunched the skirt up with her hands, stopping when the hem of her soiled skirt touched the very top of the bandage.

"It hurts," she rasped. "All the time. Not just when I move it."

"I'll bet it does." He unwound the bandage, his hands somehow the perfect combination of gentle enough not to hurt her, yet brisk enough she knew his mind was focused on treating her injury and nothing more. "You cut a hole in your leg three times bigger than you needed to."

"I didn't want to take any chances."

His eyes met hers. "Except for infection?"

Her face warmed again. "Don't suppose I was thinking about that overmuch, and I didn't know what else to do."

His eyes roved over the exposed flesh.

"I survived, though."

"You wouldn't have." He looked up and met her eyes once more, and a sudden chill traveled through her. "I'm not trying to be mean, just teach you so you'll know what to do next time."

"There's not going to be a next time." The idea terrified her. "Do you know of anyone who's been kidnapped twice in their life?"

He pressed his mouth shut as he went back to studying the wound, prodding this and twisting that. The pain was so bad at times, she almost wanted to scream.

"Is it improving?" she finally gritted.

"It is, but there's still infection. I'm hoping I don't have to lance it, but..."

"What?"

"I'm going to need to clean it again."

"By clean it, you mean...?"

"Douse it in whiskey."

She slammed her eyes shut. "That's going to hurt."

"I'm going to need to cut into it too. There's one place where the infection is bad, and I need to make sure the whiskey gets to it."

She let out a small whimper.

"Here, take a swallow of laudanum to help with the pain."

She opened her eyes to find him holding a blue bottle out to her. "No. I hate it. It makes my brain feel mushy, and I can't think."

A small smile tilted his mouth. "I agree. The only thing laudanum is good for is amputations and digging a bullet out of a man. But if you don't want the laudanum, you best take a swallow of whiskey."

That she could manage. She took the gray flask he'd extended, then swallowed a gulp of the fiery liquid. It burned a path of fire from her mouth down her throat and chest, straight into her stomach, but it wasn't as bad as the burning she was about to feel in her leg.

"You'll want this too."

He handed her a thick, stubby stick with bite marks already in it.

She didn't want to ask what he'd needed to do the last time someone had used the stick, so she sucked in a breath, bit down, and balled her hands into fists.

The pain was sharp, slicing through the part of her leg that ached the most. Then she could almost swear Cain squeezed it before pouring whiskey fire over the entire thing. Tears leaked from her eyes, and the desire to scream rose in her chest, but she didn't dare let out a sound lest it echo into the valley below. Instead, she tried to suck air into her lungs, tried to think about how her leg might feel in a creek, with cool water running over it rather than burning liquid.

And then the pain was subsiding. Cain was patting the wound dry with a clean handkerchief and murmuring gentle things about how good she'd done, how brave she was, how well her leg would be able to heal if they could stave off infection.

She pulled the stick from her mouth and heaved in a breath, staring down at him through watery eyes. His blond hair hung in a thick curtain around his face as he tended her, but his eyes were alert and focused. Even though his movements were small, the muscles played across his forearms as he wound a fresh bandage around her leg.

Oh, if only he didn't have to be so good at rescuing people. At surviving in the desert. At being a Ranger.

Seeing him work with her like this, she didn't wonder why he'd chosen to leave Twin Rivers with the Rangers in June. Nor could she even tell him he should have stayed to be with her.

How many other women had he rescued from situations like this?

How many daughters had he brought back to their fathers, or wives to their husbands?

Just in the time he'd been in Twin Rivers, he'd rescued Keely and Gabriella.

Asking Cain to be anything other than a Ranger was nothing but selfishness on her part. Especially when Paul Fordham was showing an interest in her.

So why did her heart ache at the notion that he'd up and leave her again after he returned her to Twin Rivers?

6

Daniel stood on the porch of his office, surveying the dark shadows of the mountains to the south. It had been ten days since Anna Mae had been abducted, and five days since he'd left Cain in Mexico to keep looking for her, while he returned to Twin Rivers with the posse and the desperadoes they'd captured.

Cain had yet to return.

Was he dead on the trail somewhere?

Daniel closed his eyes, and the sickening sensation that hadn't left his gut once since his sister had gone missing twisted excruciatingly inside him. He should have just stayed with Cain. Shouldn't have let him go off on his own. Cain always thought himself so invincible, but what if it got him killed this time?

Please, God, I know it seems impossible, but if there's any way Cain and Anna Mae might still be alive...

A shout sounded from inside the jailhouse, followed by a chorus of jeers.

Daniel raised his head and looked at the squat adobe structure that butted up against his office. It was ten o'clock at night, and half the town was asleep. Of course his inmates had waited until now to make yet another ruckus. Hollering at the top of their lungs in the middle of the day would have been too normal.

He sighed. The judge wasn't scheduled to come to town for another week, which meant the four men they'd apprehended in Mexico were still inside, awaiting trial and causing all manner of problems. It was almost as though they felt that the wilder they were, the more likely they were to be acquitted.

And it just made him want to be done. Done with the jailhouse. Done with criminals. Done with the whole lot of it. He already had a missing sister to worry about. He didn't want the hassle of corralling restless inmates as well.

The door to his office opened, and out stepped Bryce, his mouth flat beneath his drooping mustache.

"What's the fuss about?" Daniel nodded toward the jailhouse.

"You tell those men to settle down for the night, and they decide to start hollering. I swear half the things they do are purely to spite us. I don't think I'll ever be so happy as to see the lot of them carted away to prison."

"You and me both."

Bryce settled his hat on his head. "I'm going to ride out west of town along the river. Want to make sure everything looks as it should."

"Take your time patrolling around Fort Ashton."

Bryce cocked an eyebrow at him. "Did you think I was going to skip it?"

No, he hadn't. They'd all been watching the fort like hawks since Anna Mae had been abducted just outside it, and that was on top of the extra guards Harrison had stationed there.

"Sorry. I'm just…"

Bryce patted his shoulder. "Reckon everyone's anxious, especially with Cain and Anna Mae still missing."

Missing. That was such a nice way to put it.

And it was only made worse by the fact she'd been abducted by accident. Initially, no one had realized the outlaws had kidnapped the wrong woman, but when they'd made camp on their way back to Twin Rivers, one of the desperadoes had mentioned Gabriella, and everything had fallen into place.

Eduardo Velez had wanted Gabriella kidnapped and brought down to Mexico City so she could marry the man she'd been betrothed to. Of course, Gabriella; her older sister, Alejandra; and Alejandra's husband, Harrison, were all against the marriage. But the Velez men weren't the type of people to care about such things, especially not when they thought a marriage between Gabriella and one of their business associates would bring the family money.

"It'll be all right, boss," Bryce said, his voice carrying out into the empty street. "You'll see. Your sister is a tough one. She'll be back in no time, quarreling with you like she never left."

Daniel swallowed. What did it matter if Anna Mae had been taken by mistake or if she'd been the target? Either way, she was likely dead. And the little bit of hope he had that she might somehow—miraculously—be alive seemed to slowly drip away with each hour that passed.

One of these days, he was going to have to let his parents know. He'd wanted to wait until he had proof she was dead, but it had been so long since she'd been kidnapped that he was procrastinating more than anything.

"I'll patrol the town," Daniel said, more out of habit than because he was actually thinking about his words. "It's just past ten o'clock now, so let's meet back here at one."

His deputy dragged in a sigh, but Daniel only squared his shoulders. "There's good reason for this, and you know it."

Usually, his men patrolled the town at night completely on their own. On the rare occasion where he did have two deputies on duty, they might go their separate ways and not return until their shift ended at seven o'clock in the morning.

But after Anna Mae was taken, he put out a call for volunteers to help patrol the town. He'd also started making his men check in every three hours during their shifts. His deputies balked at the restriction, but he wasn't going to risk not learning about someone's disappearance for twelve hours.

"I can cover more ground if we don't meet back until four," Bryce said as he tromped down the steps, almost as though he was reading Daniel's mind.

"One o'clock." Daniel descended the steps behind his deputy.

"Fine, I'll be here at one." Bryce swung atop his horse, then turned the beast to the west and galloped off.

Daniel stopped at the bottom of the steps to give his horse, Blaze, a pat on his muzzle as he passed. "I'll ride you in a few more hours, boy. Want to keep a close watch on the town for now."

Then he strode off down the street toward the cantina.

Before Harrison's father and Velez had decided to set up a massive cattle rustling operation in Twin Rivers, the cantina had been the only place trouble ever really arose. The constant stream of travelers on the Chihuahuan Trail meant there were always new faces, and it was impossible to know if any of them meant trouble.

Most saloons in Texas would have tinny piano music pouring out of their buildings at this time of night, but *La Nueva Cantina* had banjo music playing in the traditional Mexican style that was so common along this stretch of the border.

Daniel climbed the steps, nodding at a handful of men on the boardwalk in front of the building, then stepped inside.

Both he and his father before him had made a point of having a deputy stop by the saloon at least once a night, so when he pushed through the swinging double doors, business inside continued as usual, no one thinking overly much about having a lawman present.

He seated himself at a table in the back, and when the owner's wife came to serve him, he ordered himself a sarsaparilla, then sat back and watched the poker game going on in the center of the room.

Everything seemed normal. A few men gathered around the poker table as the wagers crept higher, but nothing indicated the game was getting out of hand or that there was a cardsharp playing.

On the far side of the room, a man danced with one of the two girls who worked there, and the bar was filled with ranch hands who'd trickled in from a variety of neighboring ranches. He even spotted a couple of Wes's men.

All in all, it seemed like a usual night with nary a sign of trouble.

Mrs. Garcia arrived with his sarsaparilla, the top already popped.

"*Gracias.*" He leaned back and took a sip, letting the fizzy goodness fill his mouth.

She smiled at him. "*De nada.*"

He settled back in his chair and continued to watch the movements of the people around him. A trumpet and guitar joined the banjo to fill the cantina with a tune he'd heard countless times growing up on the border.

Yes. Everything was as it should be, which meant he'd better finish his drink and...

Wait. Was that movement outside the window? Had the window been facing the street, he wouldn't have thought anything odd about seeing shadows. But this window faced the barbershop, and there was only a small sliver of ground between the two buildings.

Why would anyone be loitering there after dark?

He sat up straighter and watched through the corner of his eye. Yes, a shadow had shifted. It was too vague and dark for him to tell what it was, but only a person would be tall enough to create such a shadow.

Daniel stood and caught the owner's eye behind the bar, then jerked his head toward the back. The Hernando gave a small nod, then went back to serving drinks.

Daniel moved casually toward the door that led to a small hallway. Once through it, he kept his gait light and tried to control any noise his boots might make against the wood floor as he headed to the back door. Once there, he paused and listened.

Nothing.

Slowly he cracked open the door, then attempted to peer into the darkness.

Still, nothing.

No sounds or shadows or movements. Nothing indicated someone was back there.

Just to be safe, he pulled the gun from his holster and stepped into the alley.

Only after he'd shut the door behind him, blocking the trumpet and banjo music, did he hear the faint sound of whispers coming from the side of the building.

Daniel moved toward his left, in the direction of the Spanish-speaking voices.

"I don't understand. Why did Velez even bother sending you here when he's trapped inside a prison cell?"

Daniel stilled. Velez? He'd sent the men on the other side of the building to Twin Rivers?

"Just you wait," a second voice answered, lower and rougher than the first. "His plans will be apparent soon enough, and by the time he's done, you'll laugh at how foolish your idea was to kidnap the girl."

Daniel crept closer, his heart hammering against his chest.

Were they talking about Gabriella? Had Eduardo Velez sent more men back to kidnap her?

To his knowledge, there hadn't been anyone skulking about Fort Ashton, but the massive hacienda that functioned as a trading post, hotel, and restaurant always had so many travelers passing through, it was impossible to keep track of everyone.

"You call my task foolish, but what have you been sent here to do?" the first man retorted. "Skulk about the town? How is that more useful than kidnapping Gabriella Velez? Montrose is still willing to marry her. And the Velez family cannot afford to lose an alliance such as that, not considering what happened to Raul and *La Colina*."

"Like I said"—the man with the lower voice sneered—"by the time Javier is done with what he has planned, the girl isn't going to matter."

"You say that, but what can he possibly do from inside a prison cell?"

"Suppose you'll have to wait and see. Now I best be off, there's much to learn about this town, like what time the sheriff makes his rounds and how many men he has watching it."

"You go and do that. Spend until dawn counting men and recording what time you see them. Meanwhile, I'm going to figure out how to bring Gabriella Velez back to Mexico myself. No one even knows they got the wrong girl."

Sweat beaded on the back of Daniel's neck. Did the men who kidnapped Anna Mae still think she was Gabriella?

"Wait. You kidnapped some other girl instead of the Velez one?" the second man asked.

"It wasn't my fault. I wasn't the one in charge—just did what Emilio said. And it was an accident. No one in Mexico even knows the woman everyone has been searching for is really the sheriff's sister."

Searching for? Daniel straightened. As in, the desperadoes were still looking for her? Did that mean Anna Mae was still alive?

"When I bring back Gabriella, Eduardo will have no choice but to promote me," the first man continued. "Then you'll be the fool for mocking me."

Daniel leaned forward, getting as close as he could to the side of the building without giving himself away. Though the men had obviously met in Twin Rivers, different Velez men must have sent them—Eduardo, who was still interested in kidnapping Gabriella, and Javier, who seemed to be able to get messages to his men from inside his prison cell.

"You kidnapped the sheriff's sister?" The second man's voice turned darker, almost sinister. "Where is she? *El jefe* could use her more than his niece. Perhaps we can arrange some kind of trade."

"Haven't you been listening? We don't know where she is. She escaped us, and no one has found her. Except for the Ranger. We think he found her and is hiding her. It's the only way to explain why she hasn't appeared after so long."

Daniel's heart nearly stopped in his chest. Had Cain found Anna Mae? Was it really possible they were both still alive somewhere? A small bead of hope unfurled in his chest.

"I half expected the pretty one to be back here when I arrived in town," the first man said in a low voice. "Because the Ranger who's with her is wily. They say he stopped a riot over in El Paso all on his own. And he's the one who burned down *La Colina.*"

"Cain Whitelaw is the Ranger who's with her?" The second man nearly shouted, the pitch of his voice rising in excitement. "I must tell *el jefe*. He will want to know."

The thought of Javier Velez—called *el jefe* by his men—knowing Cain was back in Mexico caused a shudder to ripple down Daniel's spine.

Fortunately, there was an easy way to prevent Velez from ever learning that bit of information.

Daniel cocked his pistol, the unmistakable sound of metal striking metal silencing the two men. Then he stepped around the side of the building, the barrel of his gun moving between them. "Actually, you won't be going anywhere—other than the jailhouse."

And they wouldn't.

But how long would it be before Eduardo Velez learned that Gabriella was still in Twin Rivers? And how long before Javier Velez discovered that Anna Mae and the Ranger who had burned down his house were lost somewhere in Mexico?

Daniel might be able to lock these two outlaws up, but the news was bound to spread eventually.

What would that mean for Twin Rivers and the people he cared about?

7

One Week Later

Anna Mae took another step up the narrow, winding trail, wincing at the stab of pain in her leg. But she'd gone too far to think about stopping now. She stepped over a small pile of rocks, following the dusty boot prints that had taken this same path an hour or so before.

Another flash of pain jolted up her leg, but she kept going. Just a few more steps until...

"What are you doing?"

She glanced up to find Cain peeking over the rocky ledge at the top of the canyon. "I wanted a look from the top."

In the past week that they'd been cooped up inside the canyon, Cain made the trek to the top at least once a day. At first she'd thought he was keeping watch for Velez's men, but his trips after dinner had become so regular that she couldn't quite stop herself from wondering just what Cain found so fascinating up there.

"Your leg's not strong enough to take a trail like this." Cain settled his hands atop his hips, a scowl plastered on his face.

"And it will never get stronger if I stay sequestered down there." Her foot slid on a loose pile of small rocks, and more pain shot up her leg, but she pressed on, continuing the last few feet to where Cain was waiting.

He extended his arm, then turned her toward the place he'd clearly been sitting on near the ledge, where his duster was spread on the ground. "If your leg was strong enough for that trail, you wouldn't be wincing each time you took a step."

Was she wincing? She schooled her features, though she had to admit, she was leaning a little heavily on Cain's arm. "I'll have you know that... Oh wow."

Cain had paused beside his duster, giving her a full view of the mountains surrounding them.

"It's beautiful." Shades of pink and yellow and orange that opened into the canyon below. On the opposite side of the large crevice, the plateau-topped mountain continued for what looked to be a half mile or better. Then the mountain fell away and a series of jagged peaks formed beyond it, each one with its own outline against the setting sun.

To their north lay the valley with the creek that supplied water, and then a series of mesas rose on the other side of the valley.

"Now I see why you've been coming up here every night," she breathed.

"It might be desolate, but it has its own type of beauty." Cain took a step closer to her, the heat from his chest radiating into her back, even though they didn't touch. Then his hand came up and settled on the side of her arm, just resting there while a warm silence stretched between them.

She didn't know how many times he'd touched her in similar ways over the past week and a half. Small things like smoothing her hair away from her face or squeezing her hand, opening his arms to her whenever she spoke of missing Twin Rivers or wondered how long it would take her leg to heal.

"You best sit. I don't want to wear your leg out." Cain gestured to where he'd spread his duster out on the ground, his sketchbook lying beside it.

She didn't need him to ask twice, and only half because her leg was smarting. If he kept that hand on her arm any longer, she just might not be able to stop herself from turning into his arms.

She lowered herself onto the duster, then stretched out her leg in front of her. "So, seeing how my leg is strong enough to make it to the top of the plateau, can we go home soon?"

He sat on the duster beside her and raised an eyebrow. "Is that what your little trek was about? Proving you're strong enough to make it back to Twin Rivers?"

"I made it, didn't I?"

"And how does your leg feel?"

She glanced away from him, trying to hide her grimace. "Like I said, the exercise will make it stronger."

His shoulders rose and fell on a sigh. "Twin Rivers is a two-day journey, and there are some narrow trails where we might be better off walking than riding. If you struggle to walk for a quarter hour, there's no possibility of us making it back without doing further damage to your leg."

"But don't you get tired of just sitting in the canyon, waiting?"

"It's normal to feel a little crazy after being stuck in one place for so long, especially considering how confined your injury has made you."

She slanted him a glance. "So you feel crazy being stuck here too?"

He glanced down at the sketchbook, which she could now see held an image of the view before them, drawn in shades of gray. "No. I like being out here, away from all the busyness of town life. Just me, the desert, and God."

Of course he did. It made perfect sense. He was a loner, not cut out for town life or families or anything with people. "At least you have your sketches to keep you company."

He picked up the book, a faint smile teasing the corners of his mouth. "Yes, I suppose I do."

She sighed and looked out over the mountains. "But I don't have a sketchbook to keep me company, and all I can think about is everything I'm missing back home."

"Like what?" He began shading the mountains he'd drawn.

"The Independence Day festival, for starters."

"That was two weeks ago. It's not like leaving tomorrow will prevent you from missing it."

She huffed. "I always win the shooting contest."

"What? You don't want to give up your title of champion for a year?"

"I'm sure if I have a contest with whoever won after I get back, I'll still beat him."

"I'm sure you would." He went back to sketching, shading another side of a mountain and adding a hawk to the sky.

She wasn't sure how long she sat there, watching him as he added details to his sketch, but he didn't seem to mind, and once again the quiet grew comfortable around them, almost peaceful.

But she could sit there for only so long before thoughts of home crept back in. "Do you think Charlotte's had her baby?"

"All I can tell you is that she was still pregnant when we left to search for you."

She blew out a breath, trying to imagine how her little niece or nephew would look snuggled in Charlotte's arms. "I want to be there for the birth."

"I'm sure Charlotte knows that." He set down his pencil, his eyes seeking hers. "But I can't promise leaving tomorrow would get you home in time."

"Do you think it's selfish of me to pray and ask God to wait on the babe until I return?"

Cain's hand reached out to run absently down her back, then up it, then down again, the movements long and soothing. "I don't think there's anything wrong with wanting to be present for the big things that happen in Charlotte and Daniel's life. Reckon that just means you love them."

"We were supposed to raise our oldest children together, but now she's having a baby, and I'm not even married." Oh dear. She squeezed her eyes shut. What had possessed her to say such a thing? And to Cain, no less? It wasn't as though he'd understand.

His hand paused on her back for a moment, then went right back to stroking. "Seems like the kind of thing two close friends who grew up together would decide to do."

Or maybe he did understand. "The Bible says children are a heritage of the Lord." Something thick welled in her throat, but she continued on. "Is it so bad that I want a child of my own one day?"

"Can't think of a woman who'd make a better mother."

"Really?" The breath stopped in her chest, and she turned to look at him.

"Don't act so surprised by it. You've wanted to be a wife for as long as I can remember."

She had, yes, but this was not something she could continue talking about with him. Not after how she'd told him she loved him, and he'd told her to find another man to marry. "I want to open a restaurant as well."

"Do you now?" A faint smile appeared at the edges of his mouth.

"Yes, my baked goods keep selling at the general store, so much so that I've been putting by some extra money each week. If I save hard enough—and if Mr. Cunningham hasn't found someone to replace me in my absence—I just might be able to buy my own place by the end of the year, maybe something with an apartment above it."

"So that's what you want, then? A restaurant with an apartment?"

There was something about his gaze that gave her the sudden urge to squirm. "I enjoy making food for people, yes."

"But that's not the same as having children."

"No." She licked her lips. Why were they talking about this again?

She reached out and touched his sketchbook, half because she wanted a distraction and half because the sketch was too beautiful not to touch. She absently ran a finger over the ridge of a mountain. "You've turned into quite a good artist over the years."

"Thank you."

She picked up the sketchbook, intending to flip back through the pages, but Cain planted a hand atop it.

"Oh no you don't. Last time you went looking through my sketchbook, it got us into trouble."

"It did not."

"It did so."

She huffed and tried to wriggle the book out from under his hand without tearing any of the pages. "Only because you didn't want me to figure out you had feelings for me."

"Is that what you learned by looking at my sketches?" His voice emerged deep and rough, and something about it caused a warm flush to steal over her face.

"Maybe."

"I see." He leaned close, likely planning to take the sketchbook back. But their eyes caught, and her entire body went still, the dying sunlight reflecting on his hair while his mouth lingered not an inch away from her own.

She could feel the puff of his breath on her chin and the heat from his body so close to hers; she could see the way a brown line rimmed the green and tan streaks in his eyes.

Then he snatched the book out of her hand and hopped to his feet, holding it behind his back.

"Hey, give that back." She scrambled up, but she was far from quick given her leg.

She limped toward him anyway.

He moved the book from behind his back to above his head, well out of her reach.

"And just how do you suppose you're going to get this book?" A teasing smile crossed his face.

Normally she would have tried to swipe it from him and take off running, but that would never work with her leg. If she wanted that book, she was going to have to be a little more creative.

She plastered her biggest smile on her face and batted her eyelashes, sidling closer. "I'm going to ask you very nicely for it. And you, being a gentleman, will give it to me."

He chuckled. "I ain't that much of a gentleman, sweetheart."

"No?" She batted her eyelashes again, taking another step closer. "Then maybe I'll offer to bake a batch of apple dumplings once we return to Twin Rivers. Just for you. You won't need to share a single one."

"Still not good enough." Another smile twitched at the corners of his mouth, his eyes alive with amusement.

Did the man realize how rarely he smiled? How he always seemed so aloof and serious? Even when it was just the two of them, cooped up in the canyon, trying to find ways to while away the time as her leg healed.

She let out an exaggerated sigh and closed the final step separating them. "Fine. Then I suppose I'll just have to…"

She snuck her hand up and tickled the soft skin just beneath his arm. He gasped in surprise, dropping the book and jerking the arm down that had been holding it to cut off access to the ticklish spot.

The book fluttered to the ground, landing with a new page

open. She raced to grab the book, half hoping to find another sketch of herself. After all, they'd spent so much time together down in the bottom of that canyon that he must have some new drawings of her.

But a different woman stared back at her.

Charlotte, her round, heavy belly clasped between her hands and staring out at what appeared to be a landscape along the Rio Grande. Her hair was down, and the dress she wore was long and flowy, the material thin enough to conform to her body in the wind.

Warmth crept into Anna Mae's chest. The image had to be imagined. There was no way Cain had ever seen Charlotte look like that. The only time she wore her hair down was for bed, and her dress in the sketch was a lot closer to a chemise than anything a lady would wear in public.

And yet somehow, the sketch made a lump swell in her throat.

"This..." She reached out and touched Charlotte's face. "It's beautiful. In real life, Charlotte is pregnant and hot and miserable, and no polite woman ever mentions being in the family way in public. And I know you certainly haven't seen her with her hair down or wearing just a chemise. But you found a way make her look lovely nonetheless."

Cain came up behind her but didn't take the book. "Some of that image was my imagination, yes. But as you said, 'Children are an heritage of the Lord.'"

He swallowed, his own eyes scanning the page as though seeing it for the first time. "Just because I'll never have any children of my own doesn't mean I can't see how happy your brother is, or that I don't understand this is a special time for him and Charlotte. And that's good. It's the way it should be. I don't want..." He gave his head a small shake, his throat working. "I don't want to see another child grow up like I did."

He blinked, almost as though surprised those last few words had come out of his mouth.

It wasn't something he talked about much, how he'd been raised.

She reached out and gripped his hand, squeezing it tightly. "I'm sorry."

He tugged his fingers away from her, almost as though he'd been burned, then looked out over the mesas in the distance. "You don't need to apologize. You weren't the one who looked at me the day I was born, called me a curse, and then named me after the most famously cursed man in the Bible. You think children are a heritage from God, remember?"

She tried to reach for him again, but he crossed his arms over his chest and sent her a glare.

She sighed. "It must have been hard on you, growing up that way."

A muscle pulsed at the side of his jaw as he stared out at the dying sun. "We best get back to the canyon before it grows too dark."

"Cain..."

He looked at her, and gone was all the softness from his eyes, the comfortable togetherness they'd shared. The man in front of her might well have been a stone statue for all the warmth he exuded.

He bent to pick up his duster. "I'll head out in the morning, see if I can find a horse for you to ride back to Twin Rivers. It would help the trip go faster."

"Really? Does that mean we can leave tomorrow?"

He scowled. "Did you listen to anything I said? You need to be stronger before we leave. All it will take is one wrong move, one wrong person spotting us, and we could end up captured. But that doesn't mean I can't procure a horse for when the time comes."

"Do you think Velez's men are still searching for us? I mean, it's been two weeks since I escaped. Maybe they think I'm dead and have stopped looking."

"That's what I aim to find out tomorrow. Now come on. Let's get you down this mountain."

He stalked off toward the trail at a pace she'd never be able to match.

8

From his place behind a boulder, Cain scanned the sleepy little Mexican town of El Rebote. There was little activity at this time of morning, only about an hour after dawn. The ranchers and farmers who lived in the area would all have risen with the sun and were probably partway through their morning chores. But as for the town itself, none of the businesses would open for a couple more hours.

Cain narrowed his eyes at the back of a squat, odd-shaped little building in the center of the town. The cantina.

It didn't look as though anyone was about, which made sense, since it would have stayed open from last night into the wee hours of the morning. But Cain couldn't afford to wait until people were bustling around town. He'd donned a sombrero and guayabera to help him blend in with the Mexicans, and he'd tied his hair back and tucked it beneath the collar of his shirt lest the blond color give him away.

Hopefully no one would see him enter or leave through the cantina's back doorway, and then he wouldn't need to worry about whether his disguise was enough to ward off questions for his informant.

He scanned the dusty landscape once more, then pushed himself to a standing position, rising from the desert as though he were a wraith, and strode toward the back of the cantina, where Cristobal's living quarters were.

He was careful to pace himself, slowing his steps into an even stride, not too hurried even though he wanted to rush. If someone did see him, it was important he look as though he was visiting Cristobal on normal business.

When he reached the back door, he knocked briefly, then tried the handle.

Locked.

"Cristobal," he called through the doorway, trying to raise his voice enough to be heard through the wood but speak quietly enough so as not to draw attention to himself.

Though it was still early, he hated paying visits in the daylight. They forced him to blend in with his surroundings in a way he felt he never could, not in Texas, not in Mexico, not anywhere.

But he would have needed to wait until after the cantina closed late into the night to make this call in the dark, and that would have meant leaving Anna Mae alone in the canyon all night.

"Cristobal," he called once more, though he didn't expect the man to answer. He was probably abed with his wife, having worked until the cantina closed.

Cain slipped his key ring from his belt and began trying the keys in the lock. There were only thirteen types of locks in the world, and with his set of master keys, one of them was sure to work.

The door opened on the fifth key, only for him to find the middle-aged man standing just inside the opening in his nightclothes.

"Cain." Cristobal stepped back so Cain could enter, then poked his head out the door, looking both ways before he closed and locked it behind him. "What are you doing here? Everyone is looking for you."

"You must be mistaken. No one knows I'm here." He ran his eyes down the man, one of his former informant's uncles who had turned into an invaluable informant on his own before Velez had been arrested.

Cristobal crossed his arms over his chest, the sun from the window catching the gray at his temples. "You were seen riding into Mexico with a posse two weeks ago, and you've yet to appear back in Twin Rivers. Everyone else in the posse has returned, but not you."

Cain nearly cursed. Velez was having Twin Rivers watched that closely? Why?

"Maybe Velez's informants missed me riding into town, and from Twin Rivers I continued on to Alpine, where my men are stationed, which would explain why no one has seen me there."

"That's not what people are saying. They are saying you disappeared with that woman, the one Velez's son tried to kidnap. The wrong one."

He nearly cursed again. He'd thought the safest thing for Anna Mae was to wait until her ankle healed and the search for her died down before they returned to Twin Rivers. But staying in Mexico only seemed to have drawn more attention.

"Did anyone see you come in?" Cristobal glanced out the window, even though it faced the open desert valley, not the town.

"No, I was watching from behind a boulder. I waited until no one was about and then approached from the back."

Cristobal ran his eyes over Cain's sombrero and guayabera. "I suppose you would have been mistaken for a Mexican from a distance."

"That was the plan."

The man gave his head a firm shake, the lines around his mouth grim. "You have to leave. I am happy to help you when I am able, but I have a wife to think of, and two daughters married to men in town. I can't risk bringing down Eduardo's wrath."

"Eduardo. That's Velez's oldest son, correct? Where's he running things from? There's nothing left of *La Colina*."

Cristobal shrugged. "I don't know. He was down in Mexico City, though I'm sure he's closer now. All I can say is that his men are everywhere, watching everyone. They suspect Mexicans are helping you, and they want to make an example of one of us."

That was the last thing he needed. If he was going to catch this son of Velez, then he would need as much help as he could get from people on the Mexican side of the border.

Cain rubbed the back of his neck. "I need to buy a horse from you, and then I'll disappear. You won't need to worry about me drawing more attention to you until this situation simmers down."

"You want a horse for the woman you are hiding?" Cristobal's dark eyes widened. "No. I can't sell you one. Eduardo would find out."

"Then tell me where I can get one. Surely you know of a farmer in the desert who could sell me one without Velez's men noticing."

Cristobal only shook his head. "*Lo siento.* There is nothing I can do. It's too dangerous. Eduardo will pay for any information about you, even if it means neighbors snitching on neighbors. The girl isn't the main thing he is searching for now that he knows you're in Mexico. He's put a bounty on your head."

Cain's heart gave a solid, heavy thump against his chest. A bounty on his head? It happened to Rangers every now and then, but this was a first for him.

Because when he took down outlaws, he usually did a thorough job. If his pa had taught him nothing else as a Ranger, it was that. Every criminal he came into contact with either went to prison or died. There wasn't room for any other kind of justice—at least not if he wanted to live.

He'd heard whispers about Velez's eldest son, Eduardo, after he'd captured Velez that spring, but Eduardo had been in Mexico City for well over a year. It had never looked as though he'd been involved in the rustling, and nothing in the papers they'd taken from Velez's office had linked Eduardo to any illegal activities.

Maybe those had been the papers Raul burned before Harrison killed him.

Cain's stomach felt sick. How could he have missed how dangerous Eduardo Velez was?

"Mexico isn't safe for you." Cristobal stepped away from the window, then headed through the arched wooden door that connected the kitchen of the cantina with the living quarters. "It's not like before, when everyone laughed at your attempts to find the rustlers. Velez has lost his estate, and he wants you to pay with your life."

"Which one? Javier or Eduardo?" Cain followed him into the kitchen, which had a large oven on one wall and was lined on the other with long wooden tables for preparing food.

"Either, both. Just because Javier is in prison doesn't mean he's powerless. But Eduardo will avenge his father and brother. He will consider it his duty. And he will hurt the woman too, the one you are hiding with. There are rumors about her beauty."

Cain wanted to turn stiff. Every muscle of his body begged him to coil up like a mountain lion ready to pounce on its prey. Instead, he forced himself to lean against one of the tables and stretch out his legs, then added a laid-back drawl to his voice. "She's not beautiful. She's ugly. You heard that from one of Velez's men. Spread it around tonight when the cantina opens."

Cristobal rolled his eyes. "She is the sheriff's sister from Twin Rivers. Everyone knows she is beautiful. Besides, Velez's men have been through here three times in the past week. Each time their stories of the woman's beauty grow bigger. She has Mexican blood, does she not?"

"No. Not a drop of it." The lie fell easily from his lips, and he wasn't going to feel sorry about it. He'd do whatever he could to make Anna Mae unappealing to the men searching for her. "No Mexican man would want her to wife. She'd be—"

"They do not speak of taking her to wife."

Cain clamped his mouth shut, his jaw clenched so tightly his teeth ached. Velez's men would have one purpose for a woman with Anna Mae's beauty, and after that they'd kill her.

In front of him, if they could manage to capture both of them together.

The laid-back stance drained from his body until his muscles coiled, every inch of his body tense and hard. He and Anna Mae had to get out of Mexico.

Tonight.

Once he got back to Texas, he'd send word to Austin that he and his men were needed back on the border. Surely Austin would give him permission to leave Alpine. But for now, he'd focus all of his attention on getting Anna Mae back to Twin Rivers.

"I need canvas, a cloak, a skirt, and shirtwaist. Can you give me any of those things without drawing the attention of Velez's men?"

"*Sì.* I can give you all of them." Cristobal reached under the counter and grabbed a covered basket, then plopped it down atop the worn wood. "You'll need food too."

Cain peeked inside the basket to find tamales and empanadas.

"They are made with dried meat and will keep in the heat," Cristobal answered even though Cain had asked no question.

"It's enough food for three days. I pray you will be in Twin Rivers on the fourth."

"You were waiting for me?"

A dusting of red climbed into the older man's cheeks. "There are rumors about where the girl disappeared. I figured if they were true, you'd stop here before traveling back to Texas."

Cain let the words seep in for a moment. Part of him wanted to thank Cristobal for trying to help. But did Cristobal's actions mean he was growing too predictable? Or was he a close enough friend that he could guess Cain's movements in a way Velez's men couldn't?

Hopefully the latter.

Cain pulled the leather cover back over the basket. *"Gracias."*

"No, I should be the one saying *gracias*. It's my niece you saved."

"Not soon enough, I'm afraid." Cain hadn't known about Hortencia when he'd first come to Twin Rivers with the Rangers. Her father, Cristobal's brother, owned a cantina closer to the border where the rustlers liked to stop. At first neither Hortencia nor her father was willing to share information with him about the rustlers, but when one of the desperadoes forced Hortencia to his bed, things changed.

Hortencia became one of his best informants, right up until the rustlers started to suspect her, and it became too dangerous for her to stay in Mexico. She'd given birth to a baby boy by that point, and it had taken the help of several people to get her safely out of Velez's reach.

"You just keep what happened to Hortencia from happening to the sheriff's sister, *entiendes*?" Cristobal gave him a sad smile.

"Comprendo," he muttered.

"Bueno. Let me get your things from the storeroom."

Cristobal shuffled to the far side of the kitchen, where he unlocked a wooden door, then disappeared inside the room.

A few moments later, he returned with canvas, a cloak, and a fresh set of women's clothing. "If I learn anything of use to you and can manage to send word safely, I will."

"Don't put yourself at risk. I don't want to see any danger befall you or those you love." Cain scrubbed a hand over his jaw. "I really thought that once Velez stood trial—"

"That's because you're *Americano*, no? You expect justice, that evil men will pay for their crimes. But that's not how justice works in Mexico. The eviler you are, the less you have to answer for."

Cain met the older man's eyes. "He'll pay, Cristobal, and so will Eduardo. Not just for what they did to Hortencia but for everything. I'll see to it."

Cristobal raised his chin. "And that is why I help you."

∾

CAIN LET Maverick pick his way along the abandoned trail that led high into the mountains, his eyes alert for anything that might indicate another person was close by.

This section of trail looked as though it hadn't been used in months, which was good. Taking it would allow him to enter from the back side the canyon, where he and Anna Mae had spent the past weeks hiding and he was less likely to be seen.

During their time in the canyon, he'd noticed an increasing number of people at the creek. He'd thought it odd, since the trail alongside it had shown little signs of use when he'd first found it. But if there was a bounty on his head, and Velez's men were telling everyone where Anna Mae had last been sighted, that explained the influx of travelers.

And it was one more reason why he and Anna Mae would

leave the canyon that night, even though her leg wasn't fully healed.

At least she could put weight on it for a short time, but with them both needing to ride Maverick, they would have to travel for shorter periods of time at night.

And yet, part of him knew it was time to leave—and not because of Velez.

He'd spent the past two weeks watching as Anna Mae smiled at him and listening to her laugh, seeing her brush her hair until it shone like a silky waterfall and tilt her head shyly whenever she felt embarrassed. She was entirely too sweet and enchanting.

And beautiful.

When he'd gone to get a horse from Cristobel, he'd really just wanted to get away.

No, he'd *needed* to get away.

All he could think about anymore was their kiss, the one they'd shared before he'd gone into Mexico in April.

If he closed his eyes, he could still smell the sunshine and wind, the sugar and yeast that had been on her skin. Still feel the way her body had pressed against his, warm and curvy and soft. Still remember the way he'd tilted her head at just the right angle so he could kiss her more fully.

But he'd eventually pulled away.

And then he'd told her she could never kiss him again.

Maverick nickered as they neared the canyon. The ground had turned steep, sloping down at an angle that only an experienced horse could handle with a rider.

Cain let the beast have his head, watching for any sign that something might be amiss as they headed into the narrow space between the rocky walls. Once inside, Cain stopped Maverick, then picked up a spindly mountain pine branch that he'd hidden beneath a rock and cleared the tracks from the last part of the trail before continuing through the narrow crack in the rock face. At first the walls towered so high they blocked the sun. After a hundred yards or so, the canyon widened into a space large enough for a campsite, though the walls would bend two more times before he reached the spot where they'd set up camp.

He heard her singing before the final bend, the low hum of her rich voice filtering between the cracks and crevices. He had to force his lips into a hard line lest they turn up into a smile. Had she been singing any louder, he would have cautioned her against making too much noise, but her voice was just soft enough it wouldn't travel far.

He came around the final bend, and there she was, her long black hair cascading freely about her shoulders while her skirt swayed with her motions.

Except the fabric swaying about her legs wasn't full or thick enough to be a skirt, and it didn't reach her ankles either.

"What are you doing?" he barked, swinging off Maverick.

Anna Mae whirled to face him, her eyes wide. "Cain, you're back already?"

"Of course I'm back. Were you expecting Eduardo Velez to capture me? Why are you undressed, and... Are you wet?"

The closer he drew, the more apparent her state became. Every last bit of her was wet, from the hair at the crown of her head to the fabric of the chemise that stopped at her knees.

White fabric, no less. He could all but see her skin through it.

He whirled around and stared at the yellow rock of the canyon before his eyes had a chance to wander somewhere they shouldn't.

"Anna Mae," he gritted, the words emerging rougher and coarser than the crushed desert rock beneath his feet. "Why are you wet?"

"I needed a bath, if you must know. It's been weeks since I was clean. And my clothes needed a washing too. I figured since you were gone..." Her voice trailed off, and there was a rustling sound, then... "You can turn around now. I'm covered."

He did, expecting to find her dressed. Instead, she'd wrapped the blanket from the bedroll about herself.

He slammed his eyes shut and sucked a breath. "Clothes. Where are your clothes?"

Did she think he was a saint? That she could go off kissing him and telling him that she loved him one month and then stand before him a few months later in a wet chemise and not have his mind go to... to... to...

Places it should only go if they were married.

Which they weren't.

And they were never going to be.

He peeked an eye open. The woolen blanket was still covering her, but how was he supposed to forget the image of her standing by the fire in her chemise?

"My clothes are still drying." Anna Mae jutted her chin toward where she'd piled a few of the larger rocks and had draped her shirtwaist and skirt over them. "I didn't think it would take this long, but without any sun in the canyon, they're not drying fast. If you really want me to put them on anyway, I can, though this blanket covers me just as well as my clothes would."

How was she so innocent? Did she have no understanding of the kind of thoughts that could pop into a man's mind?

He stalked to his horse, unfastened the saddlebag, and withdrew the clothes from Cristobal. "Here, put these on."

She took the skirt and shirtwaist from him, then looked down. "You bought me clothes?"

"Just get dressed. Please." He turned back around, his eyes finding a bump in the canyon wall to stare at.

More rustling sounded behind him. "Why did you buy me clothes?"

"Because yours are soiled, and I figured you'd like something fresh to wear for our journey home."

"Our journey home? Did you procure a horse for me? When do we get it?"

"We don't. Velez's men know who you are and that I'm with you, that the two of us are hiding together. They are putting pressure on the people in the neighboring towns to give any clues that might lead to finding us. That means if someone sells me a horse and Velez's men figure it out, an example would be made of their entire family."

Even with his back facing her, he could still hear her quick intake of breath.

"There's a bounty on my head too."

He felt something touch his shoulder, and he turned to find Anna Mae fully clothed and standing just behind him. The shirt was a little too large for her and hung lower on her shoulders than was proper, but the skirt seemed to fit well enough.

"I'm sorry about the bounty." Her voice was soft as she peered up into his eyes.

He scrubbed a hand over his face. "You're not the one who should be apologizing. I misread the situation. Seems staying in Mexico with you made things worse, not better like I thought."

"You had no way of knowing."

But maybe he should have. Was he a fool for thinking a prison cell would contain Velez's power? Or that his son wouldn't want revenge for all the Velez family had lost?

But how many men had he seen locked up in Texas, their crime rings broken up and reduced to ash? He'd expected the same would happen with Velez in Mexico. He'd known he'd ruffled a few feathers back in Austin simply by taking so many men over the border. But he'd thought leaving Velez in Mexican custody would help smooth over some of that, especially since he'd collected enough evidence to sentence the man to life in prison five times over.

But if he were able to go back and do things over again... "Cain?" Anna Mae rested a hand on his arm. "You can't blame yourself for this."

He sighed. "We leave tonight. Get rested up, because we're going to have to travel by night and stick to the mountains. The moon's fuller than I wanted it to be. I had thought to wait another week, when we'd have enough light to travel by, but not so much light that others could see our movements from a distance. But staying any longer is too dangerous."

"And we'll both be sharing Maverick?" She glanced at the horse.

Cain followed her gaze to where the horse was lying in the shade of the canyon.

Maverick usually seemed large and magnificent, but the saddle he wore suddenly looked awful small—at least for two people.

Now that they had to travel only by night and share a horse, the journey home was sure to take an extra day. That meant he'd spend the next three nights sitting in the same saddle with Anna Mae, her back pressed against his chest, her head tucked under his chin.

How was he going to survive it?

9

"I'd like to mark the Giffard case cold." Jonas set the file on the desk of his boss, Henry Moore, then stepped back so he didn't get any dust from the trail on the shiny wood surface.

"Cold?" Moore set down his sandwich, then picked up the report with his pudgy fingers. "Why does it need to be marked cold? You just solved murder cases for five men, and you didn't even have bodies for four of them."

"Yes, but I had a couple dozen cattle rustlers all willing to turn on each other in exchange for lesser prison sentences. Once one of them started talking, none of them could stop. With Giffard, I've got nothing. All the evidence points to Giffard disappearing into Mexico nearly a year ago, so unless you want to give me permission to go into Mexico after him, there's nothing—"

"You are *not* going into Mexico." Moore jabbed a stubby finger at him. "Do you understand?"

"Yes, sir."

"Good." Moore went back to flipping through the report. "Did you file extradition papers for Giffard?"

"Yes. If he's ever apprehended by the law in Mexico, he'll be extradited."

Moore harrumphed, and Jonas couldn't blame him. They both knew the chances of a man like Albert Giffard running afoul of the law in Mexico were slim.

Jonas had already caught the other three men who'd robbed the bank in Shreveport, Louisiana, last year, but Giffard had made off with his share of the money and hightailed it over the border.

Men in that situation didn't return to the United States. Not ever. After all, Albert Giffard had enough money to live the high life down in Mexico without ever needing to look over his shoulder or worry about the law.

Moore flipped through the file one more time, then tossed it down on the desk. "You've barely been focusing on the case a week. Before that you spent months focusing on the murders in Twin Rivers, while the Giffard case fell to the side. Head down to Laredo and see if you can find anyone who remembers him. Maybe he's got a sweetheart on the border or something, a reason to cross the Rio Grande from time to time."

"Where do you think I've been for the past week?" Jonas gestured to his clothes, which were covered in trail dust. He'd been in the office only long enough to add a few phrases to his report before coming up here to have it marked cold and get a new assignment—hopefully on a case he'd be able to solve.

"Try harder." Moore's hand landed on his desk with a heavy thud. "I want to see this solved."

"There hasn't been a single change in the case in over a year," Jonas growled. "The week I spent down in Laredo was nothing more than a wild-goose chase."

"A week's not long enough to mark it cold."

"Fine. I don't need to mark it cold. Just give me something else to work on too." It wasn't unheard of for Marshals to have multiple cases. After all, that's what had happened last year when he'd been given the murder cases down in Twin Rivers while also working the Giffard case.

"No. I want this Giffard case solved. Now. A paper in Shreveport ran an article on this case just two weeks ago. A quarter of the money from that bank robbery is still missing, and you need to find it."

Jonas threw up his hands. "There's nothing more I can do to solve it without going into Mexico."

Moore planted his meaty hands on the desk and pushed himself up to his full height, which was tall enough that he still managed to look intimidating, even though his large belly protruded well over the waistband of his pants. "No Marshal under my authority is going into Mexico. Do you understand?"

"Then at least assign me another case while I work this one. Or if you don't have another open investigation to give me, I can help Neville with the Velez case."

"Neville doesn't need any help with the Velez case." Moore settled his girth back into his chair and crossed his hands over his chest. "Last summer, you tracked down three out of the four men who robbed that bank in Shreveport. Like I said, the papers in Shreveport have forgotten nothing. They're still running articles about the robbery and Giffard disappearing, and it's making our agency look bad. I want every stone turned before that case gets marked cold. And it's clear giving you a second case to work will only distract you from this one. You probably would have tracked down Giffard sometime last fall had I not also given you the disappearances in Twin Rivers to work."

"Fine. I'll see what I can do." Jonas grabbed the report off the desk, then stormed out of the office.

No cold case? It probably had a lot more to do with Washington than newspaper articles in Shreveport.

After being out of the office for a week, Jonas didn't know

what other cases had been closed, but he could guess that more than one had been marked cold, and there was nothing Moore and Ulrich hated more than a high number of cold cases on the report they sent to Washington.

Never mind that there would be five solved cases on the report thanks to him alone, plus whatever cases Neville and any of the other Marshals had managed to close successfully.

Jonas turned at the end of the narrow hall and tromped down the stairs to the basement, his boots thundering loudly against the crude wooden steps. What was he supposed to do for the next week? Go back to Laredo?

Find something to work on and not tell Moore?

He flung open the door to his office, then stilled. A tall, lanky man sat in the chair facing Jonas's desk, his back to the door.

Jonas had thought his own clothes were dusty, but this man seemed to have dust coating every inch of him, though that hadn't stopped him from setting his boots atop the surface of the desk and crossing them.

At the sound of the door opening, the man turned his head to reveal a thin, chiseled face with high cheekbones and a firm jaw.

Blond hair streaked with silver peeked out from beneath his cowboy hat, and the pale blue eyes the man turned on him seemed to take in everything about his person in a single pointed glance.

Jonas swallowed and stepped inside, his palms suddenly damp. He'd seen pictures of that face in newspaper articles too many times to count. It was something of a legend among Texas lawmen.

But never before had he met the man in person.

"Ranger Whitelaw?" He closed the door behind him.

"You must be Jonas." The man didn't move from his seat,

keeping his boots firmly positioned on the desk, never mind the pile of dirt accumulating around them.

"Ah... what can I do for you, sir?"

"I'm here about my boy."

"Your...? Oh. You mean Cain?" He'd known Cain was the son of Frank Whitelaw, yes, but he'd never once heard Cain mention his father or seen the two of them together. Rumor was Cain's father had little to do with his upbringing but had spent a couple years training him to be a Ranger.

That had all been over a decade ago.

"I need to see the records you have for the Velez case," Whitelaw said, his voice rusty from years spent trailing criminals.

"You mean the files for the murder cases involving Velez's men?"

Whitelaw scowled. "No. I mean the tariff evasion, smuggling, and corruption case."

"I'm... ah... I'm not working that one. And I don't believe we're bringing any smuggling or corruption charges against Velez. Just tariff evasion."

Whitelaw dropped his boots to the floor with a thud, then stood, slowly unfolding his body until Jonas found himself looking up at a man whose hard eyes and taut muscles made him want to take a step backward.

"What do you mean there aren't going to be corruption and smuggling charges?" Whitelaw growled.

"I... uh..." Jonas had the sudden urge to stick his finger in his collar and tug. "You really need to talk to Neville Darrowich."

"Already did. Useless twit."

Right. Of course that was what Frank Whitelaw would think of Neville. "We can go to the evidence room and see if there are any useful files for you in there, and I can pull my old cases from the records room. Otherwise—"

"Let's do that." The Ranger started for the door, his boots echoing loudly against the basement tile.

Jonas rushed to open the door for him, then turned the corner to the hall that held both the evidence and records rooms. He stopped at the first door and unlocked it, then stepped inside and turned on the lights.

Frank let out a low whistle. "Looks like the Marshals store evidence a bit longer than the Rangers."

The man was right. Shelves filled the room, towering from floor to ceiling with any and all manner of evidence stashed in labeled crates and shoved on the shelves. The first part of the room was organized by agent, with each agent assigned a certain section of shelving at the front for ongoing investigations. The evidence for old cases was stored alphabetically by case name on the myriad shelves at the back of the room.

It wasn't uncommon for the Rangers and Marshals to share information on cases. Technically Jonas was supposed to have Whitelaw fill out a form and get it approved by Moore first, but he wasn't of a mind to have another conversation with Moore, and he'd never known a Ranger or Marshal to get in trouble for helping the other agency solve a crime.

He headed toward the long table against the far wall, where new evidence was put until the agent working the case either took it to his office or stored it on his section of the shelves. Three large boxes sat atop the table, all clearly marked "Javier Velez."

Whitelaw raised an eyebrow. "Thought you said you didn't have any files on him."

"Seems like these should be in Neville's office."

"Told you he was a twit."

Jonas took the lid off the first box and pulled out a piece of paper. "Looks like a court transcript from Velez's trial in Mexico. These must have arrived in the last day or two."

"Let me see." Whitelaw grabbed it out of his hand.

Jonas opened the second box, but Whitelaw stopped him before he pulled anything out. "Didn't you say you had records from your murder cases somewhere? Those would be the travelers killed by the rustlers for getting too close to the rustling trails?"

"They're next door in the records room."

"Well, don't just stand there, get them. And files from any other cases you have access to."

"Uh... which cases would those be?" Technically, if a case had been marked either solved or cold, he could pull records from it, even if he hadn't been the one to work it.

"Anything that occurred on the border during the past year from Laredo to El Paso."

Jonas scratched his head. "That covers nearly the entire border."

"I'm particularly concerned about Twin Rivers and Del Rio."

"I'll see what I can scrounge up."

It took him nearly forty-five minutes to collect all the records, but when he returned to the evidence room, Frank Whitelaw was still there poring over papers.

"Did you find anything useful?" Jonas asked as he approached.

"Maybe." He put several papers into a stack. "Need to borrow these for a few days."

Jonas winced. Whitelaw shouldn't be taking evidence from the building, especially evidence for an ongoing case, even though it looked like Neville had no intention of using any of the transcripts from Mexico.

But Frank Whitelaw wasn't exactly the type of man a person said no to.

There was a saying Texans used to describe the Rangers of old, the ones who had come home to Texas just after the Civil

War and worked to maintain order in a lawless land overrun with desperadoes and cattle rustlers. *One riot, one Ranger.*

These days the Rangers were organized more like the army, with frontier battalions under captains who ran missions and maintained order—like Cain and his battalion. But in those early days, each Ranger had gone out into the field alone, and Frank Whitelaw had earned a reputation as a lawman who could bring down an entire gang on his own, sometimes carting as many as four prisoners back to Austin for trial by himself.

"Are those court transcripts you're taking?" Jonas asked.

"I just want a few of the pages that talk about the border."

"You'll return them?"

Whitelaw's eyes narrowed. "You're as straightlaced as the twit upstairs, aren't you?"

"Ah, not really, sir." Once again he had the strange urge to stick his finger into his collar and tug.

He settled for clearing his throat instead. "I moved files from several old cases into my office. You're welcome to go there and read them anytime, but they probably shouldn't be removed from the building, at least not unless you want to file a formal request to have the Marshal records shared with the Rangers."

"Won't be no formal request, because I'm not the one who'll be reading them." Whitelaw pushed himself off the table, then strode toward the door.

It was something Cain would do, start walking away in the middle of a conversation. Jonas rushed to turn off the light and keep up with the Ranger as he headed down the hallway to his office.

"You want me to read through them?"

Whitelaw slanted him a glance. "Do I look like the type of feller to sit in an office all day and read?"

"Ah... no."

"Didn't think so." Whitelaw strode into the office as though it belonged to him rather than Jonas, then stopped and looked him up and down, studying him in a way that made Jonas suddenly want to fidget. "My boy trusts you, don't he?"

And just how was he supposed to answer that? "Cain and I have worked together before, most recently when I was investigating the murders by Velez's gang."

"That's not what I asked."

Jonas drew in a breath. "Yes. At least, I think he does. If my ma or older sister were in trouble, he's the first person I'd ask for help. I can't rightly say whether the opposite would be true for Cain, but I trust him."

"Good."

Whitelaw turned to the box on the desk and started rummaging through the files.

"So is all this about the sheriff's sister getting kidnapped?" Jonas walked behind his desk and sat. "About Cain getting in trouble for going into Mexico again?"

The older man's mouth turned grim. "My boy's been missing for over three weeks now, and I aim to do something about it."

Jonas blinked. "He still hasn't returned?"

"What rock have you been hiding under?"

"I've been in Laredo, trying to track down a fugitive."

Frank snorted. "Ain't no fugitive in Laredo. A man gets that close to the border, he's going to cross it and live the highfalutin life down in Mexico."

"Don't I know it."

Frank picked up one of the case files from a box and started skimming the first page.

"If you want to find Cain, why aren't you in Twin Rivers, or even Mexico?"

The man's mouth flattened into a thin line. "Let's just say the evidence I uncovered led me here first."

Jonas shook his head. "How could it possibly lead you here?"

"You hear they stripped my boy of his position as captain?" Whitelaw slapped the file down on the desk, causing a sharp smacking sound to fill the office. "For going into Mexico and trying to rescue a kidnapped woman? That make a lick of sense to you?"

"They stripped Cain of his position?" Evidently he'd missed quite a bit while he'd been in Laredo. "No, sir. None of this makes sense."

"That's what I thought, too, at first, but I've been in Del Rio for the last three months, trying to make sense of what's going on down there. And in Laredo too." Frank picked up another file, scanned the first page, then dropped it onto the desk beside the one he'd slammed down a few seconds earlier. "The Marshals might be investigating Velez for customs and tariff evasion, but he ain't just smuggling goods. He's smuggling people."

Jonas stilled. "What?"

"That's why you're going to read through these files and look for anything that mentions people."

"You want me to look for people in those files?" He eyed the four large crates, each one of them filled with papers that were sure to mention all kinds of people.

"Velez is smuggling them over the border in droves, and you're going to help me prove it."

"But why?" Jonas raked a hand through his hair. "And what does all this have to do with Cain?"

Whitelaw leveled him with a glare so cold the hairs on the back of his neck turned stiff. "You find the evidence I need, and I'll tell you the rest."

Then the man turned on his heel and left without so much as a word.

Jonas sighed. If that wasn't the most confusing meeting he'd had all year. He reached for the first file Whitelaw had put on his desk. Had the man set it down because he thought it useless or important? Whitelaw hadn't even bothered to say.

Just like he hadn't bothered to say how reading a bunch of old files would help Cain.

10

Anna Mae stared out at the landscape. Dawn peeked over the mountains to her east, the dusky, pink fingers of the sun streaking the deep indigo of the sky.

From her place in the cave at the bottom of the valley, she could just make out the towering, craggy mountains that surrounded them on all sides.

There might be a trail that ran through this valley, but no one had taken it in months. That was why they were on it now, like every path they'd taken for the last two nights. Cain chose the longest, hardest paths, keeping them as far from the roads as possible and hiding from any sound they heard.

Anna Mae rested her back against the wall of the cave where they would hide for the day and stretched out her aching leg. Cain had been right about it being too soon to travel. Her leg had done nothing but grow weaker on the journey, although they'd been able to stave off infection.

But considering what could have happened—she could have died from that rattler bite, Velez's men could have found them, or a hundred other things could have gone wrong—she'd take her leg getting sorer.

If all went according to plan, they would cross the Rio Grande sometime that night, and by this time tomorrow, she'd be tucked into bed at Doc Mullins's office, letting him tend her leg while she visited with Daniel and Charlotte and the rest of her friends.

While Cain left for Alpine.

"We should brush your hair."

She jolted, then looked up to see that Cain had appeared from deeper inside the cave, where he'd stabled Maverick. He held up the hairbrush he'd gotten from his saddlebag, his own freshly brushed hair falling long and free in the early morning light.

She reached for the brush. "It's going to be a rat's nest."

Cain kept hold of it and sat down beside her. "That's why I told you to brush it yesterday."

She winced. She'd been so exhausted when they'd made camp just before dawn that she'd fallen into bed without bothering. She had no one to blame but herself for being that tired, though. Cain had told her to sleep in the saddle, but she hadn't quite been able to let herself, not sitting that close to him, with the heat of his chest radiating into her back and the smell of his soap curling around her.

"Here. Let me help." He patted the ground beside him, indicating she should move closer and turn her back to him, but all she could do was stare.

"Are you serious? You want to brush my hair?"

"Who do you think brushed it while you were sick? It will take you forever to brush it on your own, especially without a mirror."

She glanced at Cain's long hair again. He more than anyone else would know how to comb snarls and desert dust from a person's hair.

"Fine." She scooted around, giving herself an even better view of the towering mountains and forgotten little valley.

Cain set to work, patiently taking the brush through each tangle while keeping his touch tender and gentle. The sounds of the desert coming to life floated around them. The cry of a hawk and the rustling sound of a javelina rooting around for food somewhere in the valley. A gust of wind swept through the sky above, and a jackrabbit darted out from behind a shrub.

He didn't speak, but then, he didn't need to. There was something about the way they sat there, both comfortable with each other while doing something completely mundane and ordinary.

Was this what it would be like to be married to him? Anna Mae couldn't help the lump that rose in her throat. Everyone thought he was gruff and aloof. Did no one see the side of him that held her when she trembled and brushed her hair when it was filled with snarls?

The side that bought her a skirt and shirt so that she didn't have to wear a soiled one and tended her wound more patiently than a doctor?

The lump in her throat grew bigger, and the breath stalled in her lungs. She turned around and grabbed the brush. "I want to do it."

"It will take you twice as long."

"Please, Cain. I can't have your hands in my hair. I just can't. Not when I'm trying to make myself fall out of love with you."

He stiffened beside her, his eyes finding hers in the growing light of dawn. "Now why would you go and say a fool thing like that?"

"I'm sorry. It just… came out." Oh, why hadn't she schooled her tongue and taken a moment to think before letting the first thought in her head tumble out?

"You already know I'm not husband material," he gritted.

"You've tended me for weeks, nursing me back to health,

making sure I'm adequately fed and drinking enough water, asking if I'm comfortable. Brushing my hair when I'm ill or tired. That sounds an awful lot like how a husband would treat an injured wife to me."

His jaw turned hard, the handsome lines of his face suddenly seeming to be formed of stone rather than human flesh. "I'd never be around. Is that what you want? To be married to a man who's gone seven days for each one day he's home? Who never sees his children? Who goes out into the desert with nothing but two guns and his horse, knowing that each time he does so, he might not live to see sundown?"

She swiped a strand of hair behind her ear. "No. I don't want that. It's why..."

She sucked in a breath, her tongue pausing on the words. But what was the point in hiding them? She might love Cain, but it wasn't a sentiment he'd ever return, and that meant she had to find a way to move on. "It's why I've been letting Paul court me."

∽

IT'S *why I've been letting Paul court me.*

Cain's lungs turned to stone, refusing to let him draw breath as Anna Mae's words echoed through the cave.

Behind her, the sun was painting the valley pink and orange, illuminating the mountains in a manner begging to be captured with a sketch. But all he could do was stare into the dark eyes of the woman in front of him.

"You've been letting someone court you?"

It shouldn't have bothered him. Hang it all, how many times had he up and told her to marry one of his men, just so he'd know she was unavailable?

Just so he'd know she was taken care of and protected.

Just so he'd know she'd have that little house with a yard

and the heap of young'uns she'd wanted ever since she was a girl.

But now his chest burned.

It wasn't fair of him to be jealous. He had no business laying any claim to her when he couldn't ever marry her.

But for as long as he'd known her, she'd shut down the attentions of every man who'd ever showed an inkling of interest in her—save him.

And now she was letting another man pursue her?

"Just who is this Paul fellow?" he snapped. "Never heard his name before."

"Sure you have. You know him as Fordham. He runs the trading post for Harrison."

Fordham? That's who she was talking about? Cain rubbed the back of his neck, trying to call up an image of the tall blond man who worked for Harrison. "Used to be a Ranger, didn't he?"

"Yes. He got injured last year and walks with a limp, so he had to leave the Rangers."

Cain gave a nod. "Happens to a lot of good lawmen."

"Does it?" She pressed her lips together, her eyes running down him, and he could almost guess what she was thinking.

"Don't, Anna Mae. I've made too big of a name for myself to get out of being a Ranger that easily. Every outlaw between the Mississippi and the Pacific Ocean knows better than to leave me alive."

Her eyes snapped up to meet his, two warm pools of brown that seemed to go straight down to her heart. "I would never want to see you injured."

He swallowed. No, of course she wouldn't. She was too kind and innocent to ever think such a thing.

Did she realize how beautiful she was sitting there, with the sun creeping into the sky behind her, bouncing off her hair and illuminating the delicate features of her face? It was yet another image that needed to be sketched, but this one would be lovelier than the one he did of just the landscape, because it would have the most beautiful woman in all of Texas in it. He'd draw her hair falling about her shoulders just like it was now, and the neckline of her too-large shirt dipping just a bit lower than was proper.

And her eyes. He never seemed to get them right, not in all the times he'd sketched them, because nothing he could do with his pencils ever conveyed how deep they went or the emotion churning inside them.

Cain swallowed, then reached out, fingering one of the silky locks of hair. He'd have it draped over the front of her shoulder in the drawing, just that one single lock.

"You make me wish things could be different between us." His words were so quiet the cave almost swallowed them. Never before had he thought that of a woman, let alone put voice to the idea.

But never before, in any of his travels or any of his years as a Ranger, had he met someone quite like Anna Mae.

"Maybe they can be." Her voice was soft against the stillness of the cave. "The Bible says he who desires a wife desires a good thing."

He raised an eyebrow. "I suppose that goes right along with your verse about children being a heritage from the Lord."

She nodded. "And the one about it not being good for man to be alone, so God created a help meet for him."

There was a verse in the Bible that said a man shouldn't be alone? Why didn't he know that? But he didn't doubt it was there, because if anyone would have that verse memorized, it would be Anna Mae.

"Do you ever feel lonely, Cain? Even surrounded by all your men, do you ever feel like you just don't… fit?"

He dropped her hair, his body going stiff. "What if I do? Would that change anything?"

"Maybe. Because maybe you could…"

"What? Turn in my badge? Stay in one place? And just what would I do for work in Twin Rivers? Be your brother's deputy? You can't imagine that any more than I can."

"Paul," she said, reaching up and pressing a hand to her mouth. "That's why I need to marry Paul."

"Yeah. You do." The words tasted bitter on his tongue, but he couldn't deny the truth of them. "If it's not good for me to be alone, then it's not good for Paul to be alone either, is it?"

"There's just one problem with my marrying Paul."

"What?"

"If I know he can give me the life I want, why can't I look into my future and imagine myself being happy with him the way I can with…?"

Her words trailed off, but she didn't need to finish them. It already felt as though a knife had been stabbed into his chest then yanked down, slicing through bone and flesh until all he felt was a searing, burning pain where his heart used to be.

"Maybe happiness will come in time," he offered.

"But what if it doesn't? What if I go to bed every night, and I dream of… of someone else? Someone who's not my husband."

"Then I reckon you'd feel much the same as I do now."

"Cain!" She walloped him in the arm, her punch hard enough for it to smart. "Don't say such a thing! Not when you're the one insisting we can't marry. How's that going to help me fall out of love with you?"

"It won't." He pushed himself away from the wall and moved closer, bringing his mouth a hairsbreadth from hers. "Don't reckon this will either."

He leaned forward until their lips touched.

The pull between them was magic. It always had been. He could stop himself from tilting her head to the side and deepening the kiss no more than he could stop the sun from cresting over the mountains.

Her arms came up to wrap around his neck in response, and he hauled her closer, until the warmth of her body pressed against his and their breath tangled. Her hair might be half knotted, but it still felt like silk in his hands; her clothes might be coated in dust from two days of travel, and yet she still carried the sweet smell of a woman.

It was like fire, the two of them together. He'd spent over three weeks alone with her in the desert, acting like a gentleman the entire time. He hadn't once touched her in a way that could be interpreted as anything other than doctorly. And now here he was, on their last day together, kissing her as though she was his sole source of air, as though he just might die of thirst if he didn't drink in every last bit of her.

Oh, and he was ten times a fool for kissing her.

Or maybe he was a hundred times a fool for not doing it more, because there was nothing in all the world quite like kissing Anna Mae Harding.

He finally forced himself to pull back, dragging breath into his burning lungs.

Anna Mae slowly opened her eyes, her chest heaving against that dratted shirt that always hung a little too loose on her shoulders. "You told me never to do that again."

"I know."

"You said there can't be anything between us." She pressed a hand to her mouth.

"There can't."

"So why did you kiss me like that?"

"Because I'm the biggest fool you've ever met." He pushed himself off the rocky floor of the cave. "I'm going to get some shut-eye."

She sprang to her feet as quickly as a mountain lion—never mind the pain it must have caused her leg—and raced around him, blocking his path deeper into the cave.

"Oh no you don't. I deserve a better answer than that."

"I shouldn't have done it, all right? It was wrong of me, because I've got no intention of making an honest woman out of you, not now and not ever." He raked a hand through his hair. "Just think of that kiss as a good-bye."

"Good-bye," she repeated, her eyes shooting fiery little daggers at him. "We've got to stop saying good-bye like this."

Boy howdy, did they ever.

Because the last thing he wanted was to end up standing in front of the preacher with Anna Mae beside him and her brother pointing the barrel of a shotgun at his back.

11

"Just give me the gun. I can make the shot." Anna Mae reached for the rifle resting against the boulder, but Cain repositioned himself, shifting between her and the gun so she couldn't reach it.

"No."

She peered around the rock, her eyes narrowed at the place where the lone desperado sat atop his horse in front of the Rio Grande. Texas was just on the other side of the water, so close she could almost taste it. "We won't be able to cross here if I don't shoot him."

"Not even I can make the shot from this distance," Cain whispered, his eyes pinned to where the outlaw stood guarding the river. "Why do you think I'd let you try it?"

"Because we both know I'm the best sharpshooter in West Texas. If I say I can make a shot, I can make it. Besides, how else are you planning to get past him? There's nothing to cover us once we leave this canyon."

Cain's jaw clamped shut, but he didn't tell her no. Instead, he surveyed the valley. They were tucked into one of the canyons that led through the giant wall of mountains that ran along the southern side of the Rio Grande. Barren, yellow rock covered the earth from the mouth of the canyon down to the narrow strip of grass and shrubs growing by the river. There wasn't so much as a boulder to hide behind if they tried to creep closer, which meant the best thing to do was take the shot now, while the outlaw didn't suspect anything.

Cain had thought they'd have an easier time of crossing the Rio Grande if they did so east of town, but it seemed as though Velez had stationed his men at different crossing points along the river. Anytime there was a canyon that ran through the mountains, there was a man on the bank near the river waiting for them.

The men along the river had delayed them from crossing into Texas during the night, as they thought they'd be able to find a clear place to cross if they headed farther east. But at this rate, they'd have to travel clear down to Del Rio before they just might happen to find an unguarded crossing point.

"Just let me shoot him and be done with it. We know he's all by himself, just like the others. I can shoot him, and we can cross, and that will be the end of it."

"Have you ever shot a person before, Anna Mae?" Cain's gaze whipped to hers, his voice as rough as the rocks beneath their feet. "It's not an easy thing to live with."

She scowled. "It is when the lout kidnapped you."

"I've killed my share of men, but each time it came down to a choice between either my life or the other man's. Both of us weren't going to walk out of the situation alive. But this here is a choice, and we're not going to choose killing. Shoot the horse, then I'll tie the desperado up and take him to Twin Rivers."

"You want to bring him with us?" A hard knot formed in her stomach. "It'll take an extra day to get home, especially if I shoot the horse. We can't put three riders on Maverick, meaning one of us will have to walk. And I..." She swallowed. She just wanted to be home, with Daniel and Charlotte and the rest of her friends, walking the streets of the town where she'd grown up.

Besides, each moment she spent with Cain would only make his leaving harder, especially after the kiss he'd given her yesterday morning.

"As soon as we cross the border, I can get more horses," Cain said. "If you're certain you can make the shot, then take it. Otherwise give me the rifle, and I'll sneak closer before I shoot."

She scanned the desert. There was nowhere to sneak, or at least not that she could tell. Though if anyone could creep through an open stretch of desert undetected, it would be Cain.

She held out her hand. "Let's get this done with."

He handed her the Sharps rifle, which happened to be the exact same model her father had. If she'd shot one bull's-eye with this type of gun, she'd shot a hundred. She settled the barrel in a groove on the boulder, trained the gun on the horse that was about six hundred yards away, and stared down the sights.

Then she paused, letting the air turn still around her and the sound of the wind and river fade. This was the best part about shooting. Not the pull of the trigger or the noise of the gun but the moment right before, when she trained the gun, looked down the barrel, and waited for everything around her to freeze until the only things left in the world were her, the gun, and the target—whatever that might be.

She pulled back the hammer and drew in a breath, stretching out the moment for as long as she could...

And then she pulled the trigger.

The sound of the bullet exploding from the barrel ricocheted through the canyon. The rider turned her direction a sliver of a second before the horse dropped from beneath him.

Cain grabbed the gun from her hand and darted around the boulder. "Put your hands up."

He repeated the words in Spanish, sprinting forward at a full run. Never mind that the horse had pinned one of the desperado's legs as it fell, and he was trying to scramble out from beneath the heavy beast.

Anna Mae left Cain to deal with the outlaw and headed back into the canyon where they'd tethered Maverick.

By the time she reached Cain, the outlaw was on his feet, gesticulating wildly, and Cain had holstered his gun. It seemed a little odd that he wouldn't have tied the man's hands behind his back, but Cain didn't look the least bit concerned. He just stood beside the dead horse, arms crossed over his chest as he listened.

"Please, take me into Texas with you. Take my brother and his family too. He has a wife and children to think of. But I do not want to be here. I do not want to work for Velez. I would have let you cross the river, I swear it. I'll do anything to help you, as long as you kill Velez."

Anna Mae stopped a few paces away. What was the man talking about?

"If you want Velez dead so badly, then why are you riding for him?" Cain drawled the question in that lazy voice he had, sounding as though he didn't care in the least about whatever explanation the desperado gave.

It was a ruse, a kind of shield he used against the world, because Anna Mae had no doubt that if she stepped close enough to see Cain's eyes, they would be sharp and alert, taking in every last detail about the bandit, from the inflection of his voice to the way he kept twisting his hands together to the fear in his eyes.

"He didn't give me a choice," the man blurted. "He doesn't give anyone a choice. Please, I love Mexico, but I would rather take my family to Texas and live in a place controlled by the law rather than a criminal."

"Velez is in prison."

"But his son can run things just as well as his father, and he's collecting men who can fight."

"What will his son do if you refuse to fight?"

The man swallowed. "Kill my younger brother. He's not yet old enough to fight."

"I see." Cain jerked his head toward the river, the other side of which meant freedom. "I still need to arrest you and take you to Twin Rivers with me, but we'll draw up a plea deal once we're there. Your legal testimony in exchange for your freedom."

The man probably should have smiled at the news, but worry twisted his face instead. "And my brother? My parents? What will we do about them?"

"I'll send a messenger for them. They can meet you in Twin Rivers, and you can travel north together with one of the sheriff's deputies."

"Thank you." The man fell to his knees, his hands clasped in front of him as though he were worshiping some sort of god.

Cain's jaw clenched. "Get up. I'm hardly a hero."

"But you are."

"No. I'm a lawman who needs to arrest you." Cain set about tying the bandit's hands, then knotted the other end of the rope to the saddle's pommel, forcing the man to walk the waist-deep water of the Rio Grande while she and Cain rode across on Maverick.

But the man didn't complain once.

And when they stopped at a small ranch a few miles down the river and Cain purchased a second horse, the man wanted to walk beside it instead of ride, since he was a criminal and deserved to be punished.

Cain had rolled his eyes and insisted that arresting someone wasn't going to slow him down, which Anna Mae was grateful for, because she wanted to be home so badly it hurt—almost as much as it hurt thinking about Cain leaving again.

12

He had to take a group of men into Mexico to look for Cain and Anna Mae.

Daniel stared out over the Sierra Madres towering over the southern side of the border. The first rays of dawn inched their way into the eastern sky, allowing him to survey the mountains in the distance. Most people would have considered them majestic and beautiful, rising from the flat valley of the river until they nearly blocked the sky. But all he could think about was the caves where desperadoes could hide and narrow canyons perfect for setting up an ambush.

It would be obvious he and his men were in Mexico. He couldn't creep around the way Cain could. He was a lawman, yes, but he was used to town living. Cain, on the other hand, could disappear into the desert and hunt outlaws for weeks at a time.

But that didn't change the fact that Cain had been only a two-day ride from Twin Rivers when they'd parted ways. There was no way a two-day ride would turn into three and a half weeks.

He had to at least try to find out what happened—even if

the thought of traveling south of the border caused his stomach to cramp and sweat to slicken his hands. After all, he was the sheriff.

At least no one had seen hide nor hair of any more of Velez's men around town since the two he'd captured two weeks ago. Thanks to the arrival of the traveling judge, all six outlaws from his jailhouse were now on their way to the state penitentiary outside of Houston.

Did that mean Eduardo's men had given up on kidnapping Gabriella? Or had they captured both Cain and Anna Mae and were satisfied with their revenge?

Daniel's stomach twisted. Again. That was all it seemed to do these days.

There'd been a time when he enjoyed standing on the office porch each morning surveying the town, a time when he'd taken a certain sense of satisfaction in locking up an unruly drunk or testifying at the trial of a man who'd stolen twenty dollars. But now that the Velez family had set their sights on Twin Rivers, now that almost two-dozen men had been killed, he didn't feel any satisfaction, only worry.

But none of that changed the fact that he needed to round up a posse of volunteers first thing this morning.

None of that changed the fact that as town sheriff, he was expected to—

Wait. Was that dust rising from the trail that led toward Sam's ranch?

This early in the morning?

Daniel clambered down the steps and strode into the street. It was dust all right, from two horses. He doubted Velez's men would approach the town so openly, and riding at such a fast pace, but he unholstered his pistol anyway before starting forward.

One of the horses held two riders, and the other held one.

Could it be Cain and Anna Mae?

As quickly as the thought sprang up, he tamped it down.

He had to stop doing that, letting himself hope each time someone approached the town. His sister been gone for too long to come riding into town as easily as that.

And besides, there were three people in this group, not two.

Daniel lengthened his gait as he strode forward. He still needed to know who was approaching. Maybe trouble had sprung up at Sam's ranch.

It was a bit dark to make out any specific features about the riders, but it almost seemed that there was hair flying out behind one of the riders, and it looked too light to be Sam's wife's red locks.

He glanced at the other horse, which held a rider who looked to have dark hair flying out from behind him.

Or maybe the second rider was a woman. Because that rider was far more slender than the first. Shorter too.

But if the first rider was a man—one with long, light hair—and the second rider was a dark-haired woman…

Could it be Cain and Anna Mae returning with a third person?

Daniel hurried forward, his feet breaking into a run as he holstered his gun.

This time he couldn't help the hope springing up in his chest. His heart hammered against his ribs and sweat beaded on the back of his neck. It seemed to take forever as he ran forward, closer and closer to the approaching horses until their shapes began to grow distinct in the early morning light. One of the riders definitely had blond hair, and the other had hair so dark it was almost black.

"Daniel," a shout rang out from the dark-haired rider, loud enough to wake the entire town.

His body jerked. He'd recognize that voice anywhere.

Anna Mae had returned. After all this time. A tear leaked from the corner of his eye, and he didn't bother to stop it. He increased his pace while Anna Mae's horse barreled toward him.

She showed no signs of slowing until she was nearly atop him. Then she pulled back on her reins and then jumped off the horse.

She landed with a wince, then took and couple awkward steps toward him before he swallowed her in his arms, holding the familiar form of her slender body against his and pressing his face to the top of her head.

How many times had he hugged his sister over the years? Yet never before had it felt so good.

"You're here. You're safe. I thought..." He buried his face back in her hair and held on, wrapping his arms so tightly around her that she was sure to struggle for breath, but he couldn't quite make himself care. "I was so worried."

"Charlotte? The baby?" Tears choked her voice. "How are they?"

"There's no babe yet. Charlotte's about the size of a barn, but you better not tell her I said that."

"It hasn't been born yet?" She pulled back just far enough to meet his eyes.

"No. Soon, though. The doc says any day."

"That's... I..." She sniffled, then burst into tears. "Oh, I'm so happy. I was afraid I would miss it."

"And I was afraid I'd never see you again," he croaked.

"I was coming back. I was always coming back. It just took longer than we expected."

"Longer than you expected? That's one way to put it. Because being here and waiting all that time made me think that..." His throat tightened, and he closed his eyes against the sudden burning sensation overwhelming them.

"It was Cain." She burrowed her head into the crook of his shoulder, her hands gripping his shirt so tightly the wrinkles might never come out. "He saved me. Without him, I would have died."

"She got bit by a rattler," Cain said from somewhere behind them.

"A rattler?" Daniel felt his body turn stiff.

"Yes. And then I ran out of water, and..."

He pressed his sister back against him. His heartbeat had just started to slow, but now it sped back into a full gallop. She must have been only a step from death before Cain found her. "Thank God you're alive."

"It's nothing short of a miracle." Cain came up beside him.

Daniel looked over to find that both Cain and the Mexican with him had dismounted. The Mexican's hands were in cuffs, but he didn't have the hard look on his face that many of Velez's men wore.

"But she's back safe now." Cain slung an arm over Daniel's shoulder and squeezed, never mind that he still held Anna Mae. It was the closest thing to a hug that he ever remembered Cain giving. "Reckon all those prayers you were sending to heaven worked."

"Reckon they did." Daniel nodded to the man in handcuffs. "Who is this?"

"Bernardo," Cain answered. "He's agreed to give us some information about Velez."

Daniel raised an eyebrow. The bandit should definitely be questioned, but only after he saw to his sister. Unfortunately, that meant dropping his arms from around her and taking a step back, then running his eyes down every inch of her.

She looked nothing less than disheveled. Dirt streaked her face and matted her hair, and the shirt she wore was far too big, the neckline dipping lower than it should over her shoulders and collarbone.

He wrapped her in another hug, but only half to hide her dipping neckline, because the other half of him was content to hold her all morning and well into the afternoon. "Where did the rattler bite you?"

"On my ankle. I…"

"It's not fully healed. She needs to get to the doctor." Cain took the reins of both horses and started walking toward town, flicking his hand to indicate Bernardo should follow.

"Is that true?" Daniel asked. "It hasn't healed?"

Her lips twisted. "It was mostly healed, but we had to leave Mexico early. I'm afraid it got worse on the trip."

She took a step away from him. An awkward, limping step.

"Was that why you looked like you were in pain when you dismounted?"

"It doesn't hurt overmuch." She took another limping step toward town.

"That's why she seemed to have disappeared when we took that posse into Mexico." Cain stopped walking with the horses and looked back at them. "She holed up in a shallow cave on the top of the mountain after she got bit."

"I tried to cut out the venom, but then infection set in and…" She looked down at her leg, even though it was covered by her dusty skirt.

"It got infected?" His heart dropped clear down into his stomach. How bad had her fever been? Had she been able to get water? How long had the infection lasted?

At least now he knew why it had taken weeks for her to return, not days.

"Like I said, she needs to see the doc." Cain nodded at Anna Mae. "Her leg wasn't quite strong enough for us to travel, but Velez had figured out we were hiding somewhere in the mountains, and staying any longer was too risky."

Daniel needed no other words from Cain. He swept his sister up in his arms.

"Put me down." She squirmed against his hold. "I can walk the length of the town."

"Carry her." Cain still stood in the middle of the road watching them, with Bernardo at his side. "Her leg has taken a turn for the worse in the last day or so."

Daniel's eyes snapped to his sister's. "Just how bad is it?"

She sighed and looked away. "Bad enough."

"I'm just glad you're safe." He drew her closer, pressing her against him so hard, he was sure to leave bruises while he met Cain's gaze over her shoulder. "Thank you. I can't tell you how much…" His throat closed up. "If you ever need anything, anything at all…"

And there went his throat, refusing to work yet again.

Cain tipped his hat at him. "Just doing my job."

But then Cain's gaze fell to Anna Mae, who was still curled into his arms, and a strange look crept over his face. A moment later Cain shook his head and looked toward town. "Best go take Bernardo to your office and find Harrison so we can write up a plea agreement."

And then the Ranger started off, leaving Daniel to wonder just what the strange look on his face had meant.

∽

It didn't take long for news of Anna Mae's arrival to spread. Before most people had even eaten breakfast, Charlotte, Alejandra, Keely, and Ellie had all crowded into the small sickroom where Doc Mullins had put her.

"I'm just so glad you're safe." Alejandra leaned down and wrapped Anna Mae in a hug, her long black hair silky soft against the hair and skin Anna Mae had yet to wash. "When I learned my uncle's men had you, I thought…" The woman gave her head a small shake, tears filling her eyes.

Anna Mae couldn't blame her. There was no question that if she'd been with Javier Velez's men the entire time she'd been gone, she would be in far worse condition.

"You should have seen how worried your brother was." Charlotte bent down to give her a hug of her own, her full belly pressing into her side. "How worried we all were. Each day you didn't return, it became a little harder to believe you were still alive."

"But I was." She reached out and gripped the hand of the woman she'd grown up with. "With the infection in my leg, we were waiting until I was well enough to travel. I wish there had been a way to send word back to everyone, to let you know I was all right."

The conversation continued around her, Keely and Ellie each taking turns at her bedside, hugging her and saying how worried they'd been.

She'd wanted to be back in Twin Rivers the entire time she'd been stuck in the desert, but she hadn't realized quite how good it would feel to finally know she was safe. To finally be surrounded by friends once again. She'd missed each and every one of them. And her brother and Sam and Wes.

And oh, hang it all, she might have even missed Harrison—not that she'd ever admit it aloud.

"What was it like being trapped out there in the desert?" Keely leaned down to give her a second hug, then squeezed her hand, worried lines etched across the quiet redhead's forehead. "I remember when I was hiding from the Wolf Point Gang, and it was terrifying."

"Yes." Ellie stood at the foot of the bed, bouncing her baby, Madeline, on her hip. "I've never had to hide from anyone, at least not like that, but I'm sure I would have been terrified too."

Anna Mae shifted on the bed. "At first, it was terrifying. Not the abduction part, but—"

"Wait." Alejandra squeaked, her dark eyes shining with fear. "You weren't terrified when strange men grabbed you outside Fort Ashton and carted you over the border?"

She shrugged. "I mean, I was a little scared, sure. But I was pretty certain I'd be able to escape—and I did. It was after I got bit by the rattler and was stuck on a mountain by myself that I was terrified."

Even now, if she closed her eyes, she could still remember the dryness coating her throat and the pounding in her head. The way every inch of her sunburned skin felt as though it had been singed to a crisp. How leg burned as though a fire had been kindled atop it, and her entire body had cried out for water she didn't have.

"I was beyond terrified, really. Because I thought what the rest of you did, that I was going to die. But after Cain found me..." She licked her lips. "Let's just say, I didn't wonder whether I would make it back home."

She hadn't even been scared when he'd gone into the village and found out how hard Velez's son was looking for them. Or when he returned and said they suddenly needed to leave.

"That's because he's an excellent Ranger," Charlotte said. "Daniel claims he's the best at his job, and the Ranger headquarters in Austin knows it."

She believed as much. Because even with everything that had happened, she'd never once doubted that Cain would keep her safe. She fell back onto the pillows, a yawn fighting to escape her lips while she met her dearest friend's eyes. "I'm just glad to be home. And I'm glad you didn't give birth while I was gone. I want to be here to meet my little niece when she arrives."

Charlotte smoothed her hand over her stomach, a soft smile creeping onto her face. "Daniel swears it will be a boy."

"He's wrong. It's going to be a girl."

Charlotte shook her head. "You're ridiculous, do you know that? Here you've been gone for over three weeks, leaving all of us to think you died, and then you come home ready to strike up an argument with your brother."

She rolled her eyes. "That's not my fault. If he'd just admit I'm right, there'd be nothing to argue about."

The entire room broke into laughter.

Or at least everyone but Alejandra laughed. The Mexican woman still had a serious look on her face.

"Were you treated with respect while you were gone? You were in the desert for so long, and I just want to make sure... well... you weren't compromised in some way. Were you?"

Every muscle in her body turned suddenly tense. She pushed herself up from her pillows and narrowed her eyes. "Cain might have long hair and travel around like a vagrant, but he doesn't mistreat women. I'll have you know he was a perfect gentleman the entire time."

Except for their kiss. There hadn't been anything gentlemanly about that.

Or the way he'd brushed her hair. Or...

Oh, good heavens. Most of Cain's behavior might have been respectable, but little about it had *felt* respectable. He had even made tending her leg feel intimate.

"I wasn't talking about Cain." Alejandra twisted her hands together, a frown marring her face. "My uncle's men are not kind, and they had you for two days."

"Oh. That." Anna Mae sank back against the pillows.

The Mexican woman's cheeks had turned red, probably because she was asking such a personal question, but her brow was still furrowed with worry.

And considering Alejandra's own experience with her uncle and his men, her worry made sense.

What had made her think Alejandra was talking about Cain in the first place? "I'm sorry I misunderstood. None of your uncle's men compromised me. They thought I was your sister, and they were under orders from your stepcousin, Eduardo, to treat me well because he still has plans to marry your sister off, from what I understand."

"*Sí.*" Alejandra gave a firm nod. the worry in her eyes turning into determination. "He still has plans to marry Gabriella to that monster he picked, and we are keeping her well guarded until the rest of this business can be dealt with."

"I'm glad to hear that."

Gabriella seemed far too sweet and kind to be able to escape her uncle's men if she was taken, and Anna Mae doubted the sixteen-year-old had the skills to survive in the desert either.

"Not that all this talk of kidnapping and escape isn't... er... interesting, but what does the doctor say about your leg?" Ellie stepped nearer to the foot of the bed, Madeline now curled up against her shoulder as though about to sleep. "Does he expect you to make a full recovery?"

Anna Mae looked down at her aching appendage, even though she couldn't see it beneath the cover. "He does, yes. He says I can return to my room at the A Bar W tomorrow or the day after. He just wants to make sure the infection is gone first."

"You won't be going back to the A Bar W, at least not at first," Charlotte announced. "You're coming home with Daniel and me until you've had a full recovery."

"You're about to have a babe."

"We can make do with you sleeping on the sofa for a few days."

Anna Mae slanted a glance at Keely. "It's kind of you to offer, but I'm sure Keely and Wes can take care of me."

Keely smiled. "We can, but it won't be the same as being with family while you recover. You should go home with Charlotte, at least until the babe is born."

Anna Mae sighed. Truth be told, she had little desire to keep arguing. Staying with Charlotte and Daniel for a few days felt right. Now that her parents had moved to Houston, her brother's house was as close to being at home as she could get, and she wouldn't mind letting Charlotte dote on her for a few more days. "All right. I'll go home with you."

A light knock sounded at the door. "I heard you were receiving visitors?"

She glanced up to find none other than Paul Fordham standing in the doorway, holding a small sack tied with a bow.

Every eye in the room turned to Paul, then back to her.

Anna Mae tried to smile, but it felt a bit stiff.

And was it just her, or had the air in the room turned suddenly warm?

"Paul, how nice to see you." Charlotte stepped away from the bed and smiled, her voice a bit too bright. "I didn't realize you'd be stopping by to see Anna Mae, but I'm glad you did."

Her best friend's gaze cut back to her, eyes narrowed accusingly.

Anna Mae found herself shifting on the bed. So maybe she'd been a little hesitant to tell her friends just how interested Paul Fordham was in her.

"But I best be going." Charlotte settled a hand atop her stomach as she looked back at Paul, the pitch of her voice still too forced. "The doc says I shouldn't be on my feet too much before the baby comes."

"I need to get back to the fort," Alejandra exclaimed before sending her a look similar to Charlotte's.

Anna Mae swallowed. Looked like she'd have some explaining to do with her friends later.

"I have some shopping to do at the general store." This from Keely, who was already scurrying toward the door where Paul stood.

He had to step aside so Keely could pass him, which only brought him farther into the room. The rest of her friends all rushed out on Keely's heels, leaving Paul and her alone in a matter of seconds.

Silence filled the air, and Paul shifted on his feet for a moment before approaching the bed.

"I hope you don't mind me stopping by. The doc's wife said you were taking visitors, but I didn't expect everyone to leave."

"I didn't either." She just might need to strangle Charlotte later. She could understand her other friends leaving, but Charlotte?

"I brought this for you." He thrust the small paper bag at her. "Had Mrs. Cunningham down at the general store wrap it up real pretty."

She reached out and opened the sack, then couldn't help the smile that pulled at her lips. "Peppermint sticks." They were tied together in a fancy-looking bundle with a red ribbon and a bow. "Thank you."

His cheeks turned red. "I remember you saying you liked them."

"It's a lovely gift." She stifled a yawn, then set the candy down on the bedside table.

"How are you feeling?" Paul pulled the little wooden chair from the corner over to the side of the bed and sat. "Are you in any pain?"

"More than anything, I'm tired. It's been a long journey from Mexico. As for my leg, it's been worse, but it was feeling better than this before we left Mexico."

Paul pulled off his hat and leaned forward. "When I got news about what happened, I was so worried. More worried than I've ever been about anything before in my life. I wanted to ride off into the desert and track you down myself, but my leg…"

He stretched the appendage that caused him to walk with a limp. Both the limp and the pain from his broken leg seemed to be improving, but the doctor wasn't sure Paul would ever be able to walk normally or be entirely free of the pain.

"I'm sure you were needed at the fort to keep things running."

He gave a brief nod. "It's a lot of work running the post and managing the guards."

"Of course it is." She knew from Alejandra that just about everyone at Fort Ashton considered Paul honest and gentlemanly, and he was especially well liked and respected among the guards.

And yet she couldn't imagine Paul being the one to rescue her in the desert.

Without his injury, he might have been able to track her down, but would he have known how to treat infection? Would he have found a canyon that concealed them for over a week as they waited for her leg to heal? Would he have taken command of the situation in a way that quelled her fear of being discovered?

Like Cain had?

The smile on her face suddenly felt tight.

"Do they expect your leg to heal fully?" he asked.

"They do." Though she almost felt bad saying so, considering his situation.

"Well, ah, even if it doesn't... I mean, I hope it heals an' all, but if something goes wrong..." He grimaced and rubbed the back of his neck. "What I'm trying to say is that I enjoy being with you, Anna Mae. You've got a way of brightening a room and being friendly to everyone and always trying to help others. So if your leg doesn't heal, that won't make a difference to me. I'd still like to court you and maybe, one day..."

His face colored again, but that was part of what endeared him to her. Most other men would have stormed into her sickroom and offered to marry her with the first five words out of their mouths. But not Paul. He wasn't even willing to bring the topic up fully.

She reached out and patted his leg. "That's awful sweet of

you, though there's plenty of cause right now to hope for a full recovery."

"Yes, yes, the entire town is hoping for that very thing, I'm sure." He ran his eyes down the length of her, then scooted his chair closer to the bed, his face serious. "Now tell me, what was it like being out in the desert with Cain Whitelaw. Did he treat you respectable?"

She felt her cheeks heat. Why was everyone suddenly so concerned about how she was treated in the desert? Though Alejandra's question pertained more to her uncle's men than Cain, it still felt odd having so many people ask.

Cain had been stationed in Twin Rivers for nine months and hadn't so much as looked in a woman's direction—not even hers. And he'd never once done anything that could be construed as unrespectable or ungentlemanly.

"Cain treated me with the utmost respect," she finally managed. "And I'll admit to being feverish for over half the time I was gone, so there's much I don't remember."

Paul tucked a finger into the collar of his shirt and tugged. "Right. It's just that... ah... you were alone with a man in the desert for an awful long time."

"Are you accusing me of something?" she asked, her voice soft.

"No, no. I would never... What I'm trying to say is..." He blushed, and this time the color from his cheeks spread clear up to the top of his forehead. "Just like your leg, whatever happened to you in the desert doesn't make no difference to me. I enjoy your company, and I'm not one to put much stake in what the gossips are saying."

"There's gossip?" Good heavens. She'd only been in town for two hours. How could there possibly be gossip?

Paul shifted again, almost as though the chair beneath him grew more uncomfortable with each second he stayed seated.

"It's just that I don't think anyone was expecting you and Ranger Whitelaw to be alone together for so long."

"I said it before, and I'll say it again. Ranger Whitelaw was a perfect gentleman to me."

But each time she made a declaration about Cain being a gentleman, she felt a little twinge in her chest.

Had Cain been the perfect gentleman? Not with the kiss they'd shared.

But he'd been a perfect Ranger, which meant he'd gotten her out of Mexico safely.

She pressed her palm to her breastbone, which had suddenly started to ache.

"What about the kidnappers?" Paul asked, scooting his chair just a tad bit closer to the bed. "Did they violate you?"

She stilled, the breath in her lungs constricting until the air inside them felt as cold as ice. "What?"

He cleared his throat and looked down, as though afraid to even meet her gaze. "I asked if the outlaws violated you."

The question seemed strange and invasive, never mind that it would have been one of the first questions out of her father's mouth, and he'd spent over two decades as sheriff. Daniel had probably asked Cain about it the moment the two of them were alone, and Alejandra had wanted to know as well.

Cain had even asked about it himself after he'd found her in the desert.

And yet when Paul asked, it almost felt as though the question itself was a kind of violation.

And if she couldn't answer such a question from Paul without feeling uncomfortable, how was she supposed to marry him after Cain left?

13

"You want to let him go? Even after he tried to prevent you and Anna Mae from crossing the river?" Harrison looked up at Cain from where he sat behind the spare deputy's desk in Daniel's office, drafting Bernardo's plea agreement.

"Yes." Cain lifted his coffee mug to his lips, intending to take a long sip.

"Absolutely not." Daniel pushed to his feet from where he'd been sitting at his own desk, a hard look on his face. "That man is not going free in exchange for signing a piece of paper."

"He didn't do anything illegal." Cain leaned back against the table where coffee and biscuits had been set out.

Bryce and Abe, Daniel's two deputies, looked between them. Both men had come into the office with Harrison that morning, wanting the details of what had transpired during the weeks he'd been gone.

"Seems to me like the feller in the prison there tried to stop you from bringing Anna Mae home," Abe said in a voice that half sounded like an accidental whistle. The white-haired man had been serving Twin Rivers since before Daniel was born, and he'd had one too many teeth knocked out in the line of duty to speak normally anymore.

"No. Bernardo was *supposed* to stop me from bringing Anna Mae home. But he didn't even try to put up a fight. Once he saw the business end of my rifle, he did everything he could to help me bring her back here."

"Because my sister shot the horse out from under him," Daniel muttered. "Otherwise, he wouldn't have been so helpful."

Cain grabbed one of the biscuits from off the table and took a bite, then grimaced. The thing was nearly as hard as hardtack, and it had an awful strong baking powder taste.

Abe crossed his arms over his chest and cackled. "Now you see why there's so many of them sitting on that there table. We've missed Anna Mae's baking 'round these parts."

"This thing is terrible." Cain tossed the rest of the biscuit into the wastebin.

"Don't throw it in there." Daniel scowled. "Charlotte will notice."

"Is Charlotte the one who made them?"

Daniel's scowl turned into a wince. "She's convinced she needs to learn to be a better cook."

"I can tell Anna Mae's not the one teaching her." Cain took a sip of coffee, letting the bitter brew wash the baking powder taste out of his mouth. Then he glanced at the wall that separated Daniel's office from the jailhouse where Bernardo sat locked in one of the cells.

There was a part of him that understood where the others were coming from, but he just couldn't see prosecuting a man who hadn't gone through the trouble to pull a gun on him and had been ready to confess every last detail about working for Velez.

"Bernardo doesn't want to go back to Mexico. He wants to go north. It's the first time I've met someone who wanted to get away. The men before, the rustlers, were set in their actions, angry we caught them, and determined not to give us any information until we raided *La Colina*. And it was clear everyone was going to prison."

Cain took another gulp of coffee. Hang it all, but he still couldn't get that baking powder taste out of his mouth. "Bernardo sings like a bird and wants to be as far away from Velez as possible. Says Velez's men threatened to kill his family if he didn't join them. That's not a man I want to bother prosecuting. We're better off moving him to a place where he can't be used against us again and being done with him."

"And what about his family?" Harrison tapped the end of his pen on the desk. "If he joined with Velez to protect his brother and parents, he's not going to move away and do nothing while Velez goes after everyone else."

"I said I'd send someone to collect them and escort them north of the border. That was his only condition."

Harrison set his pen down, his eyes narrowed. "Do you think Bernardo is the only person Velez has coerced into working for him?"

Cain shrugged. "Hard to tell, but I will say this—the villagers are living in fear of him. Most of them don't want anything to do with him, but there are snitches for Velez all over, and the risk of standing up to him is too great. No one wants their house burned, or their sons and daughters taken."

"You had trouble getting reliable information about Velez before, even when you offered to pay handsomely for it." Daniel rubbed his jaw. "I thought it was because everyone in northern Mexico supported him. But what if it was because they were too afraid to talk? What if Velez has been threatening them all along?"

"I'm wondering the same thing, but it's a bigger problem than we can solve by ourselves. I'm going to Alpine to get my men." Cain shoved himself away from the table. "I should be back next Monday, and I'll assign one of my Rangers to bring Bernardo's family north."

"You're coming back?" Bryce asked. The deputy with the droopy mustache had been quiet for most of the conversation, but now he was looking at Cain as though he'd grown a third ear on the middle of his forehead.

"Did you expect anything different? Eduardo Velez's men kidnapped an American, and you're guarding Gabriella night and day because you expect them to return and abduct her next. The man seems bent on revenge, and there's only one way to handle that."

Daniel rubbed the back of his neck. "I agree about Eduardo being bent on revenge, but is Austin going to let you come back here?"

"Don't see how they'll have much of a choice after I telegraph them."

"They didn't order the rest of your men here after Anna Mae was kidnapped."

"I'm sure they will once they know how big of a threat Velez is."

"No." Daniel gave a small shake of his head. "You're misunderstanding. I sent them a telegram explaining everything a few days after we returned from our search and you seemed to have disappeared. Bryce rode all the way to Alpine to send it, and I told him to wait a few hours for a response."

"I waited for two days." The side of the deputy's mustache twitched. "One never came."

Cain's shoulders tensed. "You told them I was missing, and they didn't send so much as a word in response?"

Let alone his entire Ranger unit down from Alpine? What had Austin been thinking? "I telegrammed them when I first left Alpine to help search for Anna Mae, so headquarters knew where I was. Maybe your telegram didn't arrive for some reason."

Bryce's lips pressed into a flat line beneath his mustache. "I sent a second one. Got nothing."

Cain frowned. It seemed odd. Had Bryce's telegram somehow gone to the wrong place in Austin? Or maybe there was a new clerk in the office who hadn't realized what the telegram meant. A missing Ranger was nothing to sneeze at, especially when the man was the captain of a frontier battalion and happened to have the best mission success rate in all of Texas.

"I'm sure once Austin hears from me directly, they'll give me permission to bring my men back here. Headquarters originally sent me here to handle the rustling last summer, and this mess is a direct result of that. I don't see how they could deny my request." Though he'd be lying if he claimed the story about the unanswered telegrams didn't bother him at least a little.

His legs felt stiff and jerky as he crossed the room and reached for his hat hanging by the door.

"Are you heading out now?" Daniel asked.

"Don't see any point in lollygagging." He settled his familiar, dusty hat atop his head.

Daniel came toward him, his eyes lined with concern.

For what, Cain didn't know. He wasn't the one being left to defend a town on the border with a dozen or so cowhands masquerading as deputies.

"Don't you want a meal before you go?" Daniel asked.

"That depends. Is Charlotte cooking?"

The room erupted into laughter. Or rather, everyone except for Daniel laughed.

The glare the sheriff sent him was probably cold enough to freeze the hide off most men.

"At least stop by the fort and have yourself a meal." Harrison set his pen down and slid the plea agreement across the desk. "Take any supplies you might need, too, including a horse for Bernardo. Just return it when you come back with the Rangers."

"Thanks. I'll do that. Seems simplest." Cain reached for the doorknob, then paused and turned back. "Be careful. If Velez returns before I do, he won't be easy to reckon with."

"We've got volunteer deputies coming in and guarding the town at night, and a dozen and a half men willing to come and fight at any sign of trouble. We'll protect our town." Daniel's eyes gave off a determined glint, as though almost daring Cain to contradict him.

But how many men would Velez's son have if he rode into town? More than eighteen, and some of them were sure to be hired guns who could kill a half dozen of Wes's cowhands in under a minute.

Which was why he needed to get his men and return to Twin Rivers as soon as possible.

"See you in a few days." Cain tipped his hat at Daniel, then walked out the door and started down the boardwalk.

He'd head to Fort Ashton for breakfast and supplies in a few minutes, but first he wanted to make sure Anna Mae was settled. A man didn't spend several weeks trying to save a woman without stopping by to check on her before he left town.

He passed the handful of buildings between the sheriff's office and the doc's, then knocked twice before entering the waiting room. It was empty, but the door to the small sickroom to the left was open. He crossed the simple room that had been set up like a parlor, then stopped just outside the sickroom.

Voices floated to him. The first one definitely belonged to Anna Mae, but the other voice sounded masculine.

He frowned. Who was in there? He'd just left Daniel and Harrison at the sheriff's office. Had Sam and Wes stopped by to visit with their wives?

No. He took a step closer, allowing him to see there was just one person in the room with her, and it wasn't Sam or Wes.

He took another step, bringing the man fully into view. A western-style shirt, broad shoulders, and sandy blond hair. It was none other than Paul Fordham.

Cain's jaw hardened. The lout might be sweet on her, but that didn't mean he needed to visit her as soon as she got back to town. Didn't he realize that she'd be tired and need rest?

He was sitting right beside her bed with a goofy, moonstruck look on his face. And this after Anna Mae had said she wasn't sure if she could see herself becoming his wife.

Fordham said something too quiet for him to hear, but a faint smile turned the corners of Anna Mae's mouth up.

Something twisted inside Cain's chest.

It wasn't right, another man sitting there talking to her, pulling smiles from her mouth and causing a blush to tinge her cheeks. Especially while she lay in bed, with her freshly brushed hair cascading down her shoulders and back.

Just that image alone would cause many a man's mind to wander where it shouldn't.

He leaned forward a bit, trying to hear what they were saying.

"There's no need for rumors or gossip, I assure you. Ranger Whitelaw was a perfect gentleman to me."

He straightened. Him? They were talking about him?

"What about the kidnappers?" Fordham asked. "Did they violate you?"

Cain's hands tightened into fists at his sides. As though that was any of the man's business.

"Because if they did, I want you to know that I think there's more to a woman than her virtue, especially when it's taken against her will. So even if you're not—"

"No one touched her." Cain stepped into the room. "Not the kidnappers. Not me. No one."

He'd be hanged if he was going to stand there and do nothing while another man insinuated Anna Mae had been compromised.

Both sets of eyes flew to him, then Fordham scrambled up from his chair. "Ranger Whitelaw, it's… ah… it's good to see you." The man limped toward him and extended a hand. "Thank you for bringing Anna Mae back to Twin Rivers. She was missed."

"I can see that." And the thought of the man in front of him missing her made him want to tear something apart.

"Anna Mae and I were just visiting for a spell." Fordham's face turned a full shade of red. "I didn't realize you were there."

Good thing Anna Mae wasn't planning to marry the lout. Sure, he seemed decent enough for most women, but he'd be entirely wrong for Anna Mae. She needed a man who was stronger than her, not someone she would trample into dust the first time they got into an argument.

"I'm on my way out of town, but I need to talk to her for a few minutes first, if you don't mind."

"Sure thing." Fordham bobbed his head. "I'll just step into the waiting room for a minute."

The waiting room? What was the man going to do? Stand there and time how long he and Anna Mae talked?

"Actually, I'm feeling a bit tired." Anna Mae sent Fordham another one of those smiles that looked entirely too soft and sincere. "Perhaps you could come back this afternoon."

"Right, right." The man's face turned an even deeper shade of red. "The trading post is scheduled to open soon anyway. I really should get back to the fort, but I'll see if Harrison will let me take a long lunch and come for a second visit."

"That sounds lovely." She sent him another smile.

Confound it. Didn't Anna Mae understand she couldn't go around smiling at men like that?

And Fordham had certainly noticed, because now his ears had turned red right along with the rest of his face.

"See you in a few hours." The man turned and limped back to the empty wooden chair, where he grabbed the hat hanging on the back of it. Then he moved toward the door with a lopsided gait.

The limp wasn't big enough to prevent him from walking about town, but if he were a Ranger who needed to run down an outlaw, it would mean his death.

Cain had to admire the man a bit for moving on, finding a job that suited him, looking for a wife to share his new life with —just as long as that wife wasn't Anna Mae.

Still, Cain would rather be shot dead than get an injury that prevented him from being a lawman.

The moment Fordham disappeared through the doorway, Anna Mae collapsed back into her pillows and yawned.

"How long did he keep you awake talking?" Cain moved to her bedside and pulled the covers up over her shoulders. "You should have told him you were tired."

Or better, Fordham should have noticed and left on his own.

"He was being sweet." Anna Mae's eyelids drifted halfway shut. "And I didn't want to disappoint him."

"It's not sweet to ask if you were violated," he growled.

She sighed, the breath rushing out of her in one long gust as she tugged a pillow to her chest and nestled deeper into the bedding. "It seems to be the question everyone is most interested in, even my friends."

He settled himself into the chair Fordham had vacated. "Others have asked?"

"Alejandra was concerned about how her uncle's men treated me."

"That makes sense."

"It does. And even though the question made me a bit uncomfortable, it made sense for Paul to ask too."

Paul. Did she have to call him by his first name?

He drew in a breath, and silence filled the space between them, but it didn't feel awkward. It felt comfortable, normal, almost like he was welcome to sit there and watch as she drifted off to sleep—just like he'd done in the desert.

Which was odd.

Since when did he want to sit around and watch a person fall asleep?

"I'm leaving," he barked out, his voice a bit rougher than he intended.

"I know. I would never expect anything different of you." She yawned again, then ran her gaze over him before finally bringing her eyes up to his. Two wide pools of brown stared back at him, so deep and endless that it seemed he could see into her very soul. "Tell me, do you leave broken hearts behind in every town you visit?"

His throat felt suddenly tight, the chair beneath him unbearably hard, but she was looking up at him with those wide, vulnerable eyes, as though she expected more of an explanation from him. "I don't. And I swear, in all the places I've been and all years I've been a Ranger, you're the only woman fool enough to up and fall in love with me."

"I won't argue with you about it being foolish."

"That's not what I meant." He reached out and took her hand, brushing his thumb over her knuckles.

Silence stretched between them, but that didn't stop their gazes from tangling. This time her eyes seemed to search his, as though she might find the answer she sought if she just looked hard enough.

"None of this makes sense," she finally said. "If a man desires a wife, he desires a good thing. Remember?"

"I remember." Just like he remembered the verse about it

not being good for a man to be alone. He'd even looked that one up. It was from Genesis 2, when God had created Eve to be Adam's help meet.

Anna Mae sighed. "Don't look so worried. If it's any consolation, I'm still trying to fall out of love with you."

Good. The word was there, on the tip of his tongue, and yet he couldn't quite force himself to say it. Instead, he reached out and took her hand. "And how's that working?"

"It's harder than you think."

"I'm sorry." His thumb stroked the back of her hand, the action natural and effortless. "I never meant for you... for this..."

"It's not your fault. You never did anything to show you were interested in courting me or make me think there could be a future between us. I'm the one who let feelings grow when I knew they would never be returned."

He drew in a breath. "Who said they would never be returned?"

"You, when you said you'd never marry me."

It was probably better to let her think that he didn't carry any feelings for her or dream about her every night or replay the kisses they'd shared each time he found himself with nothing to think about.

He shifted in his chair. "I need to head out, but I should be back at the beginning of the week with my men."

Her drooping eyes sprang open. "Wait. You're coming back?"

"I intend to track down Velez's son, the one running everything, and see to it his father's criminal enterprise is destroyed once and for all."

"So you'll be going back into Mexico?"

"Yes."

"But you don't have jurisdiction there."

"It doesn't matter. Eduardo Velez wants revenge, and it's my job to stop him. Unless you want to wake up one morning and find Velez's men have razed your town."

She swallowed. "Be careful."

"I will. Just as long as you agree to stay away from Paul Fordham while I'm gone."

Her lips twisted into a scowl. "He fancies me."

"And how does that make him different from every other unmarried man in Texas?"

"We talked about this. I want a husband and a family. A house. All things you'll never be able to give me as a Ranger."

Even if he wasn't a Ranger, he wasn't sure he'd be able to give them to her. He was the son of a vagabond lawman and a cantina girl, named Cain because his father considered his birth a curse.

He could leave the Rangers tomorrow and become the town barber, and he'd still never make a decent enough husband for any woman, let alone Anna Mae Harding.

That didn't stop him from sinking down onto his knees beside her and smoothing a strand of hair away from her face —just like he'd done countless times when he'd been caring for her in the desert.

Just like he'd imagine doing in his dreams later that night.

"You deserve those things, darling. Just because I can't give them to you doesn't mean you shouldn't have them. But I don't think Paul Fordham is the right man to give them to you either."

Her eyes drifted shut again, staying closed for so long he almost wondered if she'd fallen asleep. Then they opened again, slowly, brimming with tiredness and yet somehow still clear. "I understand why you have to go."

He leaned closer. "You do?"

"Yes. Because there might be another woman like me out there somewhere, in the desert with a rattler bite, needing to be rescued. Or a sheriff like my brother who ends up facing a powerful band of outlaws simply because he's trying to maintain law and order. You're good at your job. And you being anything other than a Ranger will lead to people dying, and I can't be responsible for pulling you away from that."

I love you.

The words almost slipped from his tongue, but he caught them, held them back just in time.

Then he blinked. He loved her? When had that happened?

Sure, she might be the only woman he'd ever met who understood his need to be a Ranger, but that didn't mean love...

Did it?

He gave his head a small shake. It wasn't worth thinking about. His path was already set, and Anna Mae wouldn't be walking it with him.

But he couldn't quite stop himself from leaning forward, from tucking her hair behind her ear, even though the hair had never really moved from the last time he'd smoothed it away from her face.

Then he leaned forward and placed a kiss on her forehead. Her skin felt warm and soft beneath his lips, and it made him wonder what it might feel like to—

"What's going on in here?"

Cain jumped away from Anna Mae, then scrambled to his feet and turned toward the doorway.

The doctor's wife, Mrs. Mullins, stood there with a tray of food in her hands, her face twisted into a horrified expression.

"Mr. Whitelaw, I don't know what might have happened between the two of you in the desert, but such behavior is not acceptable in this household. Both the doctor and myself are decent, God-fearing folk." She narrowed her gaze at Anna Mae. "I thought you were too."

Anna Mae scooted herself up on her pillows, her entire face now a bright shade of red. "I'm sorry, Mrs. Mullins. Cain—that is, Captain Whitelaw—was just bidding me farewell and—"

"Kissing is not an appropriate way to say farewell."

Anna Mae ducked her head. "I understand. Please forgive me."

"She's done nothing she needs to apologize for." Cain moved in front of Anna Mae, blocking her from Mrs. Mullins's stern gaze. "I was the one who kissed her forehead, not the other way around."

It was probably the wrong thing to say, because the older woman's face pinched tighter, the wrinkles around her mouth only becoming more pronounced.

"Maybe so, but she didn't put a stop to your kiss the way a respectable woman would, now did she? And if the two of you are kissing in the middle of my husband's office, I hate to think what you were doing for all those weeks in the desert."

"Staying alive," he gritted. "That's what we were doing. And that wasn't even a real kiss. It was a brush on her forehead, just like the one Daniel gave her when we rode into town earlier."

"Daniel is her brother," the woman seethed.

"And I may as well be. We grew up together."

She stomped her foot on the floor, her gaze not leaving his for so much as a second. "There was nothing brotherly about what I just witnessed."

She had him there, because the thoughts going through his head when he'd leaned forward to kiss Anna Mae's forehead had been about as far from brotherly as a man could get.

But he'd be hanged if he would stand there and let some old biddy tell him—

"Please, stop." Anna Mae pressed a hand to her forehead, as though a headache was starting to form. "I'm tired and I'd like to sleep. Mrs. Mullins, thank you for your warning about my behavior. I fully believe Cain meant the kiss in a brotherly way, but I understand how it must have looked. I will, of course, be more circumspect in the future."

The older woman stepped to the side and looked directly at

Anna Mae. "That's good to hear, but I'll still be letting your brother know about your behavior."

Anna Mae's cheeks turned red once again. "I understand. May I sleep now?"

"Of course." The older woman scowled at him. "You best take your leave, Mr. Whitelaw."

Captain Whitelaw. But Cain pressed his lips into a flat line before he blurted something he shouldn't, then turned back to Anna Mae. This wasn't the way he'd intended to say good-bye. If they were alone, he'd…

What?

Kiss her lips too? When he had no intention of making an honest woman out of her?

Maybe it was a good thing Mrs. Mullins had shown up and prevented anything more from happening.

He picked up Anna Mae's hand where it rested atop the quilt and gave it a gentle squeeze. "Stay safe and get better."

A soft smile spread across her lips. "I will. You be safe too."

"I fully intend to." He turned and strode out the door without so much as a glance over his shoulder.

Because if he let himself look back at Anna Mae just once, he was afraid he might find himself back beside her bed, unable to pull his eyes away from her as she drifted off to sleep.

14

"What have you been doing down here for the past four days?"

Jonas jumped at the sound of the voice, causing his coffee to slosh over the side of the mug he'd been carrying.

He winced at the burning liquid on his hand and set the mug down on the desk right inside the door of his office. When he looked up, he found Moore had planted himself behind his desk, the small wooden chair pushed nearly back to the wall to accommodate the man's protruding stomach.

"Well?" Moore bellowed, his voice loud enough to be heard throughout the basement of the Marshals' office. "I asked what you've been doing!"

"Working?" Jonas rubbed the side of his hand on his waistcoat, alleviating a bit of the scalding sensation on his skin.

"Not on the Giffard case, you're not. Why do you have Velez's court transcripts from Mexico? I told you to leave that for Neville."

Jonas glanced at his desk, which had not only court transcripts but also several other files he'd been going through, including the stack he was planning to give to Frank Whitelaw in another day or so.

"Neville said he didn't need the transcripts from Mexico. He told me I was welcome to them," Jonas answered.

Moore rose slowly, bringing himself to his full height, which was rather formidable, even given his bulging midsection. "And what do these have to do with Giffard?"

Jonas drew in a breath. "They don't. They pertain entirely to Velez, and I'm looking through them because..."

Should he say? Whitelaw hadn't told him to keep any of his research secret, only to come to him with the evidence. Besides, there wouldn't be much keeping of secrets now that Moore was in his office. His notes alone on the various case files were enough for Moore to piece together what was going on without Jonas saying so much as a word. And given the haphazard papers spread across his desk, it was clear that Moore had been going through things while he'd gone home for lunch.

"I don't think Velez was just smuggling goods into Texas. I think he was smuggling people too."

Moore planted his hands on the desk and leaned forward, his eyes narrowing into two thin slits. "What did you say?"

"I said, Velez was smuggling people. I think it stopped after he got arrested, but he does still have a son living in Mexico City and—"

"I don't care about the son." Moore picked up the notes lying smack in the middle of his desk—the ones that referenced various files he was using to build his new case against Velez.

The ones that Frank Whitelaw would find most useful.

"Tell me about this people smuggling. What put such a notion into your head?" Moore plopped himself back down in the rickety wooden chair and started flipping through his notes.

"I was looking at old case files from Laredo. You know, to

see if they could help with the Giffard case..." It wasn't entirely true. Jonas had looked at old files from Laredo and found evidence of men being moved across the border, but only because Frank Whitelaw had told him to, not because of Giffard. "That's where I found the first clues."

Jonas moved to the desk and slid one of the files from the bottom of the stack on the corner, then opened it.

"See here?" He pointed at one of the underlined sections. "When this caravan crossed the border in Laredo, there were seventeen men acting as 'guards,' but by the time the caravan reached San Antonio, there were only three 'guards.' And here in Del Rio..."

Jonas went on to hand Moore three more files, each of them showing large numbers of men crossing the border with one of Velez's caravans, and each of them having only a few men with them when the caravan passed back through the border several weeks later.

It had taken him a day or two to start seeing the connections after Frank Whitelaw left his office, but once he'd stumbled upon the first report that mentioned a large number of men crossing the border, he couldn't seem to stop himself from finding more.

"There does seem to be a pattern here." Moore sat back and stroked his chin with his pudgy fingers, scanning the report. "But there's nothing illegal about men coming into America."

"I know, but don't you think something is unusual about—?"

"Where did the men go?" Moore tossed the report back onto the desk. "What happened to them?"

"I don't know, but I'm sure with more time, I can—"

"More time?" Moore slammed his hand down on the desk. "You don't have any more time. You're supposed to be laying a trap for Albert Giffard. He's bound to come back to Texas at some point, and when he does, I want him caught. If that doesn't take up enough of your time, I brought you this." Moore pointed his thumb at a new file lying on the desk. Jonas hadn't noticed it before, but that wasn't too surprising given the clutter.

"What is it? Robbery? Kidnapping?" Jonas opened it.

"Embezzlement."

He snapped the file closed. Embezzlement? Moore wanted to pull him off a human smuggling case so he could crunch numbers?

Why was his boss suddenly so all-fired opposed to giving him a real case to work? "I thought Neville usually handled cases like this."

"Velez's tariff evasions turned out to be a little more extensive than we first thought. It will be another week or so until he can take the case, and I'd like it solved by then."

"Fine." Jonas set the file back on the desk. "I'll work on the embezzlement case."

"Good." Moore stood, then clamped his meaty hand around Jonas's stack of notes—the notes he needed to get to Frank. "I'll take these with me."

"For what? I thought you said there was nothing to them."

"Neville might find them useful after all." Moore picked up the stack of files from the corner of the desk too, the one that contained all the old paperwork that proved large numbers of men had been crossing the border with Velez's caravans. "I'll drop all this by his office on my way up."

"Um... all right." Not that Neville would know what to do with all the files. The man seemed woefully inadequate at accomplishing anything that didn't involve a straight tally of numbers.

But the assistant director wasn't exactly the type of person one argued with, especially not if one wanted to keep his job.

Now what was he supposed to do now? Tell Whitelaw what

he'd discovered without presenting any evidence? Would that be good enough for the rugged Ranger?

Moore lumbered around his desk toward the door. "And why don't you take the rest of the afternoon off."

"You're sending me home early?" Jonas felt his eyebrows wing up. "I thought you wanted me to work on this new embezzlement case."

His boss shrugged. "I ain't blind. I know how hard you've been working since you started investigating the missing men in the desert. Seems you're due a bit of a break. Besides, I can't help but wonder if I'll have a little better agent arriving in the office tomorrow if you take some time to step back from this whole Velez mess. There's such a thing as pushing a case too hard."

Jonas blew out a breath. That much was true. He had been pushing his cases awful hard, first with the murder investigations in Twin Rivers, and then with trying to track down Giffard in Laredo. "All right. I'll take the afternoon off and invite Harriet over for dinner."

"You do that. Bet your pretty little fiancée is missing you considering how much you've been gone." Moore headed for the door, his left arm filled with files. "And Redding?"

Jonas looked back at his boss.

Moore held up a file. "I'm not going to lie. I still don't think anything will come of this, but thanks for being so thorough."

Jonas managed a small smile. "You're welcome."

He watched as Moore disappeared down the hallway. He couldn't claim to like Moore, but the assistant director seemed to do a good job of matching the right agent to the right case and getting cases closed.

Maybe Moore was right about Velez and the extra people at the border.

Jonas raked a hand through his hair. Maybe he was too

close to the Velez case, and he was seeing connections that weren't there.

But if Moore was right, then why had Frank Whitelaw shown up in his office last week?

And why were the Rangers so irate that Cain was trying to rescue a kidnapped woman?

Jonas rolled his shoulders, stretching out the tightness that always seemed to gather there when he had trouble making headway on a case.

He'd pay a visit to Frank Whitelaw first thing tomorrow. Hopefully the seasoned Ranger could help him make sense of things.

But first he was going to spend a few hours romancing his fiancée.

∼

ALMOST THERE. Just a little farther. Cain blinked at the tents on the horizon, a dusty maze of green canvas tops amid a world of endless yellow rock.

The Ranger encampment sat just outside the little town of Alpine—if you could call Alpine a town. It was mostly uninhabited, since the train wasn't yet running this far west, but steam engines needed water to fill them, and wherever filling stations were established, little towns sprang up around them. Alpine, Texas, might not look like much at the moment, but when the railroad was finished in another year, a restaurant, general store, hotel, school, and church would all populate the ramshackle collection of roughhewn buildings.

But none of that mattered much as Cain ducked his head against the blinding afternoon sun and dug his heals harder into Maverick's side. "Come on, boy. Just a little farther."

Cain couldn't blame the horse for being slow to increase his gait. He'd ridden hard and long, cramming what should have been a two-day trip into a day and a half. And now every muscle in his body seemed to hurt. His neck, his shoulders, his thighs. Even his hindside felt like it was permanently melded to his saddle.

But it would be worth his extra aches and pains. By arriving before supper, he'd be able to gather his men and have everyone ready to ride out at first light.

"It's Captain Whitelaw!" someone shouted from the camp.

Heads turned his direction as Maverick barreled into the maze of tents.

"Looky there. He ain't dead after all," another man said.

"What kind of run-in did you have with the Mexicans?"

"Did you find Anna Mae?"

The questions swarmed around him as he pulled Maverick to a stop in front of his tent and swung out of the saddle.

The flap opened to reveal one of his lieutenants, Leighton Pearce.

Cain frowned for a moment. What had the man been doing inside his tent?

But his maps of the area, correspondence with Austin, records and reports, and anything else a person might need to run a frontier battalion were inside that tent. And seeing how he'd left Pearce in charge when he'd ridden out of camp about a month ago, it made sense the man would be in there from time to time.

"You're alive." A smile brightened Pearce's face beneath his ruddy beard, and the man slapped him on the back. "I have to admit, when Sheriff Harding sent a man up with a telegram for headquarters, we thought sure you'd been killed somewhere in Mexico."

"Is Anna Mae all right?" This from Roland Sims, his other lieutenant who'd always been a bit too sweet on Anna Mae.

"Anna Mae's fine. She escaped the kidnappers on her own, then got herself bitten by a rattler and had a mind to try cutting out the poison. By the time I found her, infection had set in and she was delirious with fever. We had to wait a couple weeks before we could leave."

"Boy howdy, we thought the both of you were dead!" Bryant Lindley, the youngest Ranger in his battalion, looked about ready to throw his arms around him.

"You hug me, boy, and I'll strip that tin star from your chest," he muttered.

The young man straightened and gave a stout salute. "Yes, sir, Captain, sir."

"So someone really kidnapped her?" Davis asked from behind him. "She didn't just go off on her own or anything."

"It was Velez's son, Eduardo, who ordered it done."

A hush fell over the growing crowd, each set of eyes riveted to him, then Pearce stepped forward. "I thought we took care of the Velez family this spring."

"There was a son down in Mexico City. He's stepped up as head of the business, and he's still got a mind to marry Alejandra's sister off to one of his fellow criminals. That's who his men thought they were kidnapping—Gabriella, not Anna Mae."

"So all that work rootin' out the rustlers and riding into Mexico was for nothin'?" Bryant crossed his arms over his chest, a worried look on his face.

"Not for nothing. We leave at dawn to go deal with what's left of the Velez family operations, and we're going to travel quick, because I've got a feeling Eduardo has his sights set on Twin Rivers."

His men had loved being stationed in Twin Rivers. The town was friendly and had plenty for them to do in their downtime. And Anna Mae was at the camp every other day handing out baked goods.

So when he announced that his men would get to leave Alpine and head back to Twin Rivers, he expected them to hoot and holler. Instead, they looked between him and Pearce, and some of them even had furrowed brows.

"Is that true, Captain?" Lieutenant Sims asked softly, his gaze pinned to Pearce. "Are we going to Twin Rivers in the morning?"

Captain? Cain looked at Pearce. He'd left the man in charge while he'd been gone, but he sure hadn't appointed him captain.

Pearce straightened and met his gaze. "Austin assumed you were dead."

"I'm not."

"I see that. But they thought you were, and—"

"They made you captain in my stead." Cain sucked in a breath. It made sense from Austin's perspective. In fact, if he were the director, and one of his captains had gone missing in Mexico for a month, he'd assume the man dead and appoint a different captain to oversee the battalion too.

But that didn't mean there wasn't a sudden, piercing stab of pain somewhere in the vicinity of his heart. This was his unit, and these were his men. He'd spent thirteen years as a Ranger, joining when he was only sixteen and lying about his age, and he had the highest mission success rate of any captain in the Rangers.

Even higher than his father's.

How could Austin have counted him as dead so easily? They hadn't even sent men to Twin Rivers to verify he'd died— or to Mexico to see if they could find his body and return it to Texas soil.

"So which one of you is in charge?" Bryant stepped closer and looked between the two of them.

"Whitelaw is, of course. He was our capt'n long before Pearce," one of the men called.

"Give me a moment," Pearce said. "I have a letter from Austin that was to be given to you in the event of your return. It should clarify things." Pearce turned and disappeared into the tent.

"In the event of my return?" Cain followed Pearce through the flap of fabric—only to find himself standing in a tent he no longer recognized.

Oh, sure, it was the same tent he had been using a month ago, with the same fabric covering the top and sides and the same posts holding it up. But the bedroll was different, as were the clothes hanging from the rope strung across the back and the small daguerreotype of a family sitting on the table beside the unrolled maps.

"What in tarnation...?"

"We thought you were dead, Whitelaw. Dead." Pearce pulled on his beard. "I took over your tent along with your command. You would have done the same if the situation was reversed."

Cain rubbed the back of his neck. "If you were so all-fired worried, why didn't you send anyone to look for me?"

Pearce handed him a letter, his face void of any emotion.

At least the man wasn't blushing and trying to stammer out an explanation. It meant somewhere in the seven years Pearce had been serving with him, he'd trained up a good enough leader to replace himself.

Cain took the paper and scanned it.

Captain Cain Whitelaw vacated his post without permission and failed to return. He is to be considered deceased, and no resources from the Texas Rangers may be used to recover him, since he was not acting in an official capacity at the time of his disappearance.

In the event he should return to the encampment, he is ordered to come directly to Austin, where he will be expected to face consequences for his dereliction of duty.

"Dereliction of duty?" The paper crinkled in Cain's hand. "I told them where I was going. You know as well as I do that I sent a telegram."

"I do. But we got a telegram in response after you left, commanding you not to go."

Cain sucked in a breath. "Why? It makes no sense. I was going back to the town where we were camped for nearly a year to tie up a loose end and bring an American woman back to the US side of the border. That's not being derelict. What kind of oath do they think I took when I became a Ranger?"

Pearce scratched the side of his beard. "I didn't say it made sense, but it's the orders I got, right along with the letter that made me a captain."

He shoved the paper back at Pearce. "I didn't become a Ranger so I could stand by while innocent women are abducted, raped, and killed."

"Was Anna Mae...?"

"No. Or rather, no to any of it except the abduction. And like I said earlier, she escaped the kidnappers on her own. By the time I got there, all that was left for me to do was track her to where she was hiding with her injured leg. If not for that rattler bite, she probably would have made it back to Twin Rivers on her own."

"She's tough. No question about that." Pearce set the letter on the table and sat in one of the two chairs beside it. "Can't rightly think of any other woman who'd be able to escape the likes of Velez's men."

Cain sank down into the chair opposite Pearce. "Me neither. But Anna Mae being tough doesn't help me make sense of this letter."

Pearce gave his head a small shake. "I'll admit, something about it seems wrong. I was to just assume you'd died? As though I didn't have men to spare that I could have sent in search of you? This posting in Alpine is the most useless assignment I've had in my entire time as a Ranger. I'm barely using half our men to cover the section of railroad we've been assigned to protect, and no one has shown any sign of trying to sabotage it."

Cain thought back to the assignment they'd first been given when headquarters moved them from Twin Rivers up to Alpine. "Maybe our presence alone is enough to scare off anyone with ill intent."

"Best I can figure it, the explosion that ruined that section of track outside of town was an accident that no one wanted to own up to. Someone probably forgot to secure the dynamite needed for blasting through the side of a hill, and the crate caught a spark and exploded. When no one admitted what had happened, it got framed as an intentional attack, and we got called in to protect the railroad."

Cain sat back. "It makes sense."

A lot of sense, actually. Because while he'd gone on his share of useless assignments before, none had ever felt quite so useless as being stationed to watch the track being laid between Alpine and the next watering station, Marfa. His men had been bored silly for the two months they'd been in Alpine.

"I just don't know what to make of the letter." Pearce's lips twitched beneath his mustache. "But while I'm glad to see you back, it sounds as though you should at least head to Austin."

"For what? Them to fire me? What did they even say I'd done in that letter?" Cain snatched it off the table and scanned it until his eyes came across the words. "Apparently I was 'derelict in my duty'? This isn't the army. It's not as though they can court-martial me or take any legal action against me. Hang it all, there are men who up and quit the Rangers every day, and no one at headquarters ever throws around words like 'dereliction of duty.'"

"So then don't go to Austin. Just write and tell them that you resign."

Resign. The word caused a sudden itch to form between his

shoulder blades. "I don't know how to be anything other than a Ranger."

"Maybe you could learn?"

"The Marshals Service might be hiring." Working as a lawman for the federal government would be the next closest thing to being a lawman for the State of Texas. The biggest differences were that he would be by himself most of the time and could cross state lines in pursuit of a criminal.

"You really think the Marshals will hire you fresh off of getting fired by the Rangers?"

Cain scrubbed a hand over his face. "Maybe yes, and maybe no. But it's a problem for another day. Velez is still a threat, which means I've got to go back to Twin Rivers, and I need you to send men with me."

While he'd been planning to bring all the men in his battalion with him, with a letter like that from Austin, Pearce would have to keep at least a few men in Alpine, or he'd end up losing his job too.

"Did you read the end of the letter?" Pearce slid it closer to him on the table. "I'm to send no men in search of you, and no men to Twin Rivers for any reason. I'm to consider our duties there concluded."

"It says that?" Cain picked up the letter for the third time and started reading again. Sure enough, it said that very thing, right above Assistant Director Weldon's signature.

He slammed the letter back down on the table. "You know this is wrong. Velez's son won't stand by and leave Gabriella where she is on the border, a stone's throw from Mexico. And I'm worried about what he might have planned for Daniel. A sheriff in a small town like that has to look like easy pickings for a man with Eduardo Velez's resources."

"I never said any of this was right." Pearce shoved himself out of the chair and began pacing, seven steps across the tent, a turn, then seven steps back the other direction. "No matter how you slice it, it doesn't make sense. But where you thought Austin would be happy you took us into Mexico in April—and again that you went to rescue Anna Mae—both of us now know that they don't want us to have anything to do with Velez. What choice do I have?"

"The choice to do what's right," Cain growled.

"Isn't obeying what's right? Pretty sure I remember hearing a sermon or two when I was in Twin Rivers about obeying those in authority over me. That would be headquarters."

"Pretty sure I remember a verse in the Good Book about obeying God rather than man, and I don't think God would cotton to allowing women to be kidnapped and a sheriff to be killed by a band of outlaws."

Pearce sighed, his shoulders slumping. "If I take the men down to Twin Rivers, Austin will just fire me and put Sims in charge. And if Sims goes to Twin Rivers, they'll send someone from Austin to take charge of the unit. Someone who'll do Weldon's bidding. So while I see the need for more men in Twin Rivers, I signed an oath to become a lawman, not a hired gun. And that's what me handing over my star and going down to Twin Rivers would make me."

The very words caused Cain's stomach to churn. Every so often, a hired gun turned out to be a hero, a man with a drive to uphold the law and do right. But more often than not, they meant trouble. They could be hired by honorable men and criminals alike, all with the purpose of using their guns to do whatever job they'd signed on to.

Is that what he'd become by going back to Twin Rivers? A gun for hire?

"The best I can offer you is a chance to ask the men if they want to go with you." It sounded like Pearce was talking from somewhere far away, his voice echoing around inside Cain's head. "I'll take their badges and accept their resignations, then rehire them as soon as they return."

Cain scrubbed a hand over his face, then looked up and met the eyes of his former lieutenant. "You'll take my badge, too, won't you?"

"I'm sure Sheriff Harding will deputize you. It won't be as bad as you being a gun for hire." Pearce's hand landed on his shoulder, the touch almost sympathetic.

Yes, Daniel would deputize him. But all the other times he'd been in Twin Rivers, he'd had the backing of the Ranger headquarters in Austin.

Now he had what?

A determination to protect the town where he grew up?

Did that really warrant giving up the badge he'd spent over a decade serving?

"Please, Cain." The side of Pearce's mouth twitched beneath his mustache. "It's the best I can do. You have to understand."

But he didn't. That was the difference between him and Pearce.

"I better go round up some men. Want to leave at first light." Cain pushed himself out of the chair and turned toward the tent flap.

"Wait." Pearce held out his hand, then stepped closer. "Your badge first."

Cain looked at his friend's open palm, then down at the star pinned to his shirt.

It was just a piece of tin. Taking it off shouldn't be so hard.

So why did his hand refuse to lift to his chest?

15

"Now tell me, are these dried apples for pies?"

Anna Mae smiled at Mr. Cunningham, who had just plopped three sacks of dried apples onto the counter inside the general store. "They sure are."

"Any pies you intend to make for my store? Because people have sure been missing your baking around these parts."

Anna Mae couldn't quite stop her smile from spreading farther across her lips. And here she'd been worried Mr. Cunningham had found another woman to sell baked goods at the general store in her stead.

"My leg's not quite strong enough to stand in the kitchen for too long, but hopefully I'll be able to start baking again by the end of next week."

Mr. Cunningham tallied up the cost of the apples. "I'm glad you're making such a speedy recovery."

She slid several coins across the counter. "Me too."

Though she had to admit, her initial recovery at the doctor's office had crept by. Part of that was due to the fact her fever reappeared on her first afternoon back in town, but when it was gone by the following morning, Doc Mullins decided it was safe to discharge her as long as she stayed off her leg at home.

Daniel and Charlotte's house was a bit cramped with her sleeping on the sofa, and the kitchen certainly wasn't big enough for her to bake up a storm the way she did at the A Bar W, but she wasn't going to complain. It was nice being with Daniel and Charlotte, especially since there had been a time in the desert when she'd wondered whether she might ever see them again.

"Do you need help?" Mr. Cunningham frowned at her as she placed the sacks of apples into her basket and slid the handles through her arm. "I can have someone carry your basket to the wagon for you."

"I should be fine. The doc says I should use my leg as much as I'm able, but rest it when it feels sore." It was true that her leg gave her a little trouble walking, but as long as she kept the distance short, she could get by well enough.

"All right then." Mr. Cunningham came out from behind the counter and opened the door for her. "I'll look forward to getting some of those apple pies into my store next week."

"Thank you." She started down the boardwalk toward Doc Mullins's office, where Charlotte had stopped to have the doctor check on her baby.

She couldn't stop the smile from spreading across her face as she surveyed the town. From the dusty street to the familiar buildings to the sounds of horses and wagons on O'Reilly Street, it felt good to be home.

Now if only Cain were here to...

No. She couldn't let herself think like that. Cain might be returning, yes, but he'd ride out of town again just as soon as he could, which was why she needed to turn her attention to Paul Fordham.

He'd come to visit her every day since her return, sometimes even multiple times a day. Now if only she could stop wishing it was a different man in a dusty cowboy hat filling the doorway each time Paul—

"Well, well, if it ain't the lovely Anna Mae Harding." A dusty man stepped onto the boardwalk in front of her. He looked vaguely familiar, but she couldn't quite place him. "I hear you're not in the market for a husband no more."

She straightened, pulling her basket with the apples higher onto her shoulder. "I beg your pardon?"

"You wanna stop by the bunkhouse later?" Another man appeared at the first man's side. He also wore the dusty clothes of a cowhand. "Got some things planned you might find entertaining."

Her face turned hot. "No, sir. I do not. Nor do I appreciate your insinuation."

She tried to duck around the men, but they only used her retreat to corner her against the wall of the closed post office as more of their friends sauntered over.

"Maybe she wants you to take her on a picnic," another man said. "She might not want an audience for what the two of you are going to do."

Raucous laughter rose up from the half-dozen men she suddenly found herself surrounded by.

Were these men talking about…? That is, they didn't think she'd…

"I don't know where you got the impression I'd be willing to do such things, but I'm not." She straightened again and met the gaze of the man who'd first approached her. "I am a lady, and I expect to be treated as such, even by a group of cowpokes like you."

"Sure ya are. Real ladylike." The man took a step closer, then raked his eyes down her in a way that made her feel as though she suddenly needed a bath.

The man beside him cackled, then hurled brown spittle filled with tobacco juice onto the boardwalk by her feet.

"I'm w-willing to marry you, Anna Mae." One of the men stepped forward, his hat held over his stomach. He was younger, with a clean-shaven face. And if she recalled correctly, he was one of the ranch hands from the Circle M who attended church on Sundays.

Was that where all the men had come from? The Circle M? It was late enough in the day that most of the cowhands were off duty. They'd probably come into town to frequent the cantina across the street.

"I swear I'll make an honorable woman out of ya," the scrawny cowhand continued. "Even if that low-down Ranger stole your virtue."

"Stole my..."

"He didn't steal nothing," one of the men snapped. "She gave it to him, willingly. Haven't you been listening to the tales?"

What tales? She looked around the faces of the hardened, dusty men. Was that really what all of them thought? That Cain had compromised her, and she was now willing to forfeit her morals?

She tried to open her mouth and ask, but the words clogged in her throat.

"And now she's going to give me everything she's got to offer." The first man curled his lips into a smile that made her stomach churn, then took another step closer.

Rather than back up until she found herself pressed against the wall, she swung her hand toward his face. It connected with a loud slap that ricocheted down her arm.

"I'll do nothing of the sort!"

The men erupted into laughter. Everyone but the man she'd slapped. His lips flattened into a firm line, and something hard glinted in his eyes.

He reached for her, and she took a step to the side.

Or rather, she would have taken a step to the side, but her sore leg wasn't that quick at moving, and when she put weight on it so suddenly, it gave out, causing her to topple backward into the post office wall.

More laugher rang out. "Looky there, Swanson. She's too injured to get away from ya."

Anna Mae scrambled back into a standing position, her heart pounding so loudly she could hear it in her ears.

Swanson came toward her, his jaw tight. She glanced around him at the man who'd offered to marry her, but he hung back, his head down.

"You think you can hit me and get away with it?" Foul breath rushed into her face. "I'll show you which one of us gets to do the hitting."

He raised his hand, and she swore she felt the skin of her cheek smart just looking at his open palm.

"What's going on here?" a voice thundered.

Swanson turned, his hand still raised, while the other men in the group shifted away from him.

Anna Mae looked toward the voice, only to find Paul Fordham standing on the steps.

"Don't tell me you're about to strike a woman, Swanson." Paul's voice rang out, loud and clear against the falling night. "We're both aware you know better than that."

Swanson's lips turned into a scowl. "Just giving the wench what she asked for."

Paul came closer, and Anna Mae sucked in a breath of relief. Never in her life had she been so happy to see him. "Anna Mae, is this man bothering you?"

"Yes, he is."

Swanson dropped his hand to his side, but something about his gaze still made her want to go home and scrub herself with soap three times over. "I ain't being no bother. Just teaching her not to go around slapping a man, is all. At least not if she don't want to get slapped around herself."

"We just want her to give us some of what she gave the fancy Ranger captain," one of the men behind Swanson said.

"I didn't give the Ranger captain anything," she rasped.

Swanson narrowed his eyes at her. "Sure you didn't."

She felt her face heat anew as she looked up at Paul. "I didn't. I swear."

He had to believe her.

His face remained impassive, but he offered her his elbow. "Come on. I'll escort you home."

She took it and allowed him to lead her down the steps and away from the men. They continued down the street while Swanson and his friends ambled across the street to the cantina.

"Where is your wagon?"

She pointed at the horse and wagon tied to the hitching post outside the doctor's office, still not trusting her voice enough to speak.

Paul led her forward, the two of them limping along in tandem until they reached the wagon, where he brought her to a stop.

"I told you people were talking." He looked down at her, his blue eyes serious in the golden evening light.

"I know." She licked her lips. "But I suppose I didn't realize how far the rumors went."

Or that so many people in town would believe them.

Or that the men in town she'd been refusing to marry since she'd turned eighteen would think nothing of approaching her after hearing she'd been compromised.

"Cain didn't compromise me." She looked up at him. "You have to believe me."

"I do." Paul patted her hand.

"But that doesn't mean anyone else will, does it?" A sour

ball formed in her stomach. She'd known her whole life that cowhands swapped stories and shared rumors, but she'd never before had those stories and rumors directed at her. How did she go about correcting them?

"Could be this rumor fades," Paul said, his voice soft against the muted hues of dusk. "But if it doesn't... well..."

He dropped to one knee, right beside the wagon, where anyone passing on the street could see them. "I'd be honored to be your husband, Anna Mae Harding. I promise to take right good care of you. To give you a roof over your head and a kitchen stocked with food for you to cook up. And I'll love and cherish you until my dying day."

She stared down at the top of his sand-colored hair. Part of her not quite believing he was proposing.

Yet the other part of her wasn't surprised at all, because he'd been hinting about marrying her ever since she'd returned.

Now all she had to do was say yes.

The word was simple, only three letters that even the youngest of children could manage to speak.

Saying it would give her everything she wanted. A house. A kitchen. A passel of young'uns someday in the future. A sweet man who was willing to make sacrifices for her, like he was doing now by proposing so suddenly, simply because he knew doing so would help her reputation.

And yet, she couldn't make herself say the word.

Instead, she tugged on his shirt, indicating that she wanted him to stand, which he did. "It's awful kind of you to offer, Paul. And I promise to think about it. But I'm going to be honest. I always... ah... expected I'd know my future husband a bit more before I agreed to marry him. Marriage is for life, and while I may be only twenty-two, I've seen a few too many miserable marriages in my day. I'd like to be certain we're a good fit first."

He pressed his lips together, almost as though he'd been

expecting her answer, then gave a small nod. "I figured you'd say something like that. But this means I can still call on you tomorrow, right? Because I fully intend to take you up on that part where we get to know each other better."

She tried to make the smile she forced onto her lips seem genuine and bright but couldn't quite manage it.

Because she couldn't really think of courting Paul without also thinking about Cain, and how she wouldn't even hesitate to tell him yes if he asked to call on her.

Oh, Cain might not have ruined her in the desert, at least not in the way those cowhands had suggested. But in some ways, he'd ruined her even more fully, because now she couldn't imagine herself being happy with anyone other than the vagabond Ranger.

∼

"So you think the criminal in Mexico might be smuggling humans?" Harriet reached over and squeezed Jonas's hand so tightly it was almost as though she thought speaking of Velez might cause him to suddenly appear on the steps.

They sat on the swing hanging from the porch, the bench beneath them swaying slightly while they watched evening fall around them.

He hadn't intended to bring any of this up. It was hardly the kind of conversation a man wanted to have with a fiancée he never saw. But after dinner, Harriet had asked about work, and everything had tumbled out.

"I do think the criminal is smuggling people—or at least he was." The trouble was, at the moment he had more questions than answers. Which was why he was going to track down Frank Whitelaw first thing tomorrow, before he went to the Marshals' office.

"You disappeared on me again."

He blinked, then looked over at Harriet, only to realize she was patting his hand. "I'm sorry. I guess I'm just distracted."

"It's all right." She offered him an understanding smile. "I would be, too, if I was worried about a criminal smuggling people out of Mexico."

"He's in prison now. I don't have any evidence it's still happening."

Her delicate blond eyebrows winged up, and she blinked clear blue eyes at him. "He is?"

"Did I forget to say that?"

"Yes."

"Oh, well, Javier Velez was caught for cattle rustling this spring and went to trial down in Mexico, where he was convicted on multiple counts of fraud, embezzlement, and conspiracy for crimes committed down there. He'll be moved here for trial in September, and we're in the process of building a case against him."

Harriet settled deeper into the swing, her entire body seeming to relax. "It's a relief to know he's in prison."

He smiled. "Isn't it?"

"Indeed."

Jonas blew out a breath. "I guess I still can't help from wondering why Velez would be bringing men into the country and then not return with them."

"What do you think the men might be doing once they're here?"

"I don't know."

Harriet tilted her head to the side. "Didn't any of the reports you were looking at give clues?"

He shook his head. "No. Unless..."

Unless the clues weren't in the reports from the border. Maybe the clues were in records from towns farther north. He might not know exactly why Velez was bringing Mexican men into the US, but one thing was clear, they weren't staying near the border. What if he looked at reports from Midland or maybe Marathon, where the railroad track had just been laid? And what was the name of the new town north of Twin Rivers? Aspen? Adder?

Alpine. That was it.

Cain Whitelaw's Ranger battalion was stationed at Alpine, wasn't it? Maybe the Marshals' office even had some reports from there.

Jonas stopped the swing abruptly and stood. "I need to go back to the office."

"Now?" Harriet frowned at him. "But I thought..."

"I'm sorry, you're right. I promised you a walk down by the river. Here. Let's do that first. I can always go into the office after you leave."

Moore might have taken the files he'd compiled earlier, but if he could find files that proved where the men were ending up, he could at least have some information to hand over to Frank Whitelaw in the morning.

Jonas extended his hand to Harriet. She took it and stood but shook her head. "If you need to go back to the office, you should. Don't worry about me. I'll head inside and help your ma clean up supper."

"But..."

"It's all right. I promise. I don't want to stand in the way of you solving a case, especially one that sounds so serious." She reached up onto her tiptoes and gave him a soft kiss on the cheek.

He responded by wrapping his arms around her and drawing her close. The silkiness of her blond hair felt soft against his cheek, and the faint scent of rose water twined around him. "You're too good to me."

She took a step back from him. "I'm not. Your job's important. Go solve this case, and we'll take that walk by the river in a few more days after all this is cleared up."

He could look the whole world over, and he wasn't sure he'd ever find a woman as patient or understanding as Harriet Leighman. He might not have a burning passion for her the way some of his friends who'd up and married seemed to have for their wives, but he had contentment and comfort and genuine caring.

The thought made him smile as he left her standing on the porch and started down the side street lined with houses.

Most of his friends who decided to marry left the Marshals Service before their wedding, claiming that a traveling lawman couldn't make a good husband. But Harriet had never asked him to consider such a thing, and he didn't think she ever would.

In his mind, he could see his future playing out with Harriet. It involved a cozy home to come back to after he finished a case, and quiet evenings sitting on the porch swing. At some point, it would probably involve a couple young'uns to pile on his lap too.

It wasn't a long walk to the Marshals' building, and before Jonas realized it, he was climbing the steps and unlocking the door.

The entire building was empty at this time of night, but the dying light filtering through the windows was just bright enough he could weave his way through the maze of halls without turning on any lights.

He passed by Neville's office when he turned a corner, but he'd only look at the files in there if his search in the records room yielded nothing. The last thing he needed was to get Moore upset with him again.

When he reached the stairs leading to the dark basement, he turned on the lights, causing the dull glow of the bulb above the stairway to hum with electricity. He tromped down the steps and followed the basement hallway past his office, then turned and headed to the records room.

It took him little more than an hour to collect the information he needed. Once he knew to look at the towns north of the border, everything became clear. The men Velez had brought north were working on the railroad. Of course they were. New railroad line was being laid all across the Southwest, and the railroads were desperate for workers.

He couldn't prove all of the men Velez brought north were going to the railroads, but most of them seemed to be. Not that there was anything illegal about Mexicans coming into Texas to work for the railroads. And he sure didn't know why Velez's caravans were moving the men instead of them crossing the border on their own. But at least he knew why the men were headed north.

Jonas tucked the records he intended to show Whitelaw under his arm and headed for the door.

There was barely enough sunlight left for Jonas to navigate his way through the first floor of the Marshals' building, but he eventually found his way to the door.

It was too dark to take Harriet on that walk, but she might still be at home, visiting with his mother. Maybe they could play a game together, or even sit on the porch swing again and talk some more as night fell over the city.

He started toward home, then stopped. The acrid smell of smoke floated through the air. Was something burning?

He looked to the sky. In the gathering darkness, a cloud of black smoke billowed against the inky expanse of blue. Something had caught on fire, and it looked to be awful close to his mother's house.

Dear God, please don't let the fire spread. With the houses and buildings in Austin packed so closely together, one small fire could turn into a blaze that devoured half the city.

He hurried toward the smoke. A lawman could always be

used at a fire. Whether he'd be dousing a building in water or pinning the tin star in his pocket onto his shirt and controlling the crowd, he didn't know. He only knew that the part inside him that had sworn an oath to protect and defend the American people wanted to see that fire put out as quickly as possible.

16

If Velez's men decided to attack Twin Rivers, where would they do it from? Daniel stood back and studied the map tacked to the wall—the map he'd taken down three months earlier after assuming the Velez family had been dealt with.

Hopefully Cain would return with his men quickly, and the presence of the Rangers would deter Velez from attacking. But if Cain was delayed, or if Eduardo Velez rode into town tonight or tomorrow...

Daniel's stomach twisted, and it was all he could do not to clamp his hand over it like some weakling.

What was wrong with him? Why did his body seem to revolt each time he thought about defending Twin Rivers or protecting the women in his town from more kidnapping attempts? Why did every last rational thought leave his mind when it came to Velez?

No. He couldn't let himself be weak. He was the sheriff, the sole person who had been elected to protect Twin Rivers.

The trouble was, when he ran for office, he thought he'd be

protecting it from petty thieves and drunkards. Not from a former Mexican governor with a vast criminal empire.

But he couldn't let that matter, not right now with Cain gone and everyone looking to him to protect the town.

He took a drink of water from the glass on the desk, though it did little to assuage the sick feeling in his stomach. Then he forced his eyes back to the map, studying the canyons and trails that led through the towering mountains guarding the Mexican side of the border.

When Cain had been trying to catch the rustlers before, he'd mapped out every path he found through the rugged terrain, marking the places that were good for ambushes and the ones that offered safety while traveling but were also easy for Velez to watch.

Daniel rubbed the back of his neck. If he were Velez, what would he do?

He ignored the trembling in his hands and pushed tacks into the places that marked the two most obvious trails for Eduardo to take. They were not well hidden, meaning they didn't lend themselves to ambushes, but it would also be easy for villagers and scouts to spot the men as they approached.

Besides, nothing about Eduardo Velez felt secretive. He'd tried abducting Gabriella, started a manhunt in Mexico for Cain and Anna Mae, and sent men to catch them if they attempted to cross the border.

If Eduardo wanted revenge on Twin Rivers, he likely wasn't going to try hiding it.

The door to his office opened, and Wes stepped inside.

Daniel frowned, then looked up at the clock on the wall. "Didn't expect to see you here this late."

"Just spent the day on the range with my men, moving cattle to some of the northern pastures."

"Away from the border?"

"I'm not going to risk losing more cattle now that Velez's son has decided to run things in his father's stead."

It was probably a wise choice, except for one thing. "If Velez's son comes to Twin Rivers, it won't be for cattle."

Wes sighed. "It still makes me feel better to have them farther away from the border."

Daniel leaned against the desk by the map. "Did you find any cattle tracks while you were on the range? Anything that might indicate rustling is still going on?"

"No. That's not what I came here to talk to you about."

Daniel quirked an eyebrow. "What, then?"

Wes pulled the hat off his head and hung it on the hook inside the door, then raked a hand through his hair. "It's how my men were talking."

"How they were talking?" Daniel frowned. "About what?"

"Not about what, about who." Wes heaved in a breath and plopped himself into the chair behind the deputy's desk that Daniel was still leaning on. "It's your sister."

He blinked. "Anna Mae? Why would they be talking about her?"

"Evidently there's a rumor going around about her and Cain, and uh…" Wes rubbed the back of his neck, a grimace crossing his face. "Things that may have happened between the two of them in the desert."

Daniel's jaw hardened. "Cain would never take advantage of Anna Mae—or any other woman, for that matter. You know full well that he conducts himself like a gentleman around women, even if he looks like an outlaw."

"I know, I know. But my cowhands seem pretty convinced that something did transpire. And… uh…" Wes scrubbed a hand over his face, which suddenly looked a bit red. "That also makes them pretty certain Anna Mae would… well… would be willing to do such things again. With… with one of them."

A muscle pulsed at the side of his jaw. "You told them they were wrong."

"Yes. I said that Anna Mae was a lady and to be treated with respect, and if they couldn't do that, then they'd find themselves looking for another job no matter how good of a hand they are or how long they've worked for me." Wes met his gaze, his eyes dark and serious. "I won't hear another word about it, I'm sure. But that doesn't mean they won't be talking about it at the bunkhouse."

"Great. Just great." Daniel pressed his eyes shut. Ranch hands around these parts could be about as bad as seventy-year-old gossips at a quilting ring. Once they got an idea in their heads, they'd talk about it down at the cantina, where the story would then make its way to the hands who worked at all the other ranches in the county.

"There's more."

Daniel's eyes sprang open, and he leaned forward over the desk, planting his hands on the worn wood as he glared at Wes. "What do you mean, more?"

Wes met his eyes evenly. After all, it wasn't Wes he was mad at. He was mad at whatever ruffian decided to start a twisted and terrible rumor about his sister.

"I think this rumor came from church," Wes answered.

"Church?" The word exploded out of his mouth. "What old biddy would dare take the house of God and turn it into a den of lies? So help me, when I find her—"

"The doctor's wife."

Daniel dragged in a breath, or rather, he tried to drag in a breath, but his lungs suddenly refused to work.

"Keely went to the quilting club at church yesterday and overheard some women talking," Wes went on. "She wasn't sure who they were discussing, but it was about immoral behavior. Mrs. Mullins had said she'd seen a Ranger kissing a woman in her husband's clinic, and you and I both know Cain's the only Ranger who's been in town recently."

Daniel flattened his palms on the desk. "Doc Mullins has treated more than just my sister in the past week."

"I know, but when combined with what my ranch hands were saying, it seems—"

The door to his office opened, and Paul Fordham stepped inside, his face grim. "Sheriff Harding, do you have a minute?"

"Of course," Daniel gritted, his voice coming across overly rough, even to his own ears. "Was there a problem when you escorted the women home earlier? Maybe with my sister?"

He'd thought something was a bit off when the man had shown up at his office with Anna Mae, insisting on riding in the wagon with both her and Charlotte to escort them home, but Charlotte was feeling tired and had wanted to leave, so he hadn't asked too many questions.

Fordham blinked at him, the back of his neck growing red. "There was a problem, all right. But I wouldn't say it's your sister's fault, and it didn't happen on the way home. It happened before that, just outside the post office…"

∽

IT TOOK Daniel over an hour before he rode Blaze into the yard. The lights from his house glowed warm in the gathering darkness, telling him that both women were probably still awake. If he was lucky, Anna Mae might have even baked something with the dried apples she'd gotten at the store earlier.

But he wasn't home to eat dessert, and he needed to ride back into town as soon as he was done.

After Wes had left, he'd gone on a hunt for Geoffrey Swanson. As expected, he'd found the cowpoke down at the cantina, surrounded by a group of men. After hearing the things about Anna Mae that had poured out of the other man's filthy mouth firsthand, he hadn't wanted to wait until morning to come home and find out what Anna Mae had to say about the rumor.

He opened the door with a hard twist and marched inside. Both Anna Mae and Charlotte looked up at him in surprise. Charlotte was curled onto the couch with a book on horse breeding, while Anna Mae sat at the table with her stationery and pen.

"Daniel." Charlotte stood and came toward him, a smile brightening her face. "I thought you were working through the night. What changed?"

"Nothing. I'm here on official business."

Charlotte's smile drooped until it formed a frown, but she still came up to his side and wrapped her arms around him, the bulge in her stomach nestled comfortably between the two of them.

"What's wrong?" Anna Mae lifted her pen from the paper before her, brows furrowed.

"You tell me." He released Charlotte and leveled a stare at his sister.

She gave her head a small shake. "I don't know."

"Really? Is that why Paul Fordham escorted you home earlier? Because you don't know what's wrong?"

She stilled, the pen in her hand clattering to the tabletop. "He told you?"

"I'd have throttled him if he hadn't," Daniel gritted. "It's what any decent man would do when his sister is accosted walking down the street."

"You were accosted?" Charlotte gasped. "Are you all right? Why didn't you say anything?"

Anna Mae ducked her head, causing her long black hair to fall like a curtain around her face. "I didn't do what they're saying. With Cain, that is. I didn't do it with anyone, but especially not with Cain."

Daniel came forward, his boots thumping overly loud on

the tile floor. "I didn't think you did, but that doesn't explain why Mrs. Mullins is telling everyone she saw you and Cain kissing."

"She what?" Charlotte asked from behind him, then came up and scooted out the chair across from Anna Mae, settling herself at the table.

Anna Mae slanted them both a glance from beneath the thick curtain of her hair, her face flooded with color. "He may have, um, kissed my forehead when he was saying good-bye to me. And Mrs. Mullins may have walked into the room... and... and the whole situation may have become a little misconstrued."

"He what?" Daniel rasped.

"Just on the forehead. It was brotherly, like something you would do."

"What were you thinking?" Daniel threw up his hands. How could his sister be so foolish? Especially being an unmarried woman who'd spent several weeks alone with a man in the desert?

She'd been a rumor waiting to happen the second she rode back into town, and then she went and let Cain kiss her forehead?

"I was thinking I'd miss him, is all." Tears filled her eyes. "I wasn't thinking someone might come into the room or start a rumor. I was just thinking I didn't want him to go back to Alpine."

"Wait. You didn't want him to leave?" Daniel sat down in one of the chairs. He couldn't help it. His knees had suddenly decided they didn't want to hold him up any longer.

"No." Anna Mae said the words like it was completely normal to not want a Ranger to ride out of town. Never mind that was the one thing a person could always count on a Ranger to do—leave.

"In the desert you were alone together for almost a month."

Daniel planted his hands on the table and leaned forward. "Did he kiss your forehead then too? Your cheek? Your mouth?"

"He saved my life. He treated my leg and fed me and kept me warm. He—"

"Answer the question. Was the doctor's office the first time he kissed you?"

Every inch of her face turned red, and she dropped her gaze back to the table. "I don't see what that has to do with anything."

His hands involuntarily curled into fists. "It has to do with all the rumors flying around town. Now did he kiss you or not?"

Her lips clamped shut.

Daniel pushed himself up from the table. If only Cain was still in town. Then he could stalk out into the night and put his fist where it belonged—in the side of Cain's jaw. "I'm going to kill him."

"No. You can't." She stood so abruptly her chair nearly toppled backward. "He didn't mean anything by it."

Daniel narrowed his eyes. "He took advantage of you, and he'll have to answer for it."

"He saved my life."

"That doesn't mean he can turn around and ruin your reputation!"

"He didn't ruin anything. That's all Mrs. Mullins. And besides, you can't be that mad at him because... because I wanted him to kiss me."

Charlotte let out a little whimper, but Daniel could see only red. It crept in around the edges of his vision until even his sister's black hair looked like a mix between a tomato and a plum. "What did you just say?"

"I..." Anna Mae licked her lips. "I wanted him to kiss me. And don't look at me like I did something wrong. You pined for Charlotte for years before she even looked your way. You know as well as anyone that we can't always help our feelings."

"But we sure can help what we do about them," he growled. "Like whether or not we kiss someone. How could you be daft enough to let Cain Whitelaw kiss you?"

She raised her chin. "Are you saying you and Charlotte didn't kiss before you got married?"

"Of course we kissed, but we're married now, whereas you and Cain—"

"There's no hope for marriage between us. I know." She rose and walked around the far side of the table, neatly avoiding where he stood. She picked up the blanket off the back of the couch and plopped onto the cushions. "I don't want to talk about it anymore."

"But do you love him?" Charlotte followed her around the table and sank onto the cushion beside her.

"I don't know what you're talking about." Anna Mae pulled her knees up and rested her forehead on them.

But there was something about the sorrowful way Anna Mae slumped her shoulders, about the way she sat curled into herself on his couch that made him not quite able to dismiss her words. His sister wasn't normally one to back away from a question or hide her face, but hang it all, she'd looked away from him and Charlotte more during this single conversation than she had in the past five years combined.

"Oh, this is all just stupid." Anna Mae drew in a breath and straightened her shoulders. "Why am I even bothering to hide it anymore? Fine, you want to know how I feel about Cain? Maybe I do love him. And maybe I haven't just loved him for a month or since he came to town again last year. Maybe I loved him long before that."

"You... you... what?" How could he have missed something like that? Daniel approached the back of the couch, his chest growing heavier with each moment this conversation went on. "When Cain was here eight years ago, when Pa lost his leg, did you have feelings for him then?"

Anna Mae looked up at him, her eyes two wide, vulnerable pools of brown. "I think I've had feelings for him my entire life, ever since I first saw him in school. I know he was ridiculously old for me then, and I thought the feelings would go away as I grew up, or that I'd meet someone else who'd make me forget all about him. But instead, no other man I've come across has ever measured up."

Daniel blew out a breath. What a mess. "You'll have to marry him now."

Anna Mae shot up from the couch. "What? No. He needs to be a Ranger. And besides, just because I feel that way about him doesn't mean he feels that way about me."

"Then he should have thought about that before he up and kissed you."

"It was on the forehead!"

"What about the other times?"

Her cheeks turned pink yet again, but Daniel only leaned forward over the back of the sofa. She'd been alone in the desert with Cain for weeks. While he was quite certain his sister still had her virtue, there was plenty a man and a woman could do without taking things that far. "How many times has he kissed you? On the cheek, the forehead, the hand, the lips? I want to know about every single time."

She drew in a breath. "He may have kissed my cheek or forehead a couple times, especially while I was feverish, but I was feeling so poorly that I really don't remember. Then he kissed me once on the lips. Two days before we got here. And before that, when he was in town this spring, I... I kissed him."

Daniel could feel the muscle on the side of his jaw start to pulse.

"He got angry and told me to never do it again. I thought he hated it and wanted nothing to do with me, but... but now I think he was just trying to protect me, because he can't settle down as long as he's a Ranger, and he was trying not to break my heart."

Daniel closed his eyes. He couldn't imagine a bigger mess if he tried. And he didn't have the first clue what to do about it.

Other than drag Cain and his sister down to the church the second the scoundrel rode back into town and force him to marry his sister.

Or ask Cain how he felt about his sister. Because what if the dispassionate Ranger had as many feelings for his sister as she did for him?

But either way, this would have to wait until the scoundrel returned to Twin Rivers before it could be resolved.

17

Jonas rounded the corner of a street as the ringing of fire bells filled the night. Other men started filling the street around him, each one traveling in the direction of the acrid smoke. Each one aware of just how dangerous a fire could be in a cramped city full of wooden buildings.

The smoke grew heavier in the air as Jonas sped into a run. He weaved down streets and through back alleys, getting closer and closer to the smoke. But something was wrong. It almost looked like... like... like the fire was on his street.

Dear Father, no. Please don't let it be my street.

He raced down two more blocks, then came to a sudden halt as a sick sense of dread filled his chest.

It wasn't just that the fire was on his street; it was only a block away, almost close enough to be his mother's house.

But surely it wasn't Ma's house. Surely it was the neighbor's house that caught fire. Surely...

His feet carried him forward, closer and closer to the lapping orange flames and the crowd gathered in front of it.

Sweat broke out along the back of his neck, and his mouth turned dry.

It had to be the neighbor's house burning. Not that he wanted anything to befall poor Mrs. Timmins, but he'd just been at home, and everything had seemed normal. The evening had been too warm to even light the stove, so it wasn't as though there was a way for a fire to start.

But the closer he drew, the clearer he could see that it wasn't Mrs. Timmins's house lit up with bright orange flames.

It was his own.

He increased his pace, not stopping when he reached the edge of the crowd surrounding the fire wagon. Instead, he shoved his way forward, barking at the crowd to move as he fought his way through the maze of people to the nearest police officer.

"My mother?" His heart thundered against his chest as he rasped the words. "My fiancée? Where are they?"

He couldn't stop staring at the house. It was completely engulfed in flames. They had already licked up the sides of the walls to engulf the roof. The fire wagons were being used to pump water toward the neighbors' houses, not to quell the flames eating his mother's house.

The police officer moved closer to him. "Who are you looking for?"

"I'll take him." A man appeared at his side and gripped him by the shoulders, then pulled him back into the crowd.

"Wait. Stop. I need to find..."

A hand clamped over his mouth, and two hard, pale eyes stared down at him.

Frank Whitelaw. He was here. In the crowd. As his house was burning to the ground.

"Keep your mouth shut, son. I need to get you out of here."

"Out of where?" He looked around wildly, his chest heaving. "Do you know where my ma is? Harriet?"

"What are you holding?" Frank snapped. "Evidence? Is it for me? About the human smuggling?"

"I..."

"Come on, we've got to go. No more talking. Just pretend like you're walking down the street with your old man." Frank steered him back through the crowd, the man's grip so tight he didn't dare fight it.

"What about my mother?" he asked as they finally broke free of the throng. "Harriet?"

Whitelaw kept his grip firm on his arm, his eyes facing forward as he plowed down the side of the road. "You already know the answer."

Tears filled his eyes, and his knees suddenly gave out. He stumbled, only to have Frank haul him upright.

"Stop it. Now. Unless you want to end up like your ma and fiancée."

"But..."

"Everyone who works for both the Ranger headquarters and the Marshals Service thinks you're dead. It's in our best interest to keep it that way." Frank glared down at him.

Jonas stared up into Frank's face. Everything about the man was hard. His eyes looked as though they'd been made of ice, his jaw of steel. It was almost as though the good Lord himself hadn't used flesh and bone and blood when he'd formed Frank.

"Shut up and let's go. I've got a horse you can borrow." Frank shoved him forward.

Nor had God given Frank any kindness or compassion, evidently.

"I've got my own horse."

"And if you take it, everyone will realize you're not dead, and then they'll start looking for the papers missing from the Marshals' building. Won't take them long to figure out that you're still alive, and you know what they're up to."

"Wait. You think someone inside the Marshals' office did this? Or was it the Rangers?" Heat pricked his eyes, and he shook his head. "I don't understand. Who would want to hurt me?"

"Velez. And the people he's paying to do his bidding."

"But..."

"Do you want to live through the night?"

He nodded.

"Then shut your yap and hold your head up high. The best way to get you out of here is for you to act like you don't care a lick about the burning house. You understand?"

Jonas clamped his mouth shut and gave a single nod. He might not understand everything that was going on, but it was pretty plain that if he didn't get ahold of himself, he would end up dead along with his mother and Harriet.

"Good. Now let's go." Frank gave his arm a jerk and started walking.

It had never been so hard to hold his head up before, to put one foot in front of the other or stifle the cry that kept trying to claw its way out of his chest.

It had never been so hard to refuse to let the tears come that were scalding his eyes.

Frank led him to a livery, where the Ranger strode in and took two horses. Whether they belonged to Frank or he had just committed horse theft, Jonas didn't know. He merely swung astride the horse, even though every part of him wanted to slide off the beast and let the ground swallow him.

Whitelaw rode ahead of him through town, the black smoke against the sky growing smaller and smaller as they trotted toward the rolling hills surrounding Austin.

Frank kept his back straight and shoulders set the entire time, as though he hadn't just seen a house burn to the ground, as though two women hadn't just died, as though the man beside him hadn't just had his heart shatter into a thousand jagged shards inside his chest.

They rode long into the night, silence filling the air between them.

Finally, just before dawn, they stopped by a deserted stream to water their horses.

Jonas slid to the ground beneath a cottonwood, his eyes hot and tired, and his head pounding, though he couldn't say whether from the tears he'd accidentally let slide down his face or his constant attempt to hold them in.

Frank knelt by the stream to fill his canteen, then looked over at him. "I'm sorry, son. I should have realized... Let's just say, I'm sorry."

Jonas dribbled the last drops of water from his canteen onto his neck and shirt but didn't attempt to refill the metal bottle. Moving seemed like entirely too much work.

"Do you know how they found out you were aware of the human smuggling?"

Jonas rubbed the side of his head. "If by 'they' you mean Moore, then yes. He invited himself into my office yesterday and looked through the records on my desk—records I had set aside for you."

Frank swore.

"You could have told me he was corrupt," Jonas said.

"I didn't think Moore would figure out what you were up to."

"I'm not sure it was intentional. I think he honestly came down there to give me a new case, but once he saw what was on my desk, he figured it out pretty quick."

Frank shook his head, a new string of curse words falling from his lips.

"I should never have gone back to the office." Jonas slumped forward, resting his head in his hands as he stared at the dusty ground. "Maybe if I had been there, I could have put the fire out before—"

"It wasn't a fire; it was an explosion. The house caught fire afterward, but the explosion itself was so severe no one would have survived it."

Jonas's head shot up, and he narrowed his eyes at Frank. "How do you know?"

"I was a few houses down, waiting for you to take your fiancée on a walk. Planned to come up and meet with you, say a few words in a way that didn't seem suspicious. I wasn't sure I could trust visiting you at the Marshals' building a second time."

"You didn't see me leave and go back to the Marshals' building on my own?"

"You were headed the opposite direction. There was no way to catch you without running, and that would have defeated my purpose of acting natural." His shoulders rose and fell in a lanky shrug similar to the one Cain always gave. "Besides, I figured if you were going back there after work, then there was something important you needed."

"Before Moore found the reports in my office, I'd set aside several accounts of eighteen to two dozen men crossing the border with Velez's freighters, but I couldn't figure out what was happening to them afterward. Then Harriet said something that made me wonder if I was looking for answers in the wrong place."

"What did you find out?" Frank dipped his bandana in the stream, then held it over the back of his neck and wrang it out, letting the water soak into his shirt.

"That the men are working for the railroad. I don't know why or what—"

"Because they don't have a choice."

Jonas blinked. "How could they not have a choice?"

"One of two ways. Either they're lied to and promised a good job, or they're threatened and told they need to leave if they don't want Velez's men to kill their families."

Jonas scowled. "I don't understand."

"Ever heard of the Chinese Exclusion Act?"

He shrugged. The words sounded vaguely familiar, but for someone who worked for the federal government, he paid little attention to politics.

"Congress passed it four years ago, and it bars Chinese people from immigrating to America."

"And that has to do with the railroads because...?" Jonas pulled off his boots, pushed himself off the ground, and stumbled toward the creek.

"Because who do you think laid all the railroad track west of the Mississippi? Then Congress up and decides there are too many Chinese people arriving in California, so they ban them, never mind the railroad companies have all taken out loans to expand their lines and need those workers to lay new track."

"So the railroads are what? Paying Velez to bring them workers?" Jonas dipped his bandana into the creek, then wrung it out over his neck, causing the cool water to soak the top of his shirt and trickle down his chest.

"Something like that."

"Is that illegal?"

Frank shrugged. "Could be, depending on how it's done. But with Velez involved, I guarantee there ain't nothing good about it."

Jonas dipped the bandana into the creek again, this time drenching his hair as he wrung it out above his head. "So how does Moore play into this? What's Velez paying him to do?"

"Moore assigns cases for the Marshal's Austin office. Velez has been paying him for years to redirect Marshals' attention away from him and bury any incriminating information."

Jonas stilled, his canteen halfway to the water. Moore had been on Velez's payroll for years? The claim seemed too wild to be true.

"That's why Moore's got that twit Neville Darrowich working only on tariff evasion charges." Whitelaw sloshed out of the creek and back up to the shore. "Moore knows he can't just ignore Velez's doings this time around, because he's already been convicted in Mexico. But Moore can make sure the charges remain as narrow as possible and put an imbecile on his case."

"Neville isn't an imbecile. He just can't see anything beyond numbers." Jonas took a gulp of water. Evidently he couldn't either, otherwise he would have figured out a criminal was paying off his boss.

Frank pulled one of his boots back on. "It's the same thing in this situation. Moore has an agent working on the case, so nothing will look suspicious. But in reality, he's arranged things to get Velez off on the smallest charges."

Jonas stared at Whitelaw, letting the full scope of what he was saying sink in. It made sense. Velez. Moore. The railroad workers. "You started piecing everything together this spring, didn't you? After Cain rode into Mexico, and Austin was more concerned about diplomatic ties than bringing Velez to justice."

"Velez is doing the same thing to the Rangers that he's doing to the Marshals. The assistant director, James Weldon, who is in charge of case assignments is on Velez's payroll."

Whitelaw tugged on his other boot. "I was somewhat aware of Velez before my boy was sent to the border. He's been operating a criminal empire in northern Mexico for years, and it's not a secret he's got men paid off on both sides of the border. But when they sent Cain down to Twin Rivers to deal with the cattle rustling, I don't think anyone in Austin expected Velez to ultimately be behind it. Had Austin known that..."

"They still would have had to do something," Jonas said. Neither the Rangers nor the Marshals Service can look the other direction while that many cattle are moved over the border, especially not when the Westins own one of the ranches being targeted. That family's influential enough to go to the state capitol and raise a fuss."

"Velez bit off more than he could handle with the rustling. Just you wait. It'll prove to be his fatal mistake."

"Fatal?" A sharp pain seared his chest. "How many more people are going to die before this ends?"

"This is why a lawman shouldn't get married." Whitelaw pushed himself to his feet, his face grim. "You need time with a woman, you visit a brothel. Maybe even pay to keep one in a town you frequent if you like her well enough. But you don't go getting yourself tangled up with her. Always ends poorly."

Jonas's eyes burned anew as he sloshed out of the water. "That's a horrible thing to tell a man who just lost his ma and his fiancée."

"It's true. Told the same thing to my boy, Cain, and look at how good of a Ranger he turned out to be."

Jonas stared absently over the rolling hills, their trees and shrubs painted gold by the rising sun. "I'm not going to apologize for loving Harriet. I've known her my entire life. The two of us grew up together."

"Then you're a fool." Whitelaw turned and started for his horse. "If you wouldn't have loved her, she'd still be alive. If you'd rented your own rooms, then your ma would be alive too."

The words stung, causing another bout of tears to rise up inside him, but he wasn't about to let them out, not in front of a man like Frank Whitelaw. Instead, he started for his horse and swung up into his saddle.

This spring when Cain had ridden into Mexico, Velez had lost his house, one of his sons, and a good portion of his wealth.

Jonas aimed to get down to Twin Rivers and make sure he lost everything else.

18

Anna Mae shifted on the pew beneath her, but the movement did little to make her more comfortable, and not because the wood was hard and unpadded.

Never before, in the twenty-two years she'd been sitting in the fifth pew from the front of the small clapboard church, had she known other people there were talking unkindly about her.

But there was no question who or what the group of women perched across the aisle and two pews back were talking about. Mrs. Mullins sat smack in the middle of them. Every so often, one of the women surrounding the doctor's wife glanced her way, and it wasn't the kind of look that made Anna Mae feel happy and welcome after being gone for four Sundays.

"Don't pay them any mind," Charlotte whispered from where she sat beside her, the heavy girth of her stomach making it almost impossible for her to move. "This will pass soon enough, and things will get back to normal. You'll see."

Anna Mae bit the side of her lip. Would it pass? She'd only ventured into town one other time since she'd been stopped on the boardwalk, and it had seemed as though everyone in the entirety of Twin Rivers was either gossiping about her or staring, or both.

Maybe if Daniel were here, the women on the other side of the church would be a little more circumspect. Her brother had a look that was stern enough to freeze the tongues off most people—church gossips included. But he'd put together a regular schedule of men to patrol the area around Twin Rivers, and both Daniel and Harrison were on duty that morning.

"Anna Mae." Ellie entered pew behind them and gave Madeline a little bounce on her hip. "It's good to see you."

"See?" Charlotte nudged her. "Ellie's happy to see you."

"Ellie's not who I'm concerned about," she muttered.

"What's going on?" Ellie stepped forward until she was pressed against the pew where they sat, allowing her string of eight siblings to file in behind her.

"Gossip. If you want to hear all the details, just go join Mrs. Mullins's party over there." Anna Mae jerked her head toward the group of women.

Ellie looked in their direction, then frowned. "Whatever's happened?"

"There might be a rumor or two about Anna Mae." Charlotte wrapped an arm around Anna Mae's shoulders and gave her a little squeeze. "Nothing to be believed, of course, but for a woman to be alone with a man as long as she was with Cain, well, things can get twisted rather easily."

"Cain kissed me on the forehead at the doctor's office when he was saying good-bye before he left town," Anna Mae blurted. There was no point in trying to hide what had happened. If Ellie didn't hear it from her first, she was sure to hear it from the good doctor's wife the moment the church service ended. "Mrs. Mullins happened to see it, and, well, you can guess the rest."

"Cain kissed you?" This from Keely, who had slid into the pew in front of where they were sitting.

Alejandra and Gabriella joined Keely in the pew.

"Did you slap him?" Alejandra asked.

"On the forehead! He kissed me on the forehead!" The words rang through the church a bit louder than intended, but before she could say more, something yanked on her hair. Hard.

She turned to find Madeline had fisted one of her locks in her tiny hand.

"I'm sorry." Ellie worked to untangle the hair from her daughter's determined fist.

"It's all right. Here, if she wants to play with my hair, you might as well let me hold her." Anna Mae held out her hands for the babe. "Oh goodness, she feels like she doubled in size while I was gone."

"So back to Cain's kiss." Keely leaned forward over the pew. "He might have kissed you on the forehead, but did you want it to be on the lips?"

"What?" Anna Mae swallowed. Where had that question come from? Sure, she'd told Charlotte about kissing Cain, but Charlotte knew better than to go blabbing her business to everyone else. "I think we should all focus on the service. Looks like it's about to start."

Indeed, Pastor Russell was at the front of the church, and the choir was taking their seats in the loft.

"Oh, I'd better go." Keely stood abruptly. "I didn't realize it was so late."

"Us too," Alejandra said as she stood with her sister.

The three of them filed their way into the choir loft as the pianist began the opening prelude.

On Anna Mae's lap, Madeline smiled and giggled.

"Do you like the music?" Anna Mae smiled down as she bounced the child to a lively rendition of "And Can It Be, That I Should Gain." Madeline really was the happiest little thing, with a smile that seemed to light up the entire room.

"I can't wait until your babe is born." Anna Mae glanced down at Charlotte's belly, which she couldn't imagine getting any larger, then she pulled Madeline close for a kiss on the cheek. "Then I'll have two babes to dote on instead of one."

"Anna Mae?"

She looked up to find Mrs. Cunningham had stopped by her pew.

"Yes, ma'am." She plastered on the sweetest smile she could manage—which probably wasn't all that sweet considering the woman had been speaking with Mrs. Mullins for the past quarter hour.

"It's nice to see you back home safe." The woman offered her a small, if tight, smile. "The entire town was praying while you were gone. We were all worried."

"Thank you." Anna Mae's smile blossomed into something genuine. "Cain and I needed every last prayer we could get, I'm afraid. And I have no doubt those prayers helped bring us back home."

"Yes, well." The woman gave a curt nod. "That said, I'm a bit surprised to see you at church this morning."

"It's kind of you to be concerned, but my leg is healing just fine, almost back to normal."

"Not because of your leg." Mrs. Cunningham looked pointedly at the babe. "Will you be expecting a child of your own in about eight months?"

"What?" Her cheeks turned hot, and she glanced around the church, only to find that everyone had gone back to their pews in preparation for the service that was about to start. Which meant everyone was bored enough they had nothing better to do than pay attention to their conversation, never mind the piano music had to be drowning out most of what they said.

Anna Mae raised her chin and met the portly woman's gaze. "Absolutely not. In order for that to happen, I would have needed to conduct myself in such a way that could result in a child—which I have *not* done. Ever."

"That's not what I've heard."

"Then you've heard wrong, and last I checked, God isn't too keen on spreading gossip, especially in His house."

"Last I checked, God's Book was quite clear on how this type of thing is to be handled. You need to go in front of the church and repent. Either that, or you can't come to church. God doesn't let sinners worship with the righteous."

Anna Mae clenched her jaw. It seemed there was little righteous about Mrs. Cunningham at the moment. "I haven't done anything I need to repent of."

"Not according to Mrs. Mullins."

She sucked in a breath through her nose. Calm. She needed to find a semblance of it before she up and punched the woman.

And then she would have something that truly did need repenting.

"I've instructed both Gertie and Lenora to stay away from you until this is straightened out." Mrs. Cunningham used her hanky to dab at her brow. "They're good girls, you know. Ones who deserve a good husband."

"Excuse me, but is this seat taken?"

Anna Mae looked over her shoulder to find that Paul had come up beside Mrs. Cunningham.

"Why, Mr. Fordham." Mrs. Cunningham turned and smiled at him. "How nice to see you on this fine Sunday morning. No one is sitting by my Gertie, if you're looking for company during the service."

A faint hint of red appeared on his cheeks, and he fiddled with the cowboy hat he held over his stomach. "And I'm sure whoever sits by her will be right lucky, but I was asking if anyone was sitting by Miss Harding, ma'am."

At his words, Charlotte scooted down, leaving space on the pew for Anna Mae to slide over.

"I'd be happy to have you sit here." Anna Mae smiled up at Paul.

Before she could slide over beside Charlotte, Mrs. Cunningham straightened, her words loud enough for half the church to hear above the piano. "First you go off flouncing around in the desert like a loose woman, then you set your cap for the honorable men in this town so that my daughters are left with nothing but ruffians wanting to court them. Why, you're no better than Cain Whitelaw's mother."

Anna Mae stiffened, though the tenseness in her muscles did little to stop heat from pricking the backs of her eyes.

She opened her mouth, but she didn't have the first clue what to say, not when Mrs. Cunningham's words had been so intentionally cruel.

Just then the piano music ended and Preacher Russell took his place behind the pulpit.

"Um, Anna Mae?" Paul stepped into the entrance to the pew. "Do you still want me to sit here?"

She blinked up at him, then looked around, only to realize she had yet to make space for him. "Right. Yes, I'd... I'd love that."

It was probably a lie, because the only thing she wanted to do at the moment was run home, curl into a ball, and cry into her pillow until the piercing sensation in her heart stopped. But somehow she managed to scoot over until she bumped against Charlotte.

Paul barely had time to settle beside her before the preacher told them to stand for prayer and their first hymn.

Anna Mae bowed her head, then raised it as the prayer finished and the opening strains of "The Old Rugged Cross" filled the small church.

"Don't let Mrs. Cunningham upset you overmuch." Charlotte shifted closer and gripped her hand, speaking softly enough that the music would drown out her words. "She's been trying to convince Paul of Gertie's charms for the better part of a month now, especially while you were away. She can't be happy to see him come up to you in church."

"I won't let her get to me." But that was yet another lie, because Mrs. Cunningham's words had burrowed down to a place deep inside her and settled in.

And she didn't wonder why. Cain's mother hadn't started out as a prostitute, but after it became clear that Cain's father had no intention of returning to Twin Rivers and making an honest woman of her, she'd opened her bed to the men in town, specifically the married men.

Many a woman in Twin Rivers had shed tears over the harm Cain's mother had caused their family. And though Anna Mae didn't know any specific names, some of those women were probably standing in church with her, singing "The Old Rugged Cross."

The song came to an end, and they sat while Preacher Russell gave announcements, but once in the pew, Anna Mae found herself only a few inches away from Paul.

Had Charlotte moved over a bit, giving her less space than before?

Or was the fact she was seated beside a man after just being compared to a prostitute making everything about her situation uncomfortable?

She glanced over at Paul, who offered her a genuine smile.

Any other time, she would have been able to smile back, but not then.

The fact he was even beside her somehow seemed wrong.

This wasn't Paul's mess. It was hers. Or rather, hers and Cain's. And Paul's willingness to help her clean it up almost made her feel as though she owed him something.

Her palms slickened with sweat, and the breath suddenly

seemed to clog in her throat.

Paul and Charlotte both stood again, and the pianist pounded out the opening bars of "Rejoice the Lord Is King."

Had she missed the announcement for the next hymn? Anna Mae numbly stood as the singing rose around her, but all she could do was stare at her feet.

Was it just her, or was Paul standing closer to her than before too? Or maybe he'd grown a foot or two larger? Because no matter where she looked or how close she tried to move to Charlotte, she felt like he was right there, almost on top of her.

"I'm sorry," she whispered. "I... need to get out. I'm not feeling well, and I..."

He took a step backward, allowing her room to slide in front of him and into the aisle. "Is something wrong? Do you need me to escort you somewhere?"

"No, I'll be fine." It seemed everyone nearby was staring in her direction. Again. "I just don't think I can..."

The rest of her words refused to come. She simply shook her head, then turned and rushed out of the church as quickly as her healing leg would allow.

She didn't stop once she reached the doors or even slow as she trampled down the steps. Instead, she kept running, but not in the direction of town. There were too many people there, so she took herself away from the church and the dusty road, toward the green grass of the river. The tears that had pricked her eyes now clouded her vision and slipped down her cheeks. Her leg ached, but she paid it no mind as she raced away...

Away from church.

Away from town.

Away from Paul.

Away from Mrs. Mullins and Mrs. Cunningham.

But she couldn't race away from the awkwardness she felt around Paul or the hurt from Mrs. Cunningham's words.

Or the feelings she still had for Cain.

When she reached the river, she slid down into the long grass, her chest struggling to heave each breath as though the air itself weighed fifty pounds.

How had her life become this much of a mess? Whether she'd been at the doctor's or Daniel's, Paul had called on her the last three days since her return. And every day she'd smiled at him and thanked him for coming. But...

But what?

She didn't know.

Would the rumors about her and Cain fade? Or would she have to marry the only honorable man willing to accept her after the rumors?

"Anna Mae?"

She looked up to find Daniel and Harrison approaching on horseback, concern lacing both their faces.

"I thought you were supposed to be at church." Daniel reined Blaze to a stop beside her and swung off his mount. "Did something happen? Everything seemed fine when we rode past a few minutes ago."

"The church is fine, if that's what you're asking." She sniffled and wiped the tears from her face. "Velez's son didn't interrupt the service and threaten to shoot everyone or anything like that."

"Then why are you here?"

She shrugged, keeping her face down so all she saw of her brother was his shoes. "Guess I just didn't feel like sitting through a service."

Daniel crouched beside her, ducking his head low enough that she had to shift away so she didn't end up looking him in the eyes. "You chattered all yesterday about how much you'd missed not being at church for the past month, then baked four pies for the meal after the service. What happened?"

"I'm going to have to marry him."

Daniel's eyebrows winged up. "Cain?"

"Anna Mae's marrying Cain?" Harrison plopped down onto the grass beside Daniel. "How did I miss that coming?"

"Not Cain, you louts. Paul Fordham. Cain's not ever going to stay in one place."

Daniel crossed his legs in front of him, settling into a spot on the grass as though he was in no hurry to end their conversation. "Since when do you want to marry Paul?"

She sniffled. "I didn't say I wanted to marry him. But I also don't see how I have much choice."

"You've always got a choice, sweetheart."

"Do I?" She wiped a tear from her cheek. "Mrs. Cunningham said I was just like Cain's ma, and loud enough for the entire church to hear it."

Daniel stiffened beside her. "She did what?"

"Don't you believe that lie for a second," Harrison spat. "You're nothing like Cain's ma."

She shook her head. "I can't see any way out of this except to marry. The entire town thinks I've been compromised, and the only honorable man who's made an offer for me is Paul, so that means..."

"It means we'll have a conversation with Cain once he returns." Daniel's eyes flashed. "Because marriage is for life. And while Paul Fordham is an honorable man, I don't think he's the right man for you."

Was Paul wrong for her? Or was he the only choice she had? She stared out over the river, as though it could somehow give her an answer. A rock poked through the surface of the water near the middle, causing white ripples to form around it.

She felt exactly like that rock, like everything around her had flowed smoothly and was going as planned, and then she'd come back to Twin Rivers and caused an upheaval that wouldn't go away. "Then what am I to do? We both know Cain isn't going to settle down and hitch himself to wife."

Daniel heaved a sigh. He knew the rest, of course, about the kisses, her feelings, the impossibility of the entire situation. But he also had sense enough not to speak of it in front of Harrison.

Harrison, on the other hand, furrowed his brow, clearly intent on finding some sort of solution. "You could always move in with your parents."

"You want me to go to Houston?" She blinked. "That's clear across the state."

Harrison used the bandana around his neck to dab at a trickle of sweat beside his ear. "I don't know that I want you to go, or that anyone else would want it either. I was just thinking, if you wanted to escape the rumors, Houston is a bit too far and a bit too big for them to follow you."

"He's right." Daniel sat back. "There're a lot more men in the city. If you're wanting to settle down, I'm sure you'd find someone to your liking there."

"But it would mean leaving the desert."

"It would." Her brother reached out and squeezed her hand. "But you're old enough to know you can't always get everything you want."

"That's easy for you to say. You have the job you want and the wife you want, all while living in the place you want. It's the same with Sam and Wes and Harrison. So am I really asking for that much?"

"I didn't want this, actually." Harrison held up his hands, gesturing to the river and grass and desert beyond. "Six months ago, I wanted to be in Austin, married to a woman named Adeline. God had other plans, obviously, and I'm glad He did. But I had to be open to those plans first. And let me tell you, I'm much happier at Fort Ashton with Alejandra than I ever was in Austin."

The smile on Harrison's face when he mentioned Alejandra was so big Anna Mae wanted to smile back at him. The two did make a rather perfect couple.

But was Harrison right? Was she too set on her own path to

see what God wanted for her?

Had she somehow wrongly convinced herself that she could be happy only in Twin Rivers, married to Cain, when God had a different plan?

She drew in a breath, letting the hot desert air fill her lungs. "Maybe you're right, and this is God's way of showing He wants me to move to Houston with Ma and Pa. Or maybe it's God's way of showing me I need to marry Paul. But then, if God's trying to show me something, why is it all so confusing?"

"Like I told you the other night, we're not going to do anything until Cain returns." Daniel squeezed her hand again. "He should be back in town tomorrow, maybe Tuesday at the latest."

She met her brother's gaze. "You really think he'll offer to marry me?"

Harrison started to laugh, then tried to cover it with a cough. "Cain's been dead set against marriage for as long as I've known him. A few rumors aren't going to change his mind."

Daniel scratched the side of his head beneath his hat brim, his face sporting the grim look he usually reserved for ruffians and criminals. "Maybe so, but he's standing smack in the middle of this mess, and we need to see if or how he plans to make it right before we make any other decisions."

Anna Mae pressed her lips together, her gaze drifting back at the rock in the middle of the river, then up to the mountains where she'd been trapped for four long weeks.

She appreciated her brother trying to be kind, to make it seem like Cain could solve things. But she'd already gotten herself into trouble by hoping for more from Cain than he was willing to give.

At this point, depending on him to solve her problems would only lead to more shattered dreams.

And if anything else in her life shattered now, she wasn't sure she'd be able to pick up the pieces.

19

Sweat trickled down Cain's back as he hunched low over Maverick, urging the beast toward the town taking shape on the horizon. It was about noon on Sunday, and he'd made the trip from Alpine to the border in under two days. Normally he'd be feeling pretty satisfied that he'd made the trip to Alpine and back so quickly, but the sight of Twin Rivers only made him wonder if Eduardo Velez had managed to abduct Gabriella or attack the town while he'd been away.

"Faster," he called to the seven men trailing behind him. That was all who had agreed to join him once it became clear they'd have to turn in their badges and resign as Rangers to come back with him to Twin Rivers.

And as frustrating as it was to have only seven men willing to help him put an end to the Velez family's criminal empire, he couldn't blame the other men in his battalion for choosing to stay in Alpine and receive their regular wages.

Cain brought Maverick to a slow gallop as he turned down O'Reilly Street. The town looked entirely deserted, with nary a person standing on the boardwalk or wagon rolling down the street.

But that was to be expected seeing how the entire town closed up for church every Sunday morning. Even the cantina.

He waved for his handful of men to follow him toward the sheriff's office rather than set up camp, but he'd passed only a couple buildings when Daniel and Harrison rushed out of the office, guns at the ready.

The sight made his gut twist. No lawman should need to pull his gun simply because he heard riders approaching.

Cain reined Maverick to a stop, then swung off, gesturing for his men to stay in their saddles. "Daniel, Harrison."

"We were hoping the noise was you." Harrison holstered his gun and smiled at him.

Daniel had holstered his gun as well, but he wore a scowl as he came out to meet him. And unlike Harrison, Daniel didn't stop walking when he was a couple feet away. He kept right on coming. Then his hand clenched into a fist, and it flew straight toward Cain's face.

Cain tried to jump back, but he was a second too late. Daniel's fist connected with his jaw, and a sickening crack filled the air.

Cain reached for his sidearm and cocked it. "What in the blazes, Daniel?" A screaming pain filled the left side of his face. "You best simmer down, or I'll send a bullet into the next fist you swing at me, and I'm told shattered knuckles hurt like the devil."

"Might be worth the pain if it means you'll answer for what you did to my sister."

"Your sister?" He uncocked the gun. "You want me to answer for saving her life?"

Daniel stepped closer, his eyes hard. "I want you to answer for ruining her reputation."

"Um, the two of you've got an audience." Harrison tipped his head to the left, and Cain looked down the dusty street to find that church had let out.

It seemed the entire town stood frozen just outside the church, watching him and Daniel while the meal that had been planned for after the service sat forgotten.

"Inside," Daniel growled. "Now."

His men started to dismount, but Cain glared at the lot of them. "Not you. Go set up camp down by the river."

"Yes, sir," Lindley squeaked before scrambling back atop his horse.

Cain stomped up the steps to the sheriff's office. "What in the blazes is going on?"

He sensed Anna Mae's presence the moment he stepped inside, even if it took a few seconds for his eyes to adjust to the dimness of the room. She was seated behind her brother's desk, her hair fanning about her shoulders like a rich, silky waterfall.

"Did you kiss my sister's forehead at the doctor's office last week?" Daniel growled, his muscles still tense enough that Cain couldn't quite trust him not to throw another punch.

"What's that got to do with anything?" he drawled, trying his best to make his voice sound laid back, casual. Trying his best not to give away how part of him ached to go to Anna Mae, kneel down beside her, and coax her into telling him why she sat with her shoulders slumped, refusing to look at him.

"After what she saw, or thought she saw, Mrs. Mullins decided to tell the entire town that you compromised me." Anna Mae kept her head down, her voice quiet. "We're... uh... working through how to best handle it."

"Because of a kiss on the forehead?" He stared at her. "Last I checked, that doesn't compromise a woman."

"But spending several weeks alone in the desert does." Daniel crossed his arms over his chest, his eyes hard. "And that's not taking into consideration the fact you actually did kiss her. Twice."

"You told him?" His gaze whipped to Anna Mae. What was she trying to do? Contrive a shotgun wedding?

But she didn't look like she was trying to contrive anything. She looked completely miserable curled into her brother's giant chair, with her body limp and her shiny hair hanging in such a way that it shielded most of her face.

It made him want to wrap his arms around her and assure her everything would be all right.

But something told him if he took so much as a step toward her, he'd get another fist to his jaw.

"Wait. You mean they actually kissed?" A voice said from behind him. "Not just on the forehead?"

Cain turned to find that Wes and Sam had entered the office.

"Yeah, did you kiss her?" Sam rubbed the back of his neck. "Because before service Mrs. Cunningham accused Anna Mae of being like your ma in front of the entire church. I thought it was all a bunch of malarkey, but if something happened between the two of you, then—"

"What did you say?" Cain narrowed his eyes at Sam.

"That if something happened between the two of—"

"About my ma."

"Oh." Sam winced. "Ah... that Mrs. Cunningham said Anna Mae was like your ma?"

"I'm going to put an end to that, here and now." He whirled toward the door.

"Cain, no." A slender hand landed on his arm, and he turned to find Anna Mae behind him, her eyes two deep, sad pools of brown.

"It's not all right that she talks about you like that. Not when you haven't done anything that Mrs. Cunningham didn't do herself before she got married."

"It doesn't matter."

"It matters, all right. A rumor like that could destroy you."

She swallowed, then lifted her chin and met his gaze. "I

know. That's why I'm going to Houston to live with my parents. The rumors will die as soon as I leave town."

"What?" No, no, no. This was all wrong. Anna Mae couldn't leave. She loved the desert, loved the wide-open spaces and sunsets and mountains. In all the times she'd talked about having a husband and a family, he'd never once envisioned her having that anywhere other than Twin Rivers, and he'd wager she hadn't either.

Hang it all, just what had happened in the three and a half days he'd been gone?

"So you decided not to marry Fordham?" Harrison poured himself a cup of coffee from the back table.

Wait. What?

"She wants to marry Fordham?" Wes's eyes lit with surprise.

"Boy howdy, Anna Mae." Sam shook his head. "You sure do have a way of complicating things. I didn't even know the two of you were courtin'."

"What's this business about marrying Fordham?" Cain growled.

She dropped her hand from his arm and sighed. "He asked for my hand. After we learned about the rumors and all, he offered to—"

"She means after she was accosted on the boardwalk by the Circle M cowhands." Daniel came up to stand behind Anna Mae, wedging her between the two of them. "Paul stepped in and stopped one of the men from slapping her, and who knows what else. That's how she found out about the rumors."

And he'd been a hundred miles away, unable to do anything about it. Sweat beaded on the back of his neck, and a hard ball formed in his stomach.

"What happened?" He ran his eyes up and down her, searching for any sign of injury. "Because if someone so much as laid a hand on you—"

"It's over and done." She looked away from him. "There's no need to worry."

"There is absolutely a need to worry." Especially if men felt as though they could take liberties with her because of him. That made just about every building in the entire town unsafe for her.

He looked at Daniel. "You locked him up, right? The man who tried to slap her? Locked him up and threw away the key?"

"He posted bail, but yes, I arrested him."

"Who was it?"

"Geoffrey Swanson." Daniel reached out and settled a hand on Anna Mae's shoulder, almost as though wanting to comfort her as he spoke the name. "He'll face trial when the judge comes to town next, which looks to be about six weeks out."

"I see." Cain stepped closer to Anna Mae, near enough that he could hear the quick inhale of her breath and smell the scent of rosewater on her skin. "Let me try to understand. There are rumors about you and me in the desert, about things we didn't do, but everyone is saying happened anyway. And your ways of dealing with the situation are either to leave Twin Rivers or marry Paul Fordham?"

Her eyes fluttered up to his, and in that moment, he swore the world turned still around him. That it was just Anna Mae and him standing there, no Daniel or Harrison or anyone else. No wagon lumbering down the street outside or children calling to each other. Nothing but the wide, brown eyes of the woman he wasn't supposed to care for, and the traitorously fast beating of his own heart.

"That's right," she whispered, her breath fanning against his face. "I don't seem to have any other choices."

He swallowed. "You can't marry Fordham to get away from this. I already told you. He's a decent enough man, but you'd never be happy with him as your husband."

"Just how many conversations have you had with my sister

about who she should or shouldn't marry?" Daniel growled from where he still stood behind Anna Mae.

"I'm more interested in knowing why you care whether Anna Mae will be happy with her husband." Harrison's voice was quiet as he spoke, but he speared Cain with a gaze that Cain had no desire to hold. "I thought you were a sworn bachelor."

"I am." A muscle at the side of his jaw pulsed. This was why it was better to do as his father said and never let himself become involved in another person's life. It made everything more difficult. "But I'm also a decent person who doesn't want any of his friends to be trapped in a miserable marriage."

"You're just as full of malarkey as Mrs. Cunningham." Sam came up behind him and slapped him on the shoulder, a wide grin splitting his face. "If you've got feelings for Anna Mae, just go ahead and say it. She deserves—"

"I don't—"

"Stop! Everyone just stop!" Anna Mae made a slashing motion with her hands. "None of this matters, because Cain's right. And Daniel's right. And Harrison's right. Paul Fordham might be a sweet man, but I'd tromp all over him if he were my husband, and we all know I'd never be happy with a man like that. I meant what I said earlier about going to live with my parents. The stage comes every Wednesday, and this week, I'll be on it."

Cain clamped his jaw shut. Everything about Anna Mae moving away from Twin Rivers felt wrong, but that wasn't a conversation he was going to have with her brother and three other men standing over her shoulder.

Unfortunately, Daniel didn't seem nearly so convinced the situation needed to be handled privately, because he reached out and touched her arm, then asked, "Do you want to marry Cain?"

Somehow, Daniel's eyes were ten shades softer when he

looked at his sister than whenever he glanced Cain's way.

"Just say the word," Daniel continued, "and we'll march him down to the church. He was the one who compromised you."

Sweat beaded on Cain's forehead, matching the sweat that had already formed on the back of his neck. Surely Daniel wouldn't go so far as to force them into a marriage based on nothing more than a rumor.

But Anna Mae was already shaking her head. "Cain didn't compromise me in a way that should lead to a shotgun wedding. Everyone here knows that, and if we're going to be honest, Mrs. Mullins and Mrs. Cunningham know that too. But as far as actually wanting to marry him..."

She looked at him, and her throat worked, then a soft sheen of tears gathered in her eyes.

He tried to draw in a breath, but it stalled in his chest.

Was she going to say yes? She'd already told him she loved him, that she couldn't imagine herself being happy married to anyone else.

And he was supposed to hate the idea, to balk and refuse to marry her and say he wanted nothing to do with a wife.

But when he thought of taking Anna Mae into his arms, of calling her Mrs. Whitelaw, of waking up beside her each morning and running his hands through her hair each night, hate was the farthest thing from his mind.

Except Anna Mae wasn't telling her brother yes, that she wanted to marry him. She was just looking at him as more tears gathered in her eyes.

Finally, she opened her mouth and said, "No. At least not like this. I'd rather move to Houston."

She ducked her head and hurried toward the door, only to have it open before she reached it.

Charlotte stood there, her eyes wide and her arms wrapped tightly around her middle. "Daniel? Anna Mae? I'm in labor."

20

Anna Mae would rather move to Houston than marry him, and he couldn't even talk to her about it. Cain blew out a breath as he paced inside his tent.

At this very moment, Anna Mae was in town waiting for Charlotte to deliver her babe. Evidently the pains had come on strong and fast, and since she'd already been in town when they started, she'd just gone straight over to Doc Mullins's office to deliver the babe.

Daniel was there too. And Alejandra and Keely and Ellie.

Hang it all, even Sam, Wes, and Harrison had followed Daniel across the road, as though they'd somehow be able to help when there was already a gaggle full of women and a doctor to keep Charlotte company.

Cain had sauntered across the road, too, and peeked his head inside the waiting room, just because it seemed like the thing to do. Everyone had been smiling, the men all slapping Daniel on the back and congratulating him while the women crowded into the small sickroom that Anna Mae had occupied a few days ago.

It wasn't the kind of place he belonged. And while he might

have wanted to pull Anna Mae aside and speak to her in private, he wasn't about to ask her to leave her best friend's side as she delivered her first child.

No. Talking to Anna Mae would have to wait.

Now if only he could figure out something to do with himself in the meantime.

"Captain?" One of the men called from outside the tent. "Are you in there?"

Cain opened the flap to his tent and stepped into the sunlight to find Roland Sims standing there, a grim look on his face.

Cain had been surprised when the lieutenant had agreed to follow him down to Twin Rivers, especially considering the man had a fondness for gambling and certainly liked his lieutenant's pay. Not only was Sims forgoing pay for the next several weeks, but if Austin decided to meddle with Sims the way they had with Cain, the man might lose his rank after he returned to the Rangers.

But Sims had insisted on coming, and he couldn't afford to turn away a man with Sims's experience.

"What is it?" Cain asked.

"You all right?" Sims surveyed his face. "You look…"

Cain raised an eyebrow.

"You just don't usually… ah…" The man swallowed, then gave his head a small shake. "That is, I was wondering how you wanted to set up patrols, seeing as how we've only got a handful of men."

Cain raked a hand through his hair. He'd been so busy thinking about Anna Mae that managing patrols hadn't even occurred to him.

The entire time his battalion had been stationed in Twin Rivers, he'd had three men on patrols every night. But he could hardly do that with only seven men—eight including himself. Half his men would be too exhausted to function during the day. "We'll have to work with the sheriff on that. I believe he's already got some volunteers doing patrols. Schedule one man per night to join them."

The lieutenant gave a stout nod, then glanced at Cain's chest. "What about our badges? Did you get those?"

Cain barely managed to hide his wince. It was yet another thing he'd forgotten in the wake of getting himself punched in the jaw, then walking into Daniel's office and learning Anna Mae had been accosted and was planning to leave Twin Rivers.

"The sheriff's wife went into labor. I'll get the badges and have the sheriff deputize the lot of you as soon as the babe's born and he's back in his office."

Sims rubbed the back of his neck. "Gotta say, I miss having that badge, but there are some things a man shouldn't be pulled away from, even if he's a sheriff."

"Exactly," Cain said, more because agreeing seemed like the thing to do than because he actually agreed. He didn't have the first clue what a man was supposed do when his wife was in labor.

And up until two hours ago, it wasn't something he'd ever thought he'd need to know. But now he couldn't quite seem to stop an image of Anna Mae from rising in his mind, her belly round and heavy with a child—his child.

The air in his lungs suddenly seemed to constrict, and he coughed.

Sims eyed him. "You sure you're all right?"

"Fine," he croaked. "Just fine. Distracted thinking about Eduardo is all."

Either that or the look in Anna Mae's eyes when she'd said she'd choose a hot, cramped city over marrying him.

"I'll bring you the patrol schedule to approve in a bit," Sims said. "Do you want me to schedule chores too?"

"Yes, and some time for us to train the locals. If we're going to be bringing cowhands with us into Mexico, then they need to know how to shoot."

Sims looked south toward the mountains rising up on the other side of the border. "How soon do you think before either Velez's son comes here or we end up back there?"

"I need a bit more information before I can decide that, so don't put Ridley on the schedule for tonight. I want him to come into Mexico with me."

"You're going to scout this soon?" Sims's eyebrows disappeared above his hat brim. "You haven't been in Twin Rivers long enough to know what you're walking into."

"That's all the more reason to go." Usually when he moved into a new area, he took a few days to get a general idea of the goings-on before forming a scouting party so his men didn't end up in trouble. But he didn't have any time to waste. "Besides, it's not all that hard to hide two men in those mountains."

"Yes, sir." Sims turned as though to leave, then stopped and nodded in the direction of town. "Looks like you've got a visitor."

Cain followed his lieutenant's gaze to find Harrison striding toward him, a grim look on his face.

Did that mean something had happened to Charlotte? He started forward, stopping when he reached Harrison beside one of the boulders outside the camp. "How is Charlotte?"

Harrison sent him a bland look. "She's trying to deliver her first babe. How do you think she is?"

Cain rubbed the back of his neck. "Yes, but is she miserable in a normal way? I mean, isn't childbirth supposed to be painful for women?"

"Since when are you concerned about what childbirth is like?"

"I'm not." Cain suddenly had to resist the urge to look down and scuff the toe of his boot in the dirt like he'd used to when getting a lecture from Miss Emmaline at school. "It's just, after what happened to Wes's first wife…"

Harrison's mouth flattened into a firm line. "There's no sign of that."

"Then why are you here?"

His friend blew out a breath. "Needed a break from all the sitting around and waiting. Figured I'd come to see if you wanted to make use of some of my guards while you're here. Two of them are Mexican, though it's pretty well known they work for me, so I'm not sure how much information they'd be able to gather about Velez's son without drawing suspicion."

"I'll keep that in mind in case I need a guide." Cain shifted enough to turn and scan the mountains south of the border. "But for what I'm doing tonight, I know the area well enough to go without one."

"You're going into Mexico this soon?"

Why was everyone suddenly questioning his decision to go into Mexico? "I need to get as much information as I can, and as soon as possible. I figure it's probably a gift from God that Eduardo hasn't done more than try to kidnap Gabriella."

"I suppose you're right." Harrison surveyed him, then raised his gaze and looked around the camp. "Where are the rest of your—"

"Do you think I'd make a good husband?" Cain blurted.

Harrison looked at him for a moment, his face unreadable.

Cain scowled. "Never mind. It was a stupid question."

"It's not stupid, but, ah…" The side of Harrison's mouth twitched up into a smile. "Yes, I have a bit of trouble imagining you as a husband."

"It's because of who my parents are, isn't it?" The collar around his shirt suddenly felt tight. "Reckon it was bound to be this way from the beginning."

The smile dropped from Harrison's face. "It's got nothing to do with your parents."

"Then what is it?"

"You don't care about anything."

Now the muscles in his shoulders felt tight too, right along with his collar. "I care plenty."

"Really? What do you care about so much?"

Cain flicked a hand toward his tent, which held his collection of maps and wanted posters and notes from the last time he'd been in Twin Rivers. "Seeing justice done. Rescuing people. Being a good Ranger."

"But you don't care if you have to lay down your life for one of the people you rescue."

He shrugged. "Not much of a life to lay down."

"And that's the part that won't make you a good husband." Harrison met his gaze, years of memories spreading between them. Of their childhood. Harrison's pa. Cain's own ma. All the things that had caused him to never desire to put down roots and have a family. "If you can't bring yourself to care about what happens in your own life, how will you ever bring yourself to care about Anna Mae? Not just what happens to her but what she cares about the most and what she wants in a relationship with you. If trouble arises, would you walk away from your marriage as readily as you'll sacrifice your own life?"

Cain pressed his eyes shut, and an image of Anna Mae filled his mind. "No. I'd never turn my back on my marriage. I'd..." He shook his head. "What if I don't know how to care about her like you describe? Or how to be part of a family? How to be a husband? You can hardly call what I grew up with a family."

Harrison shook his head, his eyes firm and shoulders tight. Nothing about him looked like a man who was excited to celebrate the marriage of a longtime friend. "While I appreciate you trying to do the honorable thing, Anna Mae is tough. She'll get this sorted out, and you certainly don't need to marry her just because some old biddies—"

"She loves me."

Harrison's eyebrows winged up. "She what?"

"She told me so this spring, before I left town."

"You're sure about that?" Harrison took a step back and rubbed his jaw, almost as though he needed a moment to absorb the information. "I suppose it makes sense."

"No, it doesn't make a lick of sense." Cain slashed the air with his hand. "It's the most foolhardy thing I've ever heard. A woman like her falling in love with the likes of me. She's beautiful. Mesmerizing. The perfect kind of woman for a man to settle down with. I swear half the men she meets fall in love with her on the spot."

"That's before they realize how much of a hoyden she is."

He sent Harrison a glare. "She's not a hoyden. She's passionate."

"She never shuts up."

"You're supposed to be giving me advice, and now all I can think about is punching you."

The side of Harrison's mouth quirked up into a smile. "I suppose that explains why she never married. Why she never even let herself be courted."

"I told her to marry one of my men," he growled.

"Of course you did."

Cain narrowed his eyes. "What's that supposed to mean?"

"It goes back to what I said before. If there's something holding you back from being a good husband, it's because you've got a wall thicker than the one surrounding Fort Ashton around your heart. You obviously care for Anna Mae; otherwise you wouldn't be asking me if you'd be a good husband. But you'd rather sidestep the responsibility and commitment yourself and see her settled with another man. Then you'd know she's safe and protected, but you wouldn't have to be personally responsible for her."

"I don't want to see her settle down with another man," Cain growled. "I thought I did, but I can't stand the idea of it now. I know Fordham could take care of her, even with his limp. But when I think of her with someone else..."

"It seems your feelings for her run deeper than I thought—or than you realize, for that matter." Harrison leaned back against the boulder, kicking his feet out in front of him. "Have you asked yourself what God wants in all of this? If maybe the rumors going around and the reason you found Anna Mae in the desert the way you did is God's way of bringing you together?"

Cain could feel the heat of Harrison's gaze boring into the side of his face, yet he couldn't quite bring himself to look at his friend. "No."

He'd had no trouble praying that God would lead him to Anna Mae when she was in danger, no trouble begging God to keep her alive. No trouble praying that God would help get them out of Mexico or that He would protect Cristobal and the other innocent people in northern Mexico from the Velez family.

And yet the one thing he hadn't done since Anna Mae had fled from her brother's office earlier was stop and ask God what He wanted.

Because God couldn't actually want him to marry Anna Mae.

Not considering how he'd grown up.

Not considering how he was little more than a vagabond with a gun rather than a bonafide lawman.

Don't let yourself get attached to a woman, not ever. It's sure to lead to your downfall. His father's words rose in his mind. Sure, it was thirteen years ago, but his father had plenty of cautionary tales to go along with those words. And in all the years his father had been a Ranger, he'd never once fallen in love—not even with the woman who gave him a son and loved him until her dying breath.

And his pa was one of the best Rangers in all of Texas.

Then there was Anna Mae.

He couldn't say how it had happened or why, only that he had feelings for her that a man like him ought not to have.

"Maybe you need to think long and hard about what comes next in your life." Harrison's words were quiet against the heat of the afternoon. "No man is a Ranger forever. The fact you've lasted thirteen years and aren't dead is pretty amazing. What if this is God's way of showing you it's time for a change?"

"Change. And just what do you think I can..."

A ripple of movement near his tent caught his eye. It was slight. Barely there. But something—or more likely, someone—had just slipped inside his tent.

He drew his pistol and stalked forward without a word, but the sound of footsteps behind him told him Harrison followed.

When he reached his tent, he flung open the flap, his gaze and pistol moving in tandem, instantly seeking out the intruder. "Don't move."

A Mexican boy's arms went up, a letter clenched in one of his hands. "Don't shoot. I won't hurt you. I just have this."

The youth before him was too old to be a child, but not yet a man, and he looked vaguely familiar.

"Then why did you wait until I wasn't in my tent?" Cain growled.

The boy looked around, his hand clenching the letter even tighter while his tongue came out to lick his lips. "I... you weren't..."

"I wasn't supposed to catch you?" Cain moved closer, his pistol still trained on the boy, though nothing about him seemed suspicious. He reached out, snatched the letter, and held it out for Harrison to read. "What does it say?"

Cain wasn't about to take his eyes off the boy long enough to read the letter. Though he really did look familiar.

Cain thought back, tried to draw up the last time he'd seen that face. It was dark, and he'd been somewhere in Mexico.

"Hortencia." The memory of his former informant's family suddenly became clear. "You're her younger brother."

The boy's eyes widened. "I don't know what you're talking about."

"Don't lie to me." He may have seen the boy only once or twice, but he'd trained himself to memorize faces. Few skills proved more useful than that for a Ranger.

If the boy was Hortencia's brother, then that would make him Cristobal's nephew, and supposedly someone he could trust.

But he trusted nothing coming from the other side of the border. For all he knew, Eduardo's men might be holding the boy's family captive, and the letter could be a trap.

"What does it say, Harrison?"

Harrison shifted behind him. "It claims Velez escaped from prison."

Every muscle in his body slowly turned into stone.

Velez. Had. Escaped.

Cain holstered his gun. At least he knew the boy didn't pose a threat. Velez wouldn't be in a hurry for a lawman to have that news. In fact, coming here to give him the information probably put the boy's family at risk.

Cain rubbed his jaw. How had he not seen this coming? He'd spent the past month either assuming Eduard was running things or wondering how Javier Velez was managing to control his empire from a prison cell, but he'd never once stopped to ask just how secure that prison cell was.

Because if Velez could wield power from there, then it made sense he could wield enough power to break out.

"How?" Cain pulled off his hat and stalked over to the table where his maps of Mexico had been set, then grabbed the closest one, unrolled it, and tapped his finger on where the prison was located just outside of Chihuahua. "How did he escape?"

Harrison handed him the letter. "It says the judge who sentenced him to prison was found murdered in his bed. Right along with his wife and youngest son."

"Youngest son? What happened to the older son, or sons, if there are more than one?"

Harrison shrugged. "It doesn't say."

"He's old enough to ride for Velez," the boy offered. He still hadn't left his spot by Cain's bedroll, where he had likely been planning to slip the note.

It was all Cain could do not to curse.

"The judge's daughter is missing too," the boy added.

Something sickening twisted in his stomach. "How old is the daughter?"

The boy understood everything he implied with the question, because color rose on the boy's cheeks. "Younger than Hortencia, but not by much."

So probably seventeen or eighteen. The sickening sensation in his stomach turned to a cold, hard ball. There was no question what was happening to that poor girl. The only unknown factor was how long Velez would bother to keep her alive—and how cruel he would be when he finally killed her.

He crossed his arms over his chest and stared at the boy again. With information like that, the boy's family would have risked more than usual to get this message to him.

But why? Hortencia was somewhere safe, and there were no other daughters her age for Velez's men to violate. Was Velez threatening the boy's family in some other way?

"Tell me about your father and mother, your older brother too, the one that's married. Are they safe? Is one of them being held captive?"

"Roberto is riding with Velez. He... he didn't want to, but he didn't have a choice. Velez's men came. They said if he didn't go with them, they would kill his wife and baby."

"And what is Roberto doing for Velez?"

"He's getting more men to join the… the… I'm not sure if you would call it an army or something else. We don't have a choice about joining. Any man who can ride a horse and shoot a gun has to go, or what happened to the judge and his family will happen to everyone else."

"I see," Cain said. And he did.

Four months ago, he'd taken a group of three dozen men to *La Colina* to raid it. Now it looked like Velez was planning to do the same to Twin Rivers.

Except the man would probably be bringing three hundred men with him when he came, not three dozen.

There was only one way to stop it.

Someone needed to kill both Javier and Eduardo Velez. Soon. Before an army was gathered and more plans could be made.

And there was no doubting who the most qualified man for the mission was.

The only question was, would he be able to kill both of them and return alive?

He and Harrison had just been talking about how easily he'd lay down his life for others. But in those situations, it was always a calculated risk. Something he had a chance of surviving if he was smart.

This time, he had only seven trained men and a couple dozen volunteers to help him. He was smart enough to know what the outcome would be.

"There's something else I should tell you." The boy licked his lips. "When I was sneaking into your camp, there was a man. He was kind of far away, but when he turned my way, I… I think there was a scar on the side of his neck. Not too many people have scars on their neck."

"And you recognized him," Cain said, that heavy feeling returning to his stomach. "Does he work for Velez?"

"*Sí.* He was by the boulder between the river and the back of the courthouse."

"*Gracias.*"

Cain turned on his heel, then stalked out of his tent and called for his men. He might have a death sentence hanging over his head, but that didn't mean he was going to let the town of Twin Rivers go down with him.

21

"I already said, I'm not going to tell you anything."

Cain narrowed his eyes at the Mexican man standing behind the prison bars inside the town jailhouse. Once they'd known to look for him, it had taken his men less than twenty minutes to find the desperado. He'd been hiding in the alley that ran between the back of the sheriff's office and a row of houses, and the fact the man had gotten so close to where Daniel worked made his stomach hard.

What had the man's intentions been?

If the boy hadn't happened to be sneaking into town at the same time, would the man have searched through Daniel's desk and found information that might help Velez? Or would he have done something worse, like hide behind the door and wait for Daniel to enter so he could shoot him? Or trap Daniel and his deputies inside the building and set it on fire?

He didn't like this, not one bit.

Daniel had already found a couple men in town while he and Anna Mae had been in Mexico. One had worked for Eduardo and the other for Javier, and the argument Daniel had overheard had proven more useful than anything either of the men had been willing to say once they'd been arrested. Now there was another man in Twin Rivers that they'd happened to catch.

Had more men been sent? Ones they hadn't caught? Ones that had returned to Mexico with valuable information?

They were going to need to increase patrols, perhaps even alert shopkeepers to report any suspicious activity.

But first, he had to find a way to get information out of the man who'd been stonewalling him for the past quarter hour.

"Why were you by the sheriff's office?" he tried again. "Were you planning to sneak inside?"

The man crossed his arms over his chest and pressed his lips together in a flat line, his eyes almost daring Cain to get a single word out of him, never mind convincing the man to tell him something helpful.

Maybe he needed take a different approach. "Fine. Don't talk if you don't want to. Just understand that no one in this town takes kindly to kidnappers."

"Kidnappers?" The man scoffed, the scar across his neck bunching and stretching with each movement of his jaw. "You think that's why I'm here? To kidnap the Velez girl? That was a waste of time. No one cares about her."

"No? They don't care about preserving the business alliance that would be forged if Gabriella weds this Montrose fellow from Mexico City?"

The man smirked. "I work for Javier, not his fool of a son. Now that *el jefe* is out of prison, he's the one in charge, and the only thing he cares about is making you pay for what you did to Raul, to *La Colina*."

"And if I refuse to let him?"

The man's eyes grew dark behind his prison bars. "After *el jefe* turns this town to rubble, taking his niece back to Mexico will be as easy as feeding candy to a baby. Taking the sheriff's sister will be easy too. It's not like there will be anyone left to stop him. Did you know he's already promised her to us?" The man bared his dirty yellow teeth in a cruel grin. "After he takes a turn with her, of course. There are rumors about her beauty."

It was all Cain could do to keep his hands loose, to not let them tighten into fists at his side. But he refused to give himself away to this man, never mind the chill working its way down his spine.

Things were exactly as he'd thought. Velez was planning to raze Twin Rivers, and the man had to be stopped...

At any cost.

∽

ANNA MAE CUDDLED the little bundle of sweetness against her chest and drew in a breath, long and deep. Her precious niece only seemed to snuggle deeper against her chest, her sandy blond hair sticking up in haphazard little tufts.

Across the room, Charlotte slept peacefully, exhausted after the work of delivering her first child into the world. Daniel had stayed in the room for several hours after the babe had been born, holding her and smiling and whispering soft words into her ear. He'd left only a quarter hour ago, when he'd handed the babe off to her and gone across the street to see to something at the sheriff's office before night fell.

It was just as well. She was content to sit here all night and hold the newest addition to the Harding family.

Especially since she'd have to leave her niece in three more days.

Anna Mae looked down at the babe's softly closed eyes, and a lump rose in her throat. Maybe she could delay her trip to Houston for another week. If she stayed at Charlotte and Daniel's to help with the babe and kept away from town, she wouldn't need to endure the rumors floating around.

But what good would one more week do when she didn't want to leave at all?

Anna Mae bit her lip, but the action did little to stop the unexpected pain from opening in her heart, right beneath the spot where her new niece was currently curled.

What had she expected would happen anyway? That Cain would waltz into Twin Rivers, learn about the rumors, and pledge to leave the Rangers and become her husband?

Oh, there had been times she'd imagined marrying Cain over the years. But never had any of those times involved her brother standing over her shoulder, and Wes, Sam, and Harrison listening to every word she and Cain said.

She still wasn't sure how all six of them had ended up in Daniel's office. Sam, Wes, and Harrison had probably thought they were helping, but she'd been the only woman in a room with five men while they talked about her like she was a porcelain doll. Something to be either given away to a worthy owner or put in storage and taken out at a later time.

But she was neither. She was a living, breathing person. With hopes and dreams and feelings.

A single tear welled in her eye, and before she realized what was happening, it streaked down her face and plopped onto Lucy's head of downy hair.

The door to the room opened, and a familiar lanky form with long blond hair stepped inside.

"What are you doing here?" She swallowed and shifted Lucy closer to her chest. "Don't tell me you came to see the babe?"

Cain's hazel eyes landed on hers, a mixture of soft browns and greens that had always seemed at odds with the hardened Ranger he presented to the world. He took a step closer, then looked down into Lucy's sleeping face.

"She's so tiny." One of his large, rough fingers came out and stroked the babe's cheek.

Anna Mae nearly melted into a puddle. Right there on the chair. She swore every last bone in her spine turned into butter, and her arms almost felt too heavy to keep holding the babe.

Never, in all her years, had she imagined Cain taking any interest in a babe, let alone touching one. But he was still looking down at Lucy, as though the tiny infant was the only other living person in the entire world.

Then his eyes came up to meet hers, warm and soft and unguarded. "Looks like her ma."

Anna Mae swallowed, her eyes unable to leave his as she answered. "Yes, yes she does."

He glanced at the bed where Charlotte still slept. "How's she doing?"

"Fine. Tired, but that's to be expected. The doc says things went well, especially with this being Charlotte's first babe."

Cain gave a curt nod. "I'm glad to hear it." He shifted his weight from one foot to the other.

"If you're looking for Daniel, he went back to his office."

Cain pulled his hat off his head, allowing that long waterfall of golden hair to hang freely around his shoulders. "I didn't come here for Daniel."

"Were you hoping to speak with Charlotte, then?" She glanced at the bed.

"Not her either." He cleared his throat, then dropped to one knee in front of her and held his hat over his heart. "Anna Mae, will you marry me?"

"What?" She looked at him, her heart suddenly deciding to leave her chest and climb into her throat. "I... uh... You already asked this earlier, and I... I said was moving to Houston, remember?"

His jaw tightened. "No, I didn't ask you anything. Your brother did the asking, and if I aim to propose to a woman, I don't need someone else to step in and start yakking on my behalf. Let alone in front of half the town."

She sighed. "It was all a bit ridiculous, wasn't it?"

Cain rubbed the back of his neck, still down on one knee before her. "I'm not gonna claim to know much about romancing a woman, but it sure seemed like that was the kind of conversation a man and woman should have without a bunch of people looking on."

"Is that what you're trying to do, romance me?" A small smile crept onto her lips.

"No. Yes." He shook his head. "Hang it all, Anna Mae. You know I don't have the first clue about any of this romance business. I just want to know if you'll marry me."

She glanced down at Lucy's peaceful face. "Why are you asking? Is it because of the rumors?"

"Maybe, at least a little." His brow furrowed. "But isn't this what you...?"

Lucy let out a small cry, squirming against her chest. The babe's eyes were still closed in slumber, but probably not for long if they kept talking.

"Let's take this conversation outside so Charlotte and Lucy can rest."

Cain pushed to his feet, leaving space for her to rise and carry Lucy to the cradle beside Charlotte's bed. The swaying motion of her steps seemed to calm the babe's discomfort, and she laid the child down, then tucked a blanket around her before meeting Cain at the door.

He offered her his arm, and she took it, then sent up a silent prayer that no one would be around to notice the two of them emerging from the doctor's office together. Another rumor was the last thing she needed.

Darkness was already falling when they stepped outside, and just as she'd hoped, the section of street where they stood was deserted. Most of the activity at this time of night happened at the other end of town by the cantina.

Cain wordlessly led her around the side of the doctor's

office and down the alley that ran behind it until they hit a path that led toward the river. They continued in silence until the last building of Twin Rivers fell away and it was just the two of them walking through the long grass that grew in the moist soil of the riverbank.

Cain stopped walking all of a sudden and turned to her, keeping his grip on her arm so that she found herself nearly on top of him, their bodies so close she could feel the heat radiating from his chest and smell the fresh scent of his soap. And see the little flecks of green and brown and tan that made up the hazel hue of his eyes, and the dark line of brown that ringed them.

It was a mistake, being out here alone in the growing darkness, because all she wanted to do was lean forward and raise up on her tiptoes until their lips met.

"What's this really about?" His breath brushed her chin as he spoke, soft and warm. "A woman doesn't tell a man on three different occasions that she loves him, then turn him down when he finally proposes."

"I told you in my brother's office, while there's a part of me that wants to marry you"—wanted it so much she couldn't let herself think about it—"I can't let it be like this. Marriage is forever, and you…"

He was standing too close, his large body too near for her to form coherent thoughts. She gave her head a small shake and took a step back, only to find her arms suddenly cold where his hands had been. "It's nice what you're doing, truly. Honorable and gentlemanly and all those things. But I'm not going to force you into a marriage you don't want."

He watched her with those clear hazel eyes but said nothing.

"There's a part of me that wants to get married something fierce. I'll be the first to admit I've got a hankering to have a family way more than I've got a hankering to own a restaurant.

But at the same time, there's a bigger part of me that knows I'd never be content with a marriage that didn't look like my ma and pa's, or Daniel and Charlotte's."

Did Cain understand? If so, he showed no sign of it. His face was void of any emotion, though he still kept his eyes pinned to her.

"I want to marry a man who loves me so much that he can't imagine living without me, not a man who sees me as an obligation. I truly meant what I said earlier in Daniel's office. It's not that I don't want to marry you. It's that I don't want to marry you this way."

"Because you don't think I'm capable of loving you the way a husband should love his wife." Cain's voice emerged rough and gravelly, almost as though he'd swallowed a fistful of crushed desert rock.

"Not capable of loving me?" Had she heard him right? She must have, because even in the gathering darkness, she could see the sincerity in his clear hazel eyes. "I'd never say that. The problem is you don't want to put down roots. You don't really want this, me and you together. You don't want a family. You'd rather ride from town to town, meeting new people and finding someone to rescue, than be committed to staying in one place and needing to return home to your wife."

She swallowed the thickness rising in her throat. "You make a good hero, Cain. You really do. But being a good hero won't make you a good husband or father. And those are the things I need most from the man I decide to marry."

He took a step closer to her, bringing him near enough she could once again see the flecks of brown and green in his eyes, once again feel the heat of his breath when he spoke. "It's not that I don't want to be committed to you. You talk about putting down roots as though it's easy, something everyone understands how to do, but I don't. I don't know how to put down roots, how to be a husband or a family man. Just look at how I grew up. Did you know Harrison's pa used to... ah... use my ma's services?"

Something twisted in her stomach. "No. I didn't."

"Well, he did. Right along with Deacon Sutherland."

She choked back a small sob, then reached up and framed Cain's face in her hands. This man. This dear, sweet man. He pretended to be so rough, but how much had he endured growing up? How much of that pain did he carry inside him to this day?

"You know how to love, Cain. You know how to make sacrifices. I've always seen that in you. But if I were to say yes, what does our marriage look like three years from now? Or five?" She pressed her eyes shut against the pain of her words. "You're here in Twin Rivers now, but as soon as you defeat Velez, you'll be gone again."

"No, I won't."

Her eyes sprang open. "So you're willing to stay in Twin Rivers with me? To resign your position as a Ranger?"

"I already resigned. After they stripped me of my rank."

She gasped. "What? Why did they take away your rank?"

"For going into Mexico after you. Headquarters was livid I went into Mexico after Velez the first time. When I left Alpine and headed back into Mexico without waiting for their approval, they stripped me of my rank and refused to send any Rangers into Mexico after me, even when it was apparent I was in trouble. This time I was told that if I wanted to come back with my men to fight Velez, I'd have to turn over my badge and resign."

"So the men who rode into town with you today?"

"I've only got seven men, and each one of them resigned from the Rangers to come here and take on Velez."

Her legs suddenly felt too weak to support her, and she stepped back until she reached the boulder sitting by the riverbank, then sank onto it. "You were forced to give up your job as a Ranger because of me. Why didn't you say so?"

"When did I have time to tell you?" Cain yanked his hat from his head, then ran a hand through his long strands of hair before dropping down onto the boulder beside her. "The second I rode into town, your brother started throwing punches. Then you said you wouldn't marry me, and Charlotte went into labor."

"You could have at least started with that when you came to the doctor's office."

"Does it make a difference? You gave quite a long speech about how I'll never be able to give you the life you want."

She drew in a breath. "It does if this means you're not planning to leave Twin Rivers again."

"I don't expect to leave Twin Rivers, but not for the reason you're thinking." He took her hands and clasped them in his own, a breath shuddering out of him. "There's already a bounty on my head, which is dangerous enough for a lawman, but I learned this afternoon that Velez escaped from prison. He's gathering men to come here, and he has to be stopped."

"And you're going to be the one to stop him."

"It's my job."

"Not if you're not a Ranger."

He reached out and smoothed his hand over her hair, his fingers weaving between the strands as they slid down through the very end. "It's still my job, darlin'."

She pressed her eyes shut, tears welling behind them. "Reckon if you were to do anything other than try to stop him, you wouldn't be the man I fell in love with."

He drew her close, wrapping his arms around her and pulling her into the lean strength of his body. "We don't need to ask ourselves what life as a husband and wife will look like five years down the road, because I won't be around in one year, let alone five. I'll be lucky to live another month."

"So you want to marry me so you can go off and die?" She swiped a tear away from her cheek. "How's that supposed to make things better?"

"I was already thinking about proposing, because as you said earlier, it seemed like the honorable thing to do. But after I learned about the prison break, it became the only thing to do. First off, if we marry, the rumors about us will go away. Your reputation will be restored, and you'll be able to stay in Twin Rivers, even if I die two days later. Second, there's my money."

"Your money?"

He shrugged lazily, his arms still wrapped around her. "I've got no one to leave it to after I'm gone, and I saved up over the years. There's not a whole lot a man needs when he's sleeping under the stars every night and the Rangers are paying for rations. I asked Harrison to invest some of it for me a while back, too, and let's just say I could probably buy the town of Twin Rivers a couple times over if I wanted."

She could only stare at him. He had enough money to buy the town? Sure, it probably wasn't as much money as Wes had, seeing how he owned the A Bar W. But it sounded like he had about enough to put him on par with Harrison.

And this from the man who seemed to never care about anything?

"I can buy us a house, which you'd get to keep after I'm gone." He kept right on talking, as though the breath hadn't just been stolen from her lungs and a giant, gaping hole hadn't opened up somewhere in the vicinity of her chest. "And there's plenty of money for you to start a restaurant. You could buy an old building in town or have one built brand new. You'd have enough to keep yourself comfortable here in Twin Rivers for the rest of your life, if that's what you wanted. Or you could give the money away to the weaving shop across the river or find some other cause to support. I know you'll do a good job with my money after I'm gone, no matter what you decide."

"I..." What did she say to that? That she'd marry him for money?

She didn't want to marry him for money any more than she wanted to marry him because of rumors. She'd known Cain had grown up with just a ma and no clue about what a real family looked like. But she'd always hoped that one day he'd love her enough to learn how to be part of a family for her.

She swallowed the lump in her throat, but it sprang right back up, forcing her to talk around it. "When you proposed to me earlier, I hoped it was because of me, Cain. Not because of money or a bounty on your head or rumors. Because I was enough. Because you just plain wanted me to be your wife and nothing more."

"Oh, hang it all, Anna Mae. That's not what I'm trying to say either." He gave his head a hard shake, then hopped off the rock and started pacing. "See, this is what I mean about not making a good husband. I'm no good at this part. I swear I feel like ten times a fool for just talking about it, but... I... there's... it's that..."

He blew out a breath, then stalked straight toward her, his hands landing like two warm, heavy weights on her shoulders. "There's you. If we marry, I'd get to have you. At least for a week, maybe two if we're lucky."

"Have me as in take me to bed?" she snapped, her eyes growing watery. "Like what all the other men in town want to do?"

He stepped even closer, though that shouldn't have been possible because he was already standing near enough for the heat from his body to radiate into hers and the scent of leather and wind and man to wrap around her.

"There's that, yes." His voice rumbled out from his chest. "I'm not going to lie about wanting that part of a marriage with you. But then there's the part where I'd get to wake up next to you in the morning and run my hands through your hair whenever I want. I could kiss you in the center of O'Reilly Street, and no one could say anything about it. I could wrap my arms around you and hold you in church or at your brother's office or whenever else I like. I could simply be with you. And that's something in and of itself, because ever since I dropped you off at the doc's last week, there's a part of me that keeps wishing we were back in the desert, just the two of us, and all so I have an excuse to be that close to you again."

"You love me." She whispered the words into the sliver of space between them.

His Adam's apple bobbed, and he ran his gaze down her quickly, then brought it back up to find her eyes. "I love you. Yes. I just ain't any good at saying it, and I don't rightly know what to do about it. Other than ask you to marry me."

"I love you too."

A smile quirked the side of his mouth, and he stroked a strand of hair behind her ear. "I know, darlin'. That makes the second time you've told me."

"You're keeping track?"

"'Course I am. A man doesn't hear words like that without remembering every last thing about them."

She drew in a breath, then jumped off the boulder and threw her arms around him. "Yes, Cain. I'll marry you."

"You mean it?"

"I do."

"So all this time, I just needed to tell you I loved you, and you would have up and agreed to marry me?"

"Yes."

"Women," he grumbled, stroking his hand over her hair in that familiar way she was coming to love. "Ain't no understanding them."

She laughed into his chest, her eyes moist, but with tears of joy rather than sorrow. "It's not that hard to understand. I'm going to pray every day that God lets you live. That you can bring justice to Javier Velez and his son and still come home to me. Because you're going to make a fine husband, and an even finer father. Just you wait."

"I can't think of anything I want more," he whispered, his voice thick. Then he nudged her head up just enough to capture her lips with his own.

22

Married. His sister was going to get married.

To Cain Whitelaw.

And this after she'd proclaimed just a few hours ago that she would move to Houston.

Daniel slumped into the seat behind the desk in his office. When Cain and Anna Mae had come to him half an hour ago, he'd been tempted to object to the wedding, even in spite of the points Anna Mae had made. After all, he had plenty of doubts that Cain would make her a good husband.

But if Cain hadn't offered to marry her after all the rumors, Daniel wasn't sure he would have been able to fight alongside the man anymore.

But what if his sister was better off in Houston? There would be lots of men in such a large city, and surely one of them could give her a life she'd be happy with—even if it wasn't in Twin Rivers.

He didn't know what had changed Anna Mae's mind about marrying Cain, only that when the two of them had tumbled into his office, Anna Mae's eyes were glowing with happiness.

He didn't doubt Anna Mae was happy at this very moment, but would she still be happy a year from now? Or two or three?

Because he wanted his sister to have a lifetime of happiness with her husband, not just a few months. And he wasn't sure Cain could give that to her.

Scuffling and a giggle sounded from just outside his office door. Or maybe it was a moan?

Daniel eyed the window, where the lantern hanging from the porch post cast a shadow of two people entwined in each other's arms.

"I thought you were going to walk Anna Mae over to the doc's," Daniel called. "Not kiss on my front porch, and under the lamp, no less. Anyone walking by can see you."

"Don't care," came Cain's mumbled rasp, followed by Anna Mae's giggle. "I'm going to marry your sister tomorrow. No point in hiding how I feel about her."

"If you can't manage to walk her back to Charlotte and Lucy's room, I will," he growled.

Another giggle floated through the door, followed by the sound of boot steps on the stairs.

He stifled a groan. When his sister and Cain had tumbled into his office, Anna Mae's lips had been swollen, and her hair was far more messy than usual. Sure signs that the two of them had been kissing just a little too intently before coming to find him.

But Anna Mae had seemed sure that marrying Cain was what she wanted.

And Cain, for his part, had almost seemed happy about it. He had a certain way of looking at Anna Mae that was different from the usual laid-back, devil-may-care front he showed the rest of the world.

Daniel scrubbed a hand over his face. He might have his concerns about the marriage—what brother wouldn't?—but Anna Mae brought out the best in Cain. And he couldn't complain about that.

Footsteps sounded on the porch, and Daniel glanced at the clock. Nine thirty. It was a little early for his men to be checking in. That usually didn't happen until closer to ten.

The door opened, and Cain stepped back into the office.

Daniel frowned. "Don't tell me you gave my sister a reason to call off the wedding already."

"Sure didn't." Cain offered him a full grin. "Left her asking why we had to wait until tomorrow to get married and couldn't just march ourselves down to the preacher's tonight."

Daniel groaned. He did not need images of his sister's wedding night running through his mind. "Thanks for that."

Cain's grin grew even bigger. "Not a problem."

"If not Anna Mae, why are you here?"

The grin dropped from Cain's face. "I need a badge. Or rather, I need eight of them."

Daniel narrowed his eyes at Cain. But sure enough, the tin star that was always pinned to his vest was gone. "What happened to your badge from the Rangers? Don't tell me you lost it kissing my sister."

The tips of Cain's ears turned the faintest shade of red, but everything else about the man stayed serious. "Turns out the Rangers aren't too happy I left Alpine to go track down Anna Mae after she was kidnapped. They don't want me or anyone else going back into Mexico either. They sent a letter. To Alpine. To Pearce. He's in charge now."

Daniel pushed himself up from his chair. "They stripped you of your rank?"

Cain met Daniel's gaze, neither denying nor confirming.

"I'm surprised you didn't go back to Austin and beg them for forgiveness. They probably would have kept you on in Alpine, even if you weren't still a captain."

"I swore an oath to protect the innocent, and when I rode into Mexico and raided *La Colina*, I drew the attention of a dangerous criminal to Twin Rivers and all the innocent people here." Cain's eyes flashed. "Reckon it's my job, as a lawman—or a former lawman—to protect those people until the threat has been dealt with."

"What do you mean, 'a former lawman'?"

"Just that. I won't let anyone tell me I can't do my job, so I turned over my badge to come back to Twin Rivers and take care of Velez once and for all."

Something hard fisted in Daniel's stomach. Cain had spent every bit of his adult life as a Ranger. Coming here had meant the death of that line of work, and yet the man was standing before him, as aloof and stubborn as ever, as though returning to Twin Rivers was as mundane a decision as putting on a shirt each morning.

"You didn't have to return," he finally said. "Or bring men with you. You could have…"

Cain held up his hand. "Don't go getting all sentimental on me. This doesn't make me some kind of hero. It means right now, I'm nothing more than a hired gun, same as the seven men who resigned their positions to come with me. If Velez were to ride into town this very moment, I'd end up in jail right along with the outlaws, because I don't have the badge that says I'm serving justice when I fire my gun."

Cain blew out a breath, his shoulders slumping. "I know you're probably not happy about me and Anna Mae getting hitched, and I can't say I'd feel any different if I were the one with the sister and you'd sparked a bunch of rumors. But please, if you never give me anything again in my life, just…" A strange expression crept into his eyes, something that looked almost soft but also resigned. "Just give me a badge until I've taken care of Velez. And give the men who followed me here badges too."

"You don't expect to get out of this alive." Daniel wasn't sure how he knew, whether it had been the low, quiet tone of Cain's voice, or the way the creases around his eyes seemed suddenly more pronounced, or the strange look in his eyes. But the realization swept over him with such force that he nearly took a step backward.

His future brother-in-law didn't plan on being his brother-in-law for very long. And that probably had something to do with why he was marrying Anna Mae.

"I might have had a chance before." Cain kept his eyes pinned to him, not hiding the truth. Not even trying to sugar-coat it. "But now that Velez has escaped from prison, no. My goal isn't to get out of this alive; it's to see Velez and his son stopped. And I will, Daniel. I'll do whatever it takes."

Daniel's throat worked. "Does my sister know? Because so help me, Cain. If you think you can talk her into marrying you while you intend to go off and die—"

"She knows. I wouldn't have it any other way."

"Right. I…"

Anna Mae must have been all right with marrying Cain, then, even under the circumstances.

And now Daniel didn't need to worry about whether she would be happy in three years' time. Instead, he needed to worry about how to best support her when she buried the body of the man she'd loved for years but would have for only a short time.

His chest suddenly felt tight, and he fumbled absently for the handle on his desk drawer, pulling it open and blindly searching for the tin stars he kept there.

His hand finally clasped one of the stars, and he tossed it to Cain. Then he picked up three others and set them on the desk. "This is all I've got for now. I'll have the smithy make more and bring them over in the morning."

"Thanks." Cain pinned the stare on his vest, then grabbed the others and walked toward the door.

"You know, there's part of me that wants to hate you."

Cain stopped walking, then turned back to face him, but the vulnerability in his expression was gone, replaced with his familiar devil-may-care attitude.

"It seems every time you're around, someone in my family ends up suffering."

Again, Cain remained silent, his eyes appearing bored and flat, though Daniel was starting to wonder if that was a front he showed the world rather than how he truly felt.

Daniel came around the front of the desk and crossed his arms over his chest. "Eight years ago, my pa lost his leg in a situation that involved you. I know it wasn't your fault, but you were there, and I'm not going to lie and say it doesn't still hurt at times. Now you've compromised my sister, and she has to either leave town or marry. Lots of men in my position would hate you."

Still, he said nothing.

"But then you go and do something like this. Sacrifice the thing that means the most to you, and all so you can try to protect a town you claim not to care about and friends you pretend not to have." His throat turned as dry as the desert dust coating the windowsill. "You're a good man, Cain Whitelaw."

The stiffness left Cain's shoulders for a fraction of a second, and his eyes softened just a bit. "Protect Anna Mae after I'm gone."

Daniel swallowed. "I will."

"Good." With that, Cain turned and stalked out into the night, leaving Daniel to do nothing but stare at the door behind him.

And pray that somehow, someway, God would spare Cain's life.

23

Mrs. Cain Whitelaw. Anna Mae stared up at the ceiling in Daniel's house, the dark wooden beams spaced in even lines, holding up the white adobe above it. In six more hours, that would be her official name. Not Miss Harding, but Mrs. Whitelaw.

There was much to do. She planned to look like an angel. Last night Ellie had gone back to Daniel's house with her to raid Charlotte's closet for a dress they could use. Then the two of them had stayed up till the wee hours of the morning hemming it and taking in the seams, since Charlotte was a good six inches taller than Anna Mae. She planned to be the most beautiful woman Cain had ever laid eyes on.

But first, she needed to have a conversation with another man, and it wasn't going to be fun.

She rose from the couch where she'd spent the past several nights, her eyes bleary from only a few hours of sleep, even though her brain couldn't stop spinning. On the other side of the room, Ellie had made up a pallet of blankets on the floor, and she slept silently with Madeline. Anna Mae didn't stop to eat after she'd dressed or do anything that might wake the others. Instead, she moved silently to the door, only to be greeted with early morning sunlight and clear skies. It had the makings of a beautiful day for a wedding.

The trip to Fort Ashton took under a quarter hour, but as she approached the guard at the gate, she slowed and asked where she might find Paul Fordham.

True to the guard's word, she located him in the kitchen, taking an early breakfast with most of the other workers who were preparing to start their shifts for the day.

The second she stepped inside, every eye turned to her. Paul's were the eyes she sought. "Can we have a word, in private?"

"Of course." He rose and limped toward her, then extended his arm and guided her out of the kitchen.

But the second they stepped into the corridor, he dropped his arm. "I know what you're going to say."

She swallowed. "Do you?"

"Yes. It's been apparent all along. You're not going to marry me because you're in love with Cain Whitelaw."

She pressed her lips together. "I didn't realize it was that obvious."

"Maybe not to everyone, but to a man trying to win your attention—your heart—it's rather clear both of those things are already taken."

A faint pressure rose in her chest. She looked down, staring at the tips of her shoes against the dusty tiles that made up the floor of the corridor. "I'm sorry, Paul. I really thought that given enough time, my fondness for you might grow."

"It might have." His voice was dry and flat. "Had Whitelaw not kept returning."

She drew in a breath and raised her eyes. "He's proposed."

"At least he's got enough sense of responsibility for that."

She couldn't argue with him. As a Ranger, Cain lived honor

and sacrifice. But the one thing he didn't seem to have was responsibility, at least not when it came to a family.

"Just answer me this, Anna Mae." Paul shifted from one foot to the other, his blue eyes clear as they searched hers. "Are you... are you sure you'll be happy with him? Because if not..."

The sincerity in his gaze almost made her look away. "I am. It might not seem like it from the outside. But there's never been a man I can imagine myself loving as much as I love Cain."

"Well, then I suppose that's your answer. Good-bye, Anna Mae." He turned to step back into the kitchen, but she reached out and placed a hand on his arm, causing him to look back at her. "What is it?"

She swallowed again. "It's just that Gertie Cunningham is nice, and she just turned nineteen last month."

"I know." He ducked his head and rubbed a hand over his hair. "Reckon the two of us are in similar spots, because whenever I try talking with Gertie, all I find myself thinking is how she's not you."

She squeezed his arm. "You're a good man, Paul. I have no doubt there's an equally good woman out there somewhere for you. It's just not me."

"Thank you, Anna Mae. Now I best get back to breakfast."

"The wedding is today. At eleven." She wasn't sure what possessed her to say it, but it seemed like he should know, even if he wouldn't particularly enjoy hearing the news.

"You're not wasting any time." His voice emerged low and raspy.

"There's no reason to waste it."

"No." The sides of his mouth turned up into a sad smile, and he scanned her face. "If I were in Cain's shoes, I wouldn't want to waste a single minute with you either."

And then he turned and disappeared into the kitchen.

His wife couldn't seem to stop smiling. Cain watched as Anna Mae leaned over the table inside the dining room at the A Bar W and raised her voice. The eye of every single person there was riveted to her as she recounted how she'd shot the horse out from underneath Bernardo when they'd been trying to cross the border into Texas. The story may have contained a rather exaggerated account of their argument about which of them should try shooting the horse, but Anna Mae spoke in such a way that everyone in the room had smiles on their faces.

And Cain couldn't stop himself from smiling either.

Their wedding ceremony a couple hours earlier should have been a small affair, just like the last-minute meal they were now having. Only friends and family had been invited, but by the time Daniel, Wes, Sam, and Harrison gathered their families and showed up at the church, they had over two dozen people.

Then there had been the townsfolk who saw a small crowd at the church and had come over to see what was happening.

Before he'd realized it, the little church had been packed to the gills for their wedding.

Fortunately, Keely hadn't invited the entire town to their wedding dinner. That had been reserved for their original gang of friends.

And their wives.

And their children.

That made for twenty people if he counted Sam's and Daniel's babies. And they were all crammed round one confounded table.

He should hate it. Hate the noise and busyness, hate the way he was stuffed into his seat without room to stretch his legs out under the table or rest his elbows near his plate.

But for some reason, he couldn't take the smile off his face to save his life.

Never mind that the last time he'd sat at this table—for Easter dinner four months ago—he'd felt awkward and uncomfortable. Conversations and smiles had swirled around him then, much as they did now, yet they only made him feel as though he had no place seated at the table with the close group of friends.

But now...

He reached under the table and settled a hand on Anna Mae's leg.

She paused her story for the briefest of minutes and looked at him. Then her smile brightened even more, and she went right back to talking.

Now he felt like he belonged.

Because of Anna Mae.

Not because he was in some all-fired hurry to have every eye pinned to him, or to tell a winding, animated story. Not because Daniel was softening up a bit and had stopped walking around with a fencepost for a spine, or because Sam had adopted a family that was so large, Cain would never be able to memorize all the young'uns' names.

No. His wife was the reason he suddenly seemed to belong, because she accepted him. As he was. Even with his terrible upbringing and current lack of a job, his dusty clothes and his long hair, she'd still wanted to marry him.

Was this what his life would look like now? Dinner with friends and enjoyable conversation? Maybe the old gang could carve out some time to go fishing down at the river or hunting together in the mountains.

Maybe he'd been missing more than he'd realized in the thirteen years he'd spent away from Twin Rivers, constantly roaming around but never settling in any one place.

He swallowed the lump that had risen in his throat and leaned closer to Anna Mae. "We should be going."

She turned to him, her brow furrowed. "So soon? We were going to play charades in the parlor, and after that, I was hoping I could get Wes to open up the ballroom. Do you know how long it's been since I've danced?"

No one paid them any mind as they spoke. Sam had taken over the conversation and was telling a story about how Ellie had been beside herself when she first came to Twin Rivers and witnessed when he and Wes and Charlotte had castrated the steers for spring roundup.

"I need to work tonight, remember?" He hated that he needed to remind her. In fact, this was probably the first time since he'd left Twin Rivers with his pa all those years ago that he resented needing to go do lawman work. But he had little choice in the matter. The Ranger in him knew that he should have gone into Mexico last night, before any of Velez's men realized he'd arrived back in town. But he hadn't been about to up and leave Anna Mae after she said yes to his proposal. It had seemed like the best thing was to delay his trip by a day and get married first. That way his money and other accounts could be settled in her name in case he didn't return.

Not that he had a mind to get himself killed so soon, but a man could never predict this kind of thing.

"I want some time alone with you before I go into Mexico," he whispered against her hair.

The most delightful shade of red climbed onto her cheeks. "When you say alone, do you mean alone in your tent?"

He couldn't stop the grin that spread across his face. "Not exactly in my tent, no. But your mind is headed in the right direction."

Their wedding had been early enough in the day that they still had about six hours before darkness fell.

"Anna Mae, are you all right?" Keely set down her glass of

lemonade and eyed them from where she sat across the table. "Don't tell me Cain's misbehaving already."

"Not at all." Cain pushed his chair back from the table and stood. "I only told her that it's time for us to leave."

"But Anna Mae said she'd play horseshoes with us after dinner." One of Sam's young'uns said, a look of pure devastation on the boy's face.

Cain pulled back Anna Mae's chair. "She can come back tomorrow."

"What about charades? Anna Mae's the best at that too." Ellie's younger sister asked from the end of the table where the children were all seated. If he remembered correctly, her name was Susanna.

"Another time."

"I'll stop by your place tomorrow before I do my baking. We can play charades and horseshoes then, all right?" Anna Mae stood.

The children erupted into cheers that probably would have resulted in a scolding from most parents for not having manners at the dinner table, but Sam and Ellie just smiled at their children.

"Plan on staying for lunch tomorrow." Ellie sent Anna Mae a wink. "It's been too long since we've visited."

Anna Mae smiled back at her friend. "All right, I will."

The children broke into another round of excited cheering.

And to think, here he'd been feeling guilty about leaving Anna Mae alone so soon after their wedding. But the entire town loved her, and there was hardly a place she was unwelcome—except for maybe the Cunninghams' and Mullins's.

But those two old biddies had come to the wedding earlier, both of them looking mollified during the ceremony and even smiling a bit after it ended.

He'd also spied Gertie Cunningham talking to Paul

Fordham as they left the church, which was sure to make Mrs. Cunningham happy.

All in all, it took about ten minutes longer than it should have for Anna Mae to say her good-byes, but she finally took the elbow he offered and let him lead her from the dining room.

"I didn't realize just how popular you were at parties." He leaned down so his breath brushed the hair beside her ear as he spoke.

"I am, aren't I?" She smiled up at him, but then a crease formed on her brow, and the smile drooped into a frown. "I really wish you didn't have to go into Mexico tonight."

"Me too."

"I had my heart set on dancing in the ballroom."

He stopped walking. "You wish I didn't have to go into Mexico so we could... dance?"

"And play horseshoes. And charades. I usually give Sam and Ellie's boys some shooting instructions too. I bet they have their rifles in the wagon."

He hauled her against him, drawing her near enough he could smell the rosewater on her skin and the fresh scent of soap in her hair. "Woman, I have better things for you to do besides play charades."

She grinned up at him, her eyes sparkling. "You do? Does it involve this?"

She rose up on her tiptoes, and then her lips were on his, right there in the middle of the corridor.

He gathered her even closer, drinking in the taste of her soft mouth and the scent of her skin. She'd gone and pinned her hair up for the wedding, and there weren't any dark locks for him to tunnel his hands into. So he tilted her chin up at the perfect angle, then spread his hand against the back of her neck, holding her in place as his lips left her mouth and trailed down her jaw, then her neck.

She gasped and tried to pull away, but he only tilted her head more, giving himself better access to the creamy skin of her throat before bringing his lips back to claim her mouth again.

"I have some guest rooms upstairs if you're in need of one."

Cain jolted at the sound of the wry voice behind him, then looked over his shoulder to find Wes standing at the other end of the corridor near the dining room, a smirk on his face.

"No, thanks." He sent his friend a glare, then scooped Anna Mae up in his arms and carried her through the wide stone archway into the sunshine.

"What are you doing?" She batted his arm. "I'm perfectly capable of walking."

"Really? Because you seemed a little more interested in distracting me than you did in getting to the horse."

She huffed. "You're too good at kissing. It's not my fault that's all I can think about whenever we're alone. Now if you kissed like Robbie Gladwin—"

"You kissed Robbie Gladwin?" he growled.

"I was fourteen. Charlotte dared me."

"I still don't like it." As far as he knew, the young man had left town years ago, but he didn't cotton to the thought of Anna Mae kissing anyone other than him.

"Here you are, Cain." Dobbs, who managed the stables for the A Bar W, had already brought Maverick out of the barn. He took one look at Anna Mae and sent him a wink. "She looks good in your arms, iffin' you don't mind me saying so."

"Not at all." He hoisted Anna Mae onto the horse without letting her feet touch the ground, then swung up into the saddle behind her.

"Thanks," he called back to Dobbs, then flicked Maverick into a trot.

They were quiet for a few minutes as they rode through the

A Bar W gateposts, the hot afternoon sun beating down on them while a jackrabbit darted across the trail.

He soaked in the silence, enjoying the simple feeling of his wife sitting in front of him while the warmth from her back seeped into his chest. Last time they'd shared a horse, they'd been trying to stay alive as they wound their way out of Mexico, and Cain had done everything he could to stay straight in the saddle, letting his chest bump into her back as little as possible and keeping everything about the situation respectable.

This time he found himself relaxing into Anna Mae, then leaning forward to get another whiff of that rosewater she'd placed right where her neck and shoulder met.

Anna Mae didn't seem to mind. In fact, she sat in silence for most of the way into town. Only when they crested the hill that revealed Twin Rivers below did Anna Mae turn back to him, her body a bit stiffer than his own.

"I'm sorry, Cain, but I need to ask you something."

Her teeth sunk into her bottom lip, leaving it puffy, and it was all he could do not to lean forward and kiss away the redness.

"Have there been other women? Before me?"

He blinked, the desire to kiss her draining from his body. "What?"

She shifted awkwardly, a flush stealing over her face. "Other women. I was wondering if you... they... there have been... a lot of them?"

He sighed. And here he thought she'd been enjoying the quiet ride into town. "You don't need to go worrying about that or comparing yourself to anyone else. I've got eyes only for you."

"Yes, I know. That is, I'm not worried that you're going to leave me tonight and go visit one of the girls who work at the cantina." She licked her lips. "But still, we're married now, and

I'd like to know before we... ah... get to the room you rented for the night."

He swallowed. Was this what husbands did? Did they talk about things like this with their wives? None of his friends had warned him something like this might come up.

But his friends were clear back at the A Bar W, and Anna Mae was sitting right in front of him, looking at him with eyes that weren't just wide and vulnerable but also appeared a bit worried.

"Yes, I've been with women before, but that was a long time ago." He rubbed a hand down her arm, trying to soothe away the stiffness that had overtaken her body. "My pa's got some pretty firm opinions about the role women should play in a lawman's life, and I don't mean settling down and getting married. So there was a time, after I left Twin Rivers, when he was teaching me how to be a Ranger, that I tried some things with women, made use of the brothel each time I went somewhere new. But it didn't take me long to realize just how empty that was."

He looked out over the desert and sighed. "I might not be a family man, but it wasn't hard for me to see Wes was far happier married than my pa ever was visiting the beds of an endless string of women. And I did spend two years living with Preacher Russell. I'd be lying if I said none of his teaching wore off on me, even if I'm not one to drag myself to church every Sunday."

"Oh." Her eyes turned soft, and she twisted farther around in the saddle so she could better face him. "I understand now. Thank you."

He tucked a strand of hair behind her ear, then lowered his head until their foreheads touched. "You have any more questions about me or anything I've done—as a Ranger or not—you ask, all right? There's nothing I plan to keep from you. Nothing at all."

He rasped the last few words but kept his eyes pinned to Anna Mae. His pa would say he was crazy for letting a woman make him soft, but Anna Mae seemed to love him for who he was, faults and all. And for some reason he couldn't explain, he wanted to open up everything inside himself and be soft with her.

"So did you rent a room for us at Fort Ashton for the night?"

"No." He kicked Maverick back into a trot. At some point while they'd been talking, the horse had stopped, though he didn't remember pulling on the reins.

"Then if we're not going to your tent—"

"I'd told you I'd buy you a house, didn't I?"

"Yes, but I don't know when you want to—"

"We're going there."

She whipped around to face him again. "You bought me a house? Already?"

He shrugged. "There was a reason I asked for the wedding to be at eleven and not nine. Needed a couple hours to get things sorted with the bank and all."

"What house did you buy?" Her brow puckered, and he could see her cataloging the empty houses in Twin Rivers—of which there were only three.

"The old Rivera one."

"You bought the Rivera place?" she squealed, her eyes dancing as she turned the rest of the way around and threw her arms around him. The sudden motion shifted the weight on Maverick's back so much that the horse sidestepped and whinnied before continuing down the trail.

Cain chuckled and wrapped his arms around her. "You haven't even seen the inside of it. You might hate it and want a different house."

"I'll like it."

The Riveras had owned a bank in town for the space of about ten years, but Twin Rivers was small, and there was already a branch for a different bank in town. So the Riveras closed up shop and moved to El Paso, where they opened another bank. For about a decade the house had sat empty.

"Figured it's big enough you could open up a restaurant on the first floor."

"I could...?" She squealed again, hugging him even tighter than before. "A restaurant in my own house? I hadn't even thought of that. It's probably big enough we could live on the second floor, and isn't there a small courtyard? I could pay the Owens boys to weave me some ocotillo mats for shade and put in outdoor seating, plus whatever the dining room will hold, and..."

Her words went on, her eyes alight with hopes and possibilities the rest of the way into town.

All he could do was smile down at her like a buffoon.

She kept talking as they turned down O'Reilly Street and then a side road leading off it, her voice loud enough that half the people in Twin Rivers probably heard everything she said. But when he pulled Maverick up to the hacienda that was located only one block off the main road, she quieted.

As far as haciendas like the A Bar W or Fort Ashton went, the Rivera House was small. But compared to the usual three-room, single-story houses that made up most of Twin Rivers, it was almost like a small mansion.

"Oh, Cain," she finally whispered. "It's beautiful."

"I hired a team of women from Mexico to come and clean it this morning. But still, no one's lived in it for ten years. I imagine there's more work to be done, especially if you're going to turn the first floor into that restaurant." He swung off his horse, then reached up for her.

She came willingly into his arms, but once again, he didn't set her on her own two feet. Instead, he carried her toward the double doors of the house.

The arched stone entrance that greeted them had definitely

been dusted and mopped, though the room still smelled as though it had been shut up for a bit too long.

Anna Mae squirmed and craned her neck, trying to see around him. "Let me down so I can look."

He tightened his hold. "Do I have to?"

She laughed. "Of course. What's the point of buying me a house if I can't look at it?"

He glanced at the stairs. He'd had a mind to carry her straight up to the bedroom, but Anna Mae would be spending the rest of her life here, and it seemed a bit brutish not to let her look around.

He set her down on her feet, and she was off, darting around the side of the entrance that opened to the courtyard and into the first room on the right. He followed her only to find her muttering about how it was the perfect size for tables for her restaurant. Then she went through the door that opened into the courtyard and the arched corridor that edged it, talking to herself about just where she wanted to set up a shaded seating area.

Standing in the courtyard, she was able to figure out which room was the kitchen, and she ran there next. A squeal echoed from the room before Cain had even sauntered inside.

"It's perfect! Look at all this space!" She spread her hands out and twirled around. "I had no idea this house had a kitchen so big. Thank you, thank you, thank you!"

She ran up to him, gave him a quick peck on the lips, and was out the door and exploring the next room before he had a chance to grab her and give her a real kiss.

She ran into the other four rooms on the first floor, coming up with ideas for how to use each room she entered. Then she dashed up the stairs and started exploring the series of bedrooms.

Cain followed her up the stairs, his gait slow as he made his way around the corridor to the door of the bedroom that ran the full length of the south wall. He leaned against the railing that opened into the courtyard below while Anna Mae explored a couple of the other rooms.

Finally, she stopped beside him.

"Is this one ours?" Her chest heaved from all the running she'd done, and a warm flush covered her face.

"It is." He nodded toward the door. "Go on. Open it."

He followed her as she walked to the door, slowly turned the knob, and stepped inside.

"Oh, Cain..." Her hands came up to cover her mouth. "It's beautiful."

"I agree. You are absolutely breathtaking." He wrapped his arms around her from behind, and she drew in a breath, relaxing against him as she stared out the series of large windows that faced the Rio Grande and the mountains jutting up from the opposite bank.

"I was talking about the view."

He didn't need to see her face to know she was smiling. Somehow he could hear it in her voice. Since the hacienda was taller than most of the other houses in town, they could see over the smattering of roofs and down to the green grass and trees of the river, then up to the pink-and-yellow-hued mountains.

"I had no idea anywhere in town had a view like this. I thought I needed to go out to the A Bar W for something so pretty."

"It's how I knew this was the right house for you. Once I saw the view, I couldn't imagine you living anywhere else."

She drew in a satisfied breath, then turned in his arms and laid a hand on his cheek. "Thank you."

He leaned forward, ready for their lips to touch.

But Anna Mae was already dropping her hand and turning toward the bed. "Where did you find this bedspread? I don't even think Keely has something this fancy in her room."

Cain glanced down at the cream-colored spread with a diamond-shaped pattern in turquoise, dark orange, and brown. There was no question it had been meticulously hand stitched. The moment he'd seen it, he'd known he had to have it for Anna Mae.

"Harrison had some people come through the fort last week. They had quite a large assortment of textiles. Harrison said they normally used Velez for transport, but after he was arrested, they broke off business dealings."

"And all this was just sitting in his storeroom, waiting to go to Austin with the next caravan?" She traced a finger over one of the intricate diamond shapes.

"It was, though I think Alejandra claimed a few things for her and Gabriella's rooms."

She peeled back the top blanket to feel the sheets beneath. "I don't think I've ever felt anything so soft."

"I have. Your hair."

That warm flush stole over her face again, and she cast him a shy smile. He was just about to step in and kiss her when she dropped the sheet and wandered to the dresser.

Was it just him, or now that they were finally alone in their room, was she trying to avoid getting kissed?

"The furniture is beautiful too. I love the carvings on the drawers." She traced her hand over the scrolling design on the top drawer. Then her foot bumped into her bag on the floor, and she looked down.

"Is this my carpetbag from Daniel's? And the trunk that I had at Wes's?" She glanced up at him, her brow furrowed. "You had them bring my things?"

He shrugged. "Some of them. Enough to get you through the night, at least. You can collect the rest tomorrow."

"So Daniel and Wes knew about this house? What about Keely and Charlotte and the others? Did everyone know except me?"

The tips of his ears turned warm. "Everyone's happy for you, Anna Mae. No one liked the rumors going around or the cowhands thinking they could take liberties with you. So when I said I'd proposed, the rest just fell into place."

She came toward him then, wrapping her arms around his middle all on her own. "People like you, too, you know."

He barked out a laugh. "I'm not so sure about that."

She frowned up at him. "I am."

He stared down at his wife, into her soft, warm eyes and the concerned crease on her brow, and felt a lump rise in his throat. "I don't need everyone in town to like me. Just you."

"I don't just like you, Cain. I love you." Then she pressed up on her tiptoes and kissed him again. All on her own.

She tasted sweet, like the frosting from their wedding cake, and warm, like a sunbaked rock. She smelled like roses, but if trust and honesty had scents, he swore he could smell them on her skin, too, just beneath the rosewater she'd dabbed under her ear.

He reached up and felt around the side of her head, then pulled a pin from her hair, but no soft, dark tresses fell into his hands. He blindly searched for another pin, his lips still pressed to hers.

Somewhere in the distance a horse nickered, then whinnied, then...

"Maverick." He pulled away from her, his chest heaving. "I forgot to stable Maverick."

In fact, he wasn't even sure that he'd tied Maverick up, as intent as he'd been on carrying Anna Mae over the threshold.

"Don't move." He took a painful step back from her.

Anna Mae's own chest was heaving, her eyes half glazed as she watched him.

"I'll be right back."

"All right." She licked her lips, which were full and red and testified to just how thoroughly he'd been kissing her.

"No. On second thought, take your hair down. I want to feel it in my hands next time I kiss you."

"Consider it done." She reached up and plucked one of the pins from her head, and a curtain of hair fell beside her cheek.

He groaned. How had she managed to do that so easily? But he didn't ask. Instead, he turned and barreled down the corridor. The sooner he saw to his horse, the sooner he could get back to their room and bury his hands in her hair.

He found Maverick nibbling on one of the shrubs in the neighbor's yard. Fortunately, the horse hadn't traveled too far, but he wasn't in a hurry to go into the small stable on the side of the house either. Even so, Maverick would have his work cut out for him when they went into Mexico later that night, which meant the beast needed his saddle off and some rest away from the heat of the sun.

It took Cain only a quarter hour to tend to his horse, but never before had fifteen minutes felt so long. By the time he climbed the stairs to his bedroom, his own neck felt hot from the heat of the sun, and he needed a glass of water.

Or at least, he thought he needed water, until he opened the door and found Anna Mae standing there in her chemise, her hair falling in soft waves around her shoulders while she stared out at the mountains.

"You're lovely," he whispered on a half breath, his feet giving him no choice but to cover the distance between them.

She whirled around, her hand clamped to the front of her chest as though trying to cover the skin just above her chemise. "Did you put Maverick away that fast? I'm not... that is... I wasn't... ready for you yet."

"And just how did you plan to get ready for me?" He jutted his chin toward the bed. "By crawling in there and pulling the covers up to your neck so I couldn't see you?"

She swallowed. "Maybe."

He grinned as he came to a stop in front of her, then peeked down at where her hand still tried to cover the creamy skin below her collarbone, never mind that her chemise itself had a rather high neckline. "Why are you so nervous? You weren't the least bit frightened when I left, and I've seen you in a chemise before."

"Yes, but we were kissing before you left, and now I... er... Stop looking at me like that. The last time you saw me in a chemise, you were rather irate, if I recall."

He bent and planted a kiss on the place where her neck met her shoulder. "Only because I couldn't touch you or see what you looked like with the chemise off."

Her breath hitched. "You shouldn't say such things."

"You're my wife. I can say those things as much as I want. Every day. Multiple times a day. For as long as my heart is still beating. And I can see you with your chemise off too."

The redness from her cheeks spread downward, over her neck and beneath her hand, then disappeared under her chemise.

"Anna Mae, I don't know how much longer I've got left on this earth, but the good Lord's seen fit to give me this afternoon with you. Let me love you the way a husband is supposed to love his wife."

Her breath shuddered out against his chin. Then she met his eyes and lifted her arms, looping them around his neck. "All right."

That was the only invitation he needed to scoop her up and carry her to the bed.

24

"Anna Mae, this is so lovely!" Alejandra smiled as she looked around the large room that would soon be used as the dining room for the restaurant. "I know you were at the fort finding dishes that you could buy from Harrison, but I never imagined you'd have the place looking like this."

"These windows let in so much light," Keely called from where she gazed out one of the particularly large windows with an arch at the top.

Anna Mae couldn't help but smile. She wasn't sure if it was because she held her precious niece curled against her chest, or because every last one of her friends were in her dining room, falling in love with her new house. Either way, for the first time since Cain left four days ago, the smile that had inched onto her face seemed content to stay there for longer than a few seconds.

"I really couldn't imagine a better house for you." Charlotte set down one of the blue-tiled plates that Anna Mae had wheedled away from Harrison and gave her a hug, never mind that Lucy lay snuggled between them.

"Did you move these tables in here by yourself?" Ellie studied the four tables that Anna Mae had found in other rooms of the house and wrestled into the dining room. "How many more do you think you'll need? I could have the boys go up into the mountains and cut down a few pine trees to make more tables for you. I bet we could even get them to all be the same size and shape."

"Could you?" Anna Mae jostled Lucy. Cottonwoods were the only trees that grew in the desert, and they grew big enough to use for lumber only if they were close to a river or stream. But the higher elevations in the mountains held pine trees aplenty.

"I can get some of our ranch hands to bring wood down from the mountains on the A Bar W too," Keely said. "If you need more trees, just ask."

"I kind of like the round tables mixed in with the rectangles." Gabriella studied the way she'd positioned the tables, two of which were rectangles while the other two were round. "It feels a little cozy and personal, not as formal as most restaurants."

Anna Mae cocked her head to the side and looked at the tables. The round ones wouldn't be able to fit more than two people, but a few smaller tables weren't a bad idea. "I really don't care, as long as I have enough tables to seat everyone when I open."

"I still can't believe Cain up and bought you a house." Charlotte ran a hand along the shelf that Anna Mae was using to display her new plates.

"Isn't it perfect?" She looked around the room, another smile creeping onto her face. It still needed some work before she could open the restaurant, but if things kept coming together, she might be able to open as soon as next week. "I always knew this place was here, but I never stopped to wonder what it looked like inside. It was so big and not something I imagined myself ever owning."

"It's not something any of us ever imagined owning," Charlotte said. "It's just been forgotten on this quiet little side street, but it's close enough to the main road that you're sure to get business, especially if you put a sign out on the corner. And everything about this just feels perfect for you."

Anna Mae grinned. "It sure beats the room I was renting at the A Bar W, doesn't it, Keely?"

Keely smiled back at her. "I already miss having you there, but yes, this is much better."

"Come on, I haven't shown you the kitchen yet." She shifted the still-sleeping Lucy onto her shoulder and headed out the door. Her friends followed her as she tromped across the middle of the courtyard straight toward the swinging double doors that marked the kitchen.

Charlotte stepped inside first, and she gasped. "I don't even like to cook, but this is gorgeous."

"Oh, I agree! It puts the A Bar W kitchen to shame." Keely headed straight to the stove and peeked inside.

Anna Mae rolled her eyes. "The A Bar W kitchen is far bigger."

"Yes, but it doesn't have counters and drawers and cupboards built directly onto the wall." Keely ran her hand over the smooth wooden surface that was, in fact, attached to the wall.

Anna Mae had never seen such a thing before. Usually shelves and hutches and cupboards were all freestanding, able to be moved around a kitchen as needed. But here the counter, cupboards, and drawers had all been built into the wall and edged with tile. Most of the tile was white, but some of it had intricate little blue designs that formed patterns.

"I love the patterns that the blue tiles make on the walls." Almost as though sensing her thoughts, Ellie stepped right up to the counter and ran her hand over one of the designs on the wall.

"And the old wood is lovely." Alejandra joined Keely at the counter. "It reminds me of some of the grand houses I used to visit when I lived with my uncle."

Anna Mae smiled as her friends explored the kitchen, opening cupboards to study just how the counter had been attached to the wall and running their hands over the intricate designs on the tiles.

Or rather, most of her friends explored the kitchen. Charlotte, on the other hand, came over to lean against the wall by her.

"Cain really did well with this house."

Anna Mae sighed and absently patted Lucy's back. "He did. Didn't he?"

"I know you've had feelings for him for a while. But your wedding seemed so hasty, and there's so much that goes into a good marriage. Yet after seeing this house, it's clear that Cain not only loves you, but he's committed to you too."

Was that what this house meant? That Cain's feelings for her went beyond love, and that he was committed to putting down roots and creating a family with her?

Or was he just trying extra hard to take care of her because he didn't think he'd be alive in another month?

She had to admit, in the four whole days they'd been married, he'd done an excellent job of providing for her, even if they'd been together for only a few hours before he left to go into Mexico.

"I think Cain's secretly loved you for years." Gabriella twirled around the kitchen, her words ending on a dreamy sigh. Then she clasped her hands together under her chin, almost as though imagining herself in a similar house one day.

"I'm quite certain he hasn't loved me for years, but it's kind of you to say so." Anna Mae smiled at the girl's antics, all romance and sunshine. She couldn't be more opposite from Alejandra, either, who was all serious practicality.

"Now I'm curious." Alejandra cocked her head to the side, leaning against the counter as though she was settling in for a long conversation. "How did you know Cain had feelings for you? He always keeps himself so aloof that I don't know how you can even tell what he's thinking."

"I'm not sure. Honestly, I didn't think he even knew I existed until I found those sketches in his book last spring."

"What sketches?" Charlotte reached for Lucy.

Anna Mae handed her niece over, her face turning warm. Had she really just said that bit about the sketches aloud? "I... uh... they were nothing, really. Just sketches for work is all."

"If they were for work, you wouldn't be blushing," Alejandra quipped.

Anna Mae licked her lips, recalling the day she'd ended up in Cain's tent last spring, listening to him lecture her about how she couldn't come to the Ranger camp anymore because all she did was distract his men.

Trying to calm him down, she'd offered him an apple dumpling, and when she set the pan down to give him one, it had been right beside one of his open sketchbooks. She'd picked it up and flipped through it. There had been a sketch of Alejandra and another of the scene where they'd found a dead body in the desert. At first, it was easy to believe Cain when he'd said they were for work, but it had been a little less easy as she flipped to a sketch of Preacher Russell, then her brother, and finally, her.

And there hadn't been just one.

She didn't know what she'd done to give herself away, but Cain must have noticed something was wrong because he took a step closer to her and peered over her shoulder, then tried to take the book.

"You best get back to town."

She couldn't make herself let go of the sketchbook as she stared down at the image with cascading black hair and happy eyes, and a wide smile. "This... this is me?"

"I said it's time to go."

He reached for the book again, but she held it away from him. "Why would you draw a sketch of me?"

"Same reason I draw sketches of everyone else. Sometimes it's work, sometimes I'm bored."

"But this... it... it makes me look... beautiful." *Far more beautiful than the reflection she saw when she looked in the mirror. Was the sketch a reflection of what Cain saw when he looked at her?*

"That's because you're beautiful." *The words were quiet inside the tent, and she couldn't stop herself from looking into his eyes, into the tiny flecks of green and brown that looked almost warm when they stood so close.*

"You think I'm beautiful?"

He groaned. "Everyone thinks you're beautiful. It's why my men can't stop fighting over you."

She set the sketchbook down and took a step closer. "I didn't ask about your men. I asked about you. Do you think I'm beautiful?"

His tongue came out to lick his lips. "I... ah... I think you're my friend's sister, and I need to watch out for you. That's what I think."

"You didn't answer the question."

"And I don't intend to. I'm only going to be in town for a few more weeks."

"Why would that matter—unless you do think I'm beautiful?" *She took another step nearer.* "Unless you're attracted to me and don't want to admit it."

She was standing close to him now. So close that the scents of sunshine and wind and leather twined around her, so close that the heat of his breath grazed her chin. So close that if she raised up on her tiptoes, her lips would brush against his.

He stared down at her for a moment. Did he feel it? The way the air seemed to hum between them? The way the breath hitched in her chest and it seemed oh so easy to simply raise up on her toes and feel the softness of his lips?

But then his eyes turned hard and he stepped away.

"I don't understand. Why won't you say whether you think I'm beautiful?" She gave a little huff and tried to step close again, just so she could smell the sunshine and wind on his shirt, see the little flecks of color in his eyes.

But Cain held out his hand, preventing her from coming any closer. "I won't say because you want to get married one day. You want to settle down and have a passel of young'uns, and I'm not the type to stay in one place for more than a few weeks, let alone speak vows and raise a family."

"Anna Mae, where'd you go on us?"

She jolted, then followed the sound of Gabriella's voice until she found the girl standing beside the sink, her head cocked as though her curiosity had been piqued.

"Nowhere. I'm right here."

"Thinking about the sketches?" That dreamy look filled Gabriella's face again.

She sighed. "Do any of you remember how Cain used to draw things when he was younger?"

"Charlotte was the only one of us who was here." Ellie tilted her head in Charlotte's direction.

Charlotte only quirked an eyebrow at her. "I never paid any attention to Cain, and I certainly never realized that you were paying attention to him, or I would have tried to talk you out of it. He was nothing but trouble as a boy."

Anna Mae licked her lips. "Well, he carried around a sketchbook. Sometimes, when he wasn't allowed to go home—I think maybe because his ma had men visiting, though he never came out and said it—he would find a place to go and draw the loveliest scenes. Of the river, of the mountains, even of the town."

She looked around to find all her friends watching her, the

intricacies of the kitchen forgotten. "So last spring when I found his sketchbook, he claimed it was all for work, but when I flipped through the sketches, there were ones of me. Lots of them."

Charlotte tilted her head to the side. "And yet you don't think he's loved you for years?"

Her face heated. "I... he never said he did."

"He's Cain." Keely shrugged. "He doesn't say anything unless someone drags it out of him."

"Those sketches are the most romantic thing I've ever heard of." Gabriella clasped her hands under her chin again and fluttered her eyelashes. "You should frame them, maybe hang them in your bedroom."

Anna Mae stiffened. "Absolutely not. I am not hanging sketches of myself around my house. That just seems odd."

"It won't look odd once they're up. Especially not if you add some of his other sketches too." Gabriella started looking at the walls, as though she could almost imagine sketches hanging on some of them. "Does he still do landscapes?"

"Yes. I mean, he claims it's all for work, but it isn't. I caught him sketching while we were stuck in the desert."

"There you have it." Keely looked around the walls as though she, too, was imagining sketches hanging there. "If he does a sketch of you and a sketch of himself, or some landscapes, or several of us together, it won't seem odd to hang them up."

"I bet you could even hang some in your restaurant," Alejandra said.

"Maybe." She tried to imagine what Cain's drawings would look like on the walls inside her dining room. The picture that formed in her mind made her belly feel warm.

Or it would, if her husband lived long enough to see the sketches hanging there. But when Cain had left four days ago, he'd told her he'd try to be back before the next night.

Not only had he not returned, but after four days, she wasn't sure she'd ever see him again.

At this very moment, he might be lying in the desert, wounded and in need of water.

Or maybe he'd already been killed, and the desperadoes were doing terrible things to his body.

She twisted her hands together while her friends chattered about the walls and whether tapestries or paintings should go in the dining room along with the sketches, but all she could think about was how Cain had spoken vows to her, then taken her to bed and loved her in a way she hadn't known was possible. After that, he'd held her in his arms as they'd lain in bed and watched the sunset fall over the mountains.

And then he'd kissed her good-bye and slipped out into the night.

Oh, this was part of the reason she hadn't wanted to marry Cain in the first place. She didn't want to be in a marriage where she was separated from her husband for long periods of time, always wondering if he was safe.

She'd tried not to let herself think about his absence overmuch, had kept herself busy the first day he was gone, then the second. She'd admit to crying when she'd gone to bed last night, but only because she wanted her husband beside her and didn't have the first clue if he was still alive.

"Anna Mae, are you all right?" Charlotte asked from beside her.

She gave her head a small shake. "I'm sorry. All this talk about sketches has me thinking about Cain. He was supposed to be back by now, and I'm starting to wonder if..."

"Come here." Charlotte slid an arm over her shoulder, then pulled her close until they were once again hugging with Lucy in between them. "Your husband went into Mexico to track down an evil, evil man. It's normal to be worried."

"I know." She wiped her eyes. "I just expected we'd have more than one day together is all."

"You'll have more than one day together. I mean, you disappeared for almost a month, remember?" Charlotte rubbed a hand down Anna Mae's arm in long, soothing strokes. "And we all thought you were dead, only to find out that you'd been waiting until you were strong enough to walk on your leg to come home."

She blew out a breath. "I suppose you're right. Maybe Cain's stuck in Mexico for a good reason. Maybe he's figured out where Velez is, and I just need to

"Trust God," Ellie said. "That's what you need to do. Trust God to keep your husband safe."

"But what if God doesn't keep him safe?" She brought her hand up to swipe at a tear that had somehow trickled down her face. "What if God allows him to die?"

"Like God did with Wes's first wife, Abigail?" Keely's voice was soft, but it had a way of filling the giant kitchen. "That was a lesson Wes had to learn before we could be together in the ways that really mattered. Not that I think God wants Cain to die, but even if he never returns from Mexico, God has still been good to you, and you can trust Him in that."

"'*Blessed is the man that trusteth in the* Lord, *and whose hope the* Lord *is*,'" Alejandra whispered. "'*For he shall be as a tree planted by the waters, and that spreadeth out her roots by the river, and shall not see when heat cometh, but her leaf shall be green; and shall not be careful in the year of drought, neither shall cease from yielding fruit.*'"

Alejandra held out her hand for Gabriella, a wistful look on her face. "I used to lie in bed at night and quote those verses in my head, all while praying that God would allow Gabriella and me to be together. Never once in all of that did I imagine how truly good God's plan would end up being for me. Never did I imagine I'd get to marry Harrison and be with my sister too."

Anna Mae only sniffled. Alejandra was probably right. She needed to trust that God had good things planned for her and Cain, but part of the reason they'd married was because Cain thought he was going to have to sacrifice his own life to bring down Velez.

And now that Cain might already be dead, the pain in her heart seemed almost unbearable.

"I know God's timing might seem off in all of this, but keep in mind none of us even realized Cain was the man God had for you up until a few days ago." Charlotte stroked Anna Mae's back. "But standing here, looking at this house he bought for you, it's kind of hard to argue that God wanted the two of you together. And you waited years for that. Now you need to wait on His timing to bring Cain back to you."

Anna Mae couldn't stop herself from looking around the beautiful kitchen. "You're right. All this makes me happy that I waited for Cain. With all those marriage proposals I got over the years, sometimes I wondered if I was a fool for not saying yes, or at least not allowing some of the men to court me. But none of them ever seemed to compare with Cain, and so I just... waited."

"You waited longer than any woman I've ever seen, and for a relationship that seemed almost hopeless." Charlotte gently patted Lucy's back. "Now you just need to wait again."

"I think there's a lot to be said about waiting for God's timing." Keely fiddled with one of the whisks on the counter. "I mean, if Wes hadn't posted that ad for a bride when he did, I never would have responded to it, or come to Twin Rivers and met any of you. But the timing was just right. Because a year earlier, I never would have been in the position to answer that ad."

"I wouldn't have been able to bring my siblings to Twin Rivers without God's timing either," Ellie said. "Everything about the situation seemed so very wrong when it was happening. I kept asking why my aunt couldn't have taken in some of my siblings like we'd originally planned, or why my mother had to die. Why my father refused to have anything to do with us afterward. It was all so hard, and I won't lie. Bringing eight siblings into a marriage certainly caused some issues between Sam and me during our first months together. But now that I look back on it all, I can see how God had a way of working everything out, even though I didn't realize it at the time."

Anna Mae drew in a breath. Her friends were right. Each and every one of them had gone through their share of trials to get to where they were, and each of them was in a good place and married to a wonderful man. Now she was the one facing trials.

But could she really trust God to bring Cain back to her, when Cain himself wasn't even sure that he'd be coming back?

25

From his position crouched behind a rock, Cain readjusted his hat against the hot summer sun. His eyes scanned the remote mountainous stretch of desert for any sign of activity, but it seemed not even the jackrabbits and javelinas paid attention to this baked stretch of land.

"Kind of makes you wonder how many canyons a place can have, doesn't it?" Ridley said from beside him, his eyes riveted to the small crevice in the towering wall of rock that jutted out from the desert floor. "Because I swear we should have done explored every canyon in Mexico twice over by now."

Cain turned his head and smiled at the man who looked almost like the spitting image of himself. Ridley was tall and lanky and had let his blond hair grow increasingly long during the year and a half he'd been a Ranger. "I don't care if we need to explore every canyon and cave in northern Mexico six times over. We're not going back to Twin Rivers until I find where Javier and Eduardo Velez are hiding."

On their first night in Mexico, they'd gathered enough information to learn that Eduardo Velez had left Mexico City to join his father. They were hiding together in the mountains, in a place big enough to conceal them and their men but remote enough that none of the local villagers seemed to know where they were.

Cain was determined not to leave Mexico without learning exactly where Velez was. And if he and Ridley could manage to avoid being discovered, then return to Twin Rivers to gather the men, he just might be able to sneak back into Mexico and kill both of the Velez men before anyone knew what was happening.

As far as he could tell, that was his best chance of surviving the border war he was stuck in the middle of.

"I sure hope Velez is hiding in this canyon," Ridley said from beside him, almost as though the younger man could read his thoughts. "Nothing against your jerky, Cap'n, but after nearly a week of trail food, a man gets a hankering for a nice, home-cooked meal."

"I understand." In the five days since they'd entered Mexico, the two of them had searched more canyons than they could count. And each time he walked away from yet another empty canyon, he had a hankering to ride straight back to Twin Rivers —to the arms of the wife who was waiting for him there—and forget Javier Velez even existed.

Cain scanned the area again, eyes peeled for anything that seemed out of place, then glanced at Ridley. "Is it safe to enter?"

The man looked around, his eyes careful and slow, examining every last pebble of the terrain. "Yes, we can go in."

"And you know that how?"

"Well, first off because there's no one around, but that's the obvious part. The way I figure it, the entrance to the canyon is the most likely place for us to be shot, but I've been watching it for nigh on twenty minutes now, and not so much as a shadow has moved."

Cain nodded. "Very good."

Ridley squinted against the glare of the sun. "If we were in the hill country, the lack of animals near the entrance might give me pause, but there's nothin' but rattlers and scorpions in the desert."

A slight feeling of pride swelled in his chest. Ridley might be relatively new to the job, but the man was shaping up to be an excellent lawman.

"Very good. Now let's go."

They crept closer, moving from boulder to boulder and trying their best to hide, even though there were precious few places to do so on the barren stretch of desert that gave way to the wall of cliffs.

Without uttering a sound, Cain drew his pistol and motioned for Ridley to follow him into the narrow entrance to the canyon. The towering walls immediately blocked out the sun, casting the sandy bottom of the canyon in shadows, but the canyon cut left at a sharp angle almost immediately, blocking his view of anything that might be farther inside.

"Cover me." Cain kept his gun at the ready as he jumped around the rocky protrusion, only to find the canyon empty for another twenty feet or so until the next sharp turn.

Ridley stepped around the wall of rock, then scowled. "I know we gotta find where the Velezes are hiding, but I gotta admit. Each time I go into one of these places, I get a sick feeling in my gut like I'm about to be shot."

"You're not the only one."

Ridley raised his eyebrows. "You nervous being in here, Cap'n?"

Cain crept toward the next bend. "You know the difference between a good lawman and a dead one?"

"Don't reckon I do."

"A good lawman can tell when to listen to his fear and when to ignore it."

"And the dead one?"

"He ignores it until it ends up killing him."

Ridley sighed. "I take it this is one of those times when we gotta ignore the fact we're sitting ducks for anyone stationed at the top of the canyon or on the other side of that bend up ahead."

Cain looked down at the sandy bottom of the canyon. "Do you see any footprints or places where prints might have been wiped away?"

"Nope."

"Then we're ignoring it until something indicates otherwise." Cain crept around the next bend in the twisty canyon, only to find the next stretch of yellow, rocky walls just as empty as the others.

"All right, so we'll search this canyon, but what if Velez takes all his men and goes to Twin Rivers before we can figure out where he's hiding?" Ridley whispered.

Cain's shoulders tightened. That was the biggest problem with his plan. "We'll give this another day or two at most, then we'll return regardless of whether we find the hideout."

Being back in Twin Rivers was something he hadn't let himself think about too much on the trip. He'd intentionally blocked thoughts of Anna Mae from his mind, because if he didn't, he just might have ridden back to Twin Rivers after that first night.

But if there was any chance he and Anna Mae could have a future together, one that lasted more than a few weeks, then he had to find a way to—

A scream echoed through the canyon, feminine and bone-chilling.

Cain's heart gave a sudden thud against his chest. He looked back at Ridley, then jerked his head in the direction of the sound.

Had he found Velez?

No. The canyon seemed woefully unguarded for a man of Velez's importance to be hiding in it.

But maybe he'd found some of Velez's men, and with enough persuading, they just might offer up information on where Velez was hiding.

"Seems like this might be one of those times we start listening to our fears." Ridley surveyed the canyon again, eyes narrowed as though he could somehow see through the walls of rock to where the scream had originated.

"Not until we know more." Cain stepped around the next bend, only to find it empty like he'd thought. He didn't know how long the canyon was, but the scream hadn't sounded close.

As quickly as he could, he made his way through the narrow twists and turns, being careful about where he stepped lest his feet make any noise that could draw attention.

Ridley did the same, flawlessly exhibiting every last bit of his training as he moved with stealth and kept his gun ready to meet any threat.

After a few more turns, a woman's sobs floated through the canyon, followed by an older man's pleas and the hard voice of a desperado.

"You hid a horse."

"I am but a humble farmer, and that was my only horse."

Cain picked his way silently toward another sharp bend, the voices near enough they could only be coming from the other side of the rock wall.

"When we say we need horses, we need horses." The desperado's voice whipped through the narrow space.

"I'm sorry. It was my fault."

Cain reached the final turn. A large slab of yellow sandstone jutted up toward the sky, blocking everything on the other side from view. He shoved his gun into his holster, whipped off his hat, and quickly used a strip of leather to pull his free hair back into a queue. He didn't know what would greet him when he peeked around that boulder, but he had a better chance of not being seen without his hat or hair calling attention to him.

Ridley came up beside him, then did the same with his own hat and hair, just like Cain had trained his men to do when trying to move undetected.

Slowly, Cain peeked around the edge of the rock, then ducked back behind it.

One of Velez's men stood with a gun trained on an older man and a woman who looked to be about Anna Mae's age. They were just on the other side of the wall, almost so close he could reach out and touch one of them, which meant he'd likely be spotted if he poked his head around the side of the rock again.

"I was the one who lied, not Maria." Panic laced the older man's tone. "Kill me if you must, but let my daughter go. She did nothing."

"Maria, is it?" A sneer dripped from the desperado's voice.

"Don't touch her!" the older man cried.

Cain couldn't stop himself from peeking around the wall again.

The man had moved a few steps away from the outcropping and was now standing beside the woman.

Did he work for Velez, or were he and his men operating on their own? Cain didn't have enough information one way or the other to tell.

The outlaw took a strand of the woman's long black hair in his hand, then lifted it to his nose and smiled cruelly.

"No!" Maria tried to lurch away from him.

Cain forced his gaze off the woman and surveyed the small opening on the canyon floor. There were six desperadoes in all. Two of them were at the back of the space cooking food over a fire and not overly concerned with what was happening to

Maria and her father. The others were watching the scene unfold.

"Don't touch me," Maria gritted, trying to step away from her captor.

"Don't touch you?" The man's hand shot out and gripped her arm, dragging her closer. "I can touch you whenever and however I want, as you're going to learn."

Cain's stomach clenched, his hand tightening around his pistol.

"You can't, Cap'n. You'll give us away." Ridley's voice came from behind him, barely a whisper.

The man was right. In a normal situation, he would have stood there for hours, listening to the men as they talked, seeing if he could learn what their next plans were or if they mentioned Velez. He might even have trailed them for a day or two if he thought he could remain undiscovered while gleaning information.

But not with Maria and her father there. "If you think for a moment that I'm going to stand by and watch while they..."

A cruel laugh echoed through the canyon.

Cain peeked back around the corner to find that the desperado holding Maria had holstered his gun, but a shorter man had stepped forward, gun trained on Maria's father and a leer on his face.

The first man fisted his hands in the front of Maria's dress, and a tearing sound filled the air.

Cain fired his gun.

He didn't think, didn't plan, didn't have the first clue how he and Ridley were going to get out of the canyon alive if they ended up with five guns trained on them.

All he knew was that he hadn't taken an oath to become a lawman so he could stand there and watch a woman be violated.

The man who'd been holding Maria fell to the ground, a

growing patch of blood soaking his shirt. Cain trained his gun on the short man who had stepped forward to guard Maria's father. The desperado had drawn his gun and was pointing wildly with the nose of his pistol as he tried to figure out where the first shot had come from.

The crack of Cain's next shot echoed through the canyon, and the man dropped to the ground. Then he fired a third shot at another desperado.

He searched frantically for a fourth man to take out, only to find one of the men standing with his hands up in surrender.

"Please d-don't shoot," he stammered, searching for where Cain was hiding.

Behind that man stood another who had his pistol trained not at Cain but at the final desperado who still sat by the fire cooking.

"We're friends," the man with his hands up called, his eyes narrowing in on where Cain peeked around the corner of the rock wall.

"Then why were you about to stand there while a woman was violated?"

The man turned pale and raised his hands higher. "We didn't want to, at least not Alfonso and me. Are you the law? You can take Pablo and question him. We don't want any more of this. We just want to go back to our families."

"Don't trust them," Maria cried. "They work for that monster, Velez. They took us from our farm and dragged us here. They stole our only horse."

Cain looked over to find both Maria and her father had taken pistols from the two men whose dead bodies were closest to them and were pointing them at the man with his hands up, all while Maria held the front of her dress clenched together with her free hand.

It was possible this was a trap, and the desperado with his gun trained on the cook would turn it on him as soon as he stepped out from where he hid, but Cain didn't think so. Both the man voluntarily putting his hands up and the man with the pistol trained at the desperado by the fire looked half sick as they watched Maria.

"Don't worry. I have no intention of lowering my gun." Cain jutted his chin toward his hat, which Ridley handed to him.

After positioning the hat on his head, Cain stepped around the canyon wall, gun trained on the man with his arms up.

"Are you the Ranger?" the man asked, eyes wide. "Ranger Whitelaw?"

"I am."

"Take him." The man with the gun nodded his head at the cook. "We don't want him. We don't want this. Can I join your men? I want to fight Velez and his son."

"You want to..." Cain stilled. Cristobal had told him villagers were hoping he could kill Velez and rid them of the terror the man was causing, but he hadn't expected the men to want to join forces.

"You join Whitelaw and you'll be shot dead," the cook sneered. "Just wait. Whitelaw's days are numbered, and now yours are too—and your families'."

Cain hardened his jaw, then glanced back at Ridley, who had stepped into the open section of the canyon behind him. He jerked his head toward the cook. "Tie him up."

Ridley strode forward, shoulders back and face serious.

"Is that true?" the man who still held the pistol at the cook asked—Alfonso, if he remembered correctly. "Do you think Velez will find out if we help the Rangers? I've got a wife to think of, and I don't want..." His gaze fell to Maria.

"Do you have an extra shirt?" Cain asked.

The man blinked. "You want a shirt?"

"*Sì*, do you have one?"

"In my saddlebag."

"Good, get it and give it to the woman."

"Oh, I..." Two splotches of red appeared on the man's face at the reminder that Maria's dress had been torn. "*Sí.*"

Cain kept his gaze on Alfonso as the man holstered his gun and went to get the shirt, then took it to Maria. There was nothing sneaky about his movements, and he didn't touch his gun again, even though Maria kept hers trained on him.

"The Velez family forced you to fight for him?" Cain still didn't drop his gun, but he was awful close to holstering it.

At the mention of the Velezes, more fear flickered in the man's eyes, but he headed to the fire, where he'd been helping the cook make some sort of meal. "Emilio showed up in our village one night. He went from house to house, then farm to farm, forcing all young men to come with him unless we wanted to see our families killed."

Cain's jaw turned even harder. "And who is Emilio?"

"He is one of Velez's most trusted men." The first man who had surrendered pointed toward the body of the desperado who'd been ready to violate Maria.

"I see." Cain rubbed his jaw. "And what's your name?"

"Hugo."

"Hugo. You don't want to fight with Velez and his son? You want to fight with me instead?"

"Yes. At least as long as my wife and daughter will be safe. Can you take them north, out of Mexico, like you did with the woman from Texas?"

Cain felt his eyebrows rise. "How do you know about that?"

Hugo pointed at Emilio again. "He was the kidnapper."

Cain looked over at the man with the pool of red on his shirt. "That's the man who kidnapped Anna Mae? Right there?"

"*Sí*. He took her, then lost her. *El jefe* wasn't happy."

"No, I'm sure he wasn't," Cain growled. Hopefully losing Emilio would weaken the outlaw.

"You want a tamale?" Alfonso approached him holding out

the food wrapped in a corn husk. "They are ready now. Cool enough to eat."

Cain blinked. "I... ah..."

"Can I have one too?" Ridley stepped closer to the fire, though he still watched the cook, who had been handcuffed. "I'm happy to eat anything that's not hardtack and jerky."

"There is enough for everyone." Alfonso placed the tamale in Cain's hand. The smell of meat and masa caused his stomach to rumble. Ridley was right. It had been too long since he'd had a decent meal.

"*Gracias.*" He bit into the food, and the spicy Mexican flavors filled his mouth.

"Can you take my family into Texas too, like Hugo's?" Alfonso looked up at him expectantly. "I will ride with you as long as I know my family will be safe. I don't need to sell my house and land. I've got a little dinero saved up. We will start again in Texas, away from Velez."

"*Sì*, I don't need to sell my house either." Hugo moved to the fire and took a tamale from the pan sitting on a rock beside it. "I will take my dinero from the bank and start again in Texas."

Cain looked between the two men, earnestness radiating from their faces. The cook sat just past Alfonso with his jaw clamped tight, hatred glinting in his eyes. But he was no longer claiming that Hugo's and Alfonso's families would be killed.

"I could move your two families to Texas, yes, but what about Maria and her father?" When he turned back to look at them, he noticed they had lowered their guns and were creeping closer to the food. "Do you want to go to Texas?"

"*Sì*," the older man said. "We will go to Texas if it means we can escape Velez. No one wants to live like this."

Cain took another bite of the tamale. "What about your neighbors? And your cousins? Do they want to go to Texas too?"

The four agreed instantly. It seemed everyone and their brother, second cousin, and grandparents wanted to leave.

He wasn't sure how he'd ended up having half the people in northern Mexico depend on him for justice when he wasn't even a Ranger anymore.

"What if Velez and his son were dead, along with his men? What if their control of this region was completely snuffed out? Would you still want to move to Texas?"

The four Mexicans looked at each other, then slowly shook their heads.

"My parents are here."

"I like my farm."

"I have grandchildren here that I'd never be able to see in Texas."

And on the reasons went, each person thinking of more and more things holding them to Mexico.

Cain popped the last bite of tamale into his mouth, then leaned back against a boulder. "It seems to me like we've got two choices. We can either move every last person living in northern Mexico to Texas, or we can kill Velez and let y'all go on with your lives."

"We can't kill Velez."

"It's not possible."

"He's too powerful."

"His son would hunt us down."

"You'll never kill him." At the sound of the cook's voice, everyone quieted. "He's guarded by a half dozen of the best men."

A half-dozen men? Cain committed the figure to memory. That information could turn out to be more helpful than the cook realized.

"Just so happens I'm a quick shot." Cain shoved himself off the boulder and approached the cook.

"Not that quick." The man spat at Cain's feet. "Besides, you'll never be able to find him."

"No?" Cain turned to Hugo. "Do you know where Velez and his son are hiding?"

The man nodded, his eyes wide and the tamale all but forgotten in his hand. "There's a canyon about an hour's ride from here."

The cook's jaw clamped shut, but his eyes burned with rage.

"How many men does Velez have hiding there?"

"Maybe fifty."

"Fifty?" Cain's eyebrows shot up. "I thought you said he was forcing all the men of fighting age to go with him?" There should be at least a couple hundred men hiding.

Hugo shrugged. "He sends most of them north. They do not stay with him."

North? That was the first he'd heard of any such thing. "What do these men do in the north?"

Hugo looked around at the others, as though he found the line of questioning rather odd. "They work for the railroad."

Cain crossed his arms, the lingering flavors from the tamale turning to dust in his mouth. "What do you mean, the railroad?"

"Velez says the railroad needs men. Last year when he started sending men north, he said it would pay well, that people would like it." Hugo shoved a bite of tamale into his mouth, then shook his head. "But then word came back to Mexico. The pay wasn't good, the working conditions were poor, and the men were away from their families. No one wanted to go anymore, but Velez says the railroad still needs workers, and men must go anyway."

"Why is he so insistent on providing men to work for the railroad?" Cain unscrewed the lid to his canteen and took a sip of water. "Is he being paid?"

"How should I know?" Hugo spoke around the tamale in his

mouth. "I hit the target when I shot my gun, so Velez's men said I needed to ride with them, not go north."

"It was the same for me," Alfonso added. "I hit the target, so Velez's men kept me. My brothers were both sent north."

"I see." Or at least he thought he did.

He leaned back against another boulder and took another sip of water, an idea taking shape in his head—one that just might put an end to Javier Velez's control over northern Mexico.

And might also leave him alive to tell about it.

26

By the time the town of Twin Rivers appeared on the horizon two days later, Cain had a plan.

The cook, who was loyal to the Velez family, had tried to escape before they left the canyon, and Alfonso had shot him before Cain had the chance to see if he could wheedle any extra information from the man. But even with losing the cook, Cain still counted it an excellent trip.

Both Alfonso and Hugo had agreed to return to Velez and feign loyalty to him, all while finding others forced into service who would be willing to fight against Velez when the time came. Also, since Velez and Eduardo were hiding out somewhere near the town of El Rebote, they were going to pass messages about Velez's actions to Cristobal. It would still take two days for those messages to reach Cain, but at least he'd have some idea what Velez was up to.

The old man and his daughter had been sent back to their village with a story of how the man and Maria had surprised Emilio with a gun and shot him when he and his men had come to their farm to take their food and commandeer their horse. Once Emilio was dead, an argument broke out among the other men, resulting in the other desperadoes who were loyal to Velez all being killed.

Hopefully Velez would believe the story and wouldn't discover who had really killed his men or that it had been in a canyon rather than on the farm where Maria and her father lived. And hopefully Velez wouldn't discover that Hugo and Alfonso weren't quite as supportive as Velez believed.

But as Maverick and Ridley's horse Thunder splashed across the murky waters of the Rio Grande toward camp, Cain couldn't help but push the grisly thoughts of Velez aside. He'd never in his life been so happy to see the town of Twin Rivers. He wanted to go straight to Anna Mae and sweep her into his arms, but a lawman couldn't exactly ignore his men after disappearing for seven days, then expect them to pick up their guns and risk their lives for him the next day.

Hopefully Anna Mae would understand.

Just like when he'd approached the camp in Alpine, his men noticed him and Ridley coming and headed to the edge of the camp.

Cain rode Maverick straight to the watering trough, with Ridley and Thunder only a few paces behind him. Cain swung off the horse as he started drinking.

"We thought the both of ya were dead, Captain." Lieutenant Sims stepped up to him and Ridley, a worried look on his face.

"I know." Cain patted Maverick's flank. "I didn't mean to worry you, but I didn't have a good way of getting news back here either."

"The Cap'n here had a mind to search every canyon in northern Mexico until we learned where Velez and his son were hiding," Ridley drawled.

"Did you kill them?" This from Bryant Lindley. The young Ranger had been the first to agree to come with him when he left Alpine.

"No. But I know they are, and I've got a plan. It's only a matter of gathering the men and getting supplies."

"Good." Sims gave a sharp nod beneath his dusty hat brim. "When do we head out?"

"Tomorrow or the day after. Need to talk to the sheriff first."

"About what?" At the familiar sound of Daniel's voice, Cain looked over to find the sheriff had walked over to the camp, along with Harrison, Wes, and Sam.

"How to kill Velez and his son," he answered.

"So it's not as hopeless as you were thinking?" Daniel stopped beside him, his eyes sharp.

"No."

Daniel sent his gaze heavenward, and Cain swore he could almost hear the silent prayer his friend was sure to be uttering. "I told Anna Mae there were only two reasons you'd be gone this long. One was extremely good, and the other was extremely bad. I'm glad to hear it was the first."

Cain straightened. "How is she?"

"She did just fine while you were gone. Better than most women would, I'm sure. You married a strong one."

"You got that right." Sam slapped him on the shoulder. "If I went missing for seven days in the desert, Ellie would be crying herself to sleep each night and making plans to sell the ranch and move back to Michigan."

"Keely too," Wes said. "Except she'd make plans to move to California with her brother."

"Anna Mae baked for us each day you were gone." Lindley patted his stomach. "Says she'll have to charge us for the food when she opens her restaurant next week, though."

"Next week?" Cain blinked. She'd be ready to open that soon?

He gave his head a little shake. Of course she'd be ready that soon. This was Anna Mae. She didn't sit still or twiddle her thumbs.

And he couldn't wait another second to take her into his arms. "If you'll excuse me, I think it's time to go see my wife."

Whoops went up from his men, followed by so much teasing he couldn't possibly respond to it all.

Which was fine. There was no question he'd married a lovely woman, and he wasn't going to apologize for wanting to hold her and kiss the breath from her lungs.

"You know you're allowed to bring her to camp, right?" one of his men said. "Maybe she can cook breakfast for us in the morning?"

Cain narrowed his eyes at Harvey, who was standing at the back of the crowd. "Let me guess. It's your turn to cook?"

The burly man raised his chin. "Don't see as how that makes any difference."

He resisted the urge to twist his lips into a smile, but barely. "Stow it. You're cooking."

"I vote Anna Mae cooks." Lindley rubbed the back of his neck, then looked at Sims. "Remember how bad Harvey burned dinner while the captain was gone?"

Cain cocked an eyebrow at the loyal Ranger who had to be one of the worst cooks he'd ever come across. "Only way a man learns to improve is by practicing."

"Aw, don't tell him that," Sims groaned. "He's been a lawman for three years, and he still hasn't learned. Maybe he can at least take a few lessons from Anna Mae."

The tips of Harvey's ears turned red.

It was true. If practice was going to teach Harvey how to cook, it would have worked by now. "Fine. I'll see if Anna Mae wants to give you a few pointers tomorrow morning, but you're the one making breakfast, not her. Am I clear?"

The man nodded, the redness from his ears spreading down to his throat.

"All right, I'm off to see Anna Mae and make some plans

with Daniel. I'll be back after dinner." Cain nodded to Lindley. "See to Maverick for me."

"Yes, Captain."

Cain started toward town, with Daniel, Wes, Sam, and Harrison walking alongside him. "Don't suppose any of you have sent word to Anna Mae letting her know I'm back?"

Daniel shrugged. "Not really. We weren't sure it was you when one of Sam's boys told us riders were approaching."

"Well, I aim to see her before we do any strategizing. I got a lot of information about Velez. If we're smart about it, there just might be a chance..." His throat tightened, and he glanced around at the others. Daniel and Anna Mae were the only ones who knew just how unlikely he was to survive this border war, and he wanted to keep it that way. "Is she at the house or with one of her friends?"

"At the house getting the restaurant ready," Harrison said. "The women have been there helping her all week."

"Got that right." Wes dipped his head. "Keely's been there so much, I almost feel like I'm a widower again."

"All right. Thanks." They were almost to O'Reilly Street, and Cain lengthened his stride. In the desert, he'd done everything he could to push thoughts of Anna Mae from his mind so he didn't get distracted. But now that he was home, all he could think about was—

"Not so fast." Sam's hand clamped down on his shoulder.

Cain glared at the hand. "What? Don't tell me I need to ride out to your ranch for something or other before I see my wife. It ain't happening."

"Oh no," Daniel said. "You don't need to do anything except stop by my office." A smile twitched at the corners of his lips.

Cain narrowed his eyes. "I told you we'd plan our attack after I see Anna Mae."

"And you can." Harrison's hand landed on his other shoulder, but there was nothing soft or friendly about the grip. "We just aim to give you a haircut first."

"If I recall, your birthday isn't for another month." Wes squashed his hat down atop his head, a smile similar to Daniel's emerging at the corners of his mouth. "And I seem to remember someone swearing an oath he wouldn't ever get married. What about the rest of you?"

"Yep, I remember it clear as day." Sam's grip on his shoulder tightened. "Said he'd never need a woman, and if he ever got himself hitched, we could shave his head."

Cain tried to step away from Sam and Harrison's hold, but all four of his friends were surrounding him, directing him across the dusty road toward Daniel's office rather than letting him turn toward his house.

There was no question he'd broken his long-ago promise when he married Anna Mae, but... "Fine. But can't we do this after I see my wife?"

"Oh no. Bet she'll think you look right pretty with a haircut." Harrison kept a firm grip on his shoulder as the lot of them marched up the steps to Daniel's office.

A chair had already been placed dead center in the room.

"It's so long, I think we'll have to cut it first, then shave it," Wes said.

Cain glanced at the straight-edged razor lying on Daniel's desk, and his gut churned. Sure, his friends might take razors to their chins every day, but shaving an entire head had to be different than shaving a jaw. "Can the barber do this?"

Daniel stepped directly in front of him, a grin on his face. "That's not what the pact said. And you've been the one torturing us with that pact for the last seventeen years. Threatened to shave my head last summer, if I recall."

Cain had an almost uncontrollable urge to slide his tongue out and lick his lips, which had suddenly turned dry. "I'm not sure getting married at gunpoint should count as part of the pact. It wasn't like I had much choice."

Daniel had been reaching for the scissors, but he stopped and turned back, his eyes serious.

"Is that really why you married her? If not for the pistol in my holster, would you have turned your back on my sister?"

Cain's chest tightened. The rumors had more to do with their marriage than Daniel's pistol. But if he said the right thing, Daniel would probably let him off the hook.

Cain looked back at the silver blade, at the sunlight slanting in from the window hitting the metal until it gleamed.

"No." The simple word filled the office. "My offer for your sister would still stand. In fact, there's a part of me that wishes I would have offered for her when I came to town last year."

"That's what I thought." The serious expression on Daniel's face turned into a taunting smile. "Now my next question is, can you hold still on your own, or do we need to tie you down?"

"Oh, we're tying him," Harrison piped up, a grin plastered across his face. "Definitely tying him."

27

Seventeen Years Earlier

"Just tell me straight, Daniel. Are you sweet on Abigail Ashton or not?"

Cain glanced up from his hand of poker cards to find Harrison sitting on the other side of the crevice studying Daniel, his own hand of cards nearly forgotten.

Daniel, for his part, seemed to be looking at his cards a little too intently.

Cain shifted against the rocky wall of the canyon that the lot of them had all sneaked off to. The summer heat caused a drop of sweat to trickle down his back even though the towering sandstone walls surrounding them provided more shade than they'd be able to find anywhere else.

"I ain't sweet on nobody," Daniel retorted. "Why do you keep asking?"

Cain had to agree. If anyone seemed taken with Abigail Ashton, it was Wes, not Daniel. He'd wager Harrison's question had more to do with distracting Daniel from his hand so that

Harrison would have a better chance of winning than it did with any true interest in the Ashton girl, pretty as she was.

"Quit your yakking, Harrison," Cain drawled. "You in or you out?"

Harrison blew out a breath and studied his cards, which all but told Cain he was right. Harrison was only trying to buy time and distract Daniel. And it might work—for Daniel. But then Harrison would still have to beat him and Wes, and that wasn't going to happen, no way, no how.

"If you're not sweet on her, then why did the two of you sneak off during the church picnic on Sunday?" Wes was the one staring at Daniel now, the look in his eyes serious.

"Wait, you and Abigail snuck off together after church?" Cain grinned, then reached out and slapped Daniel on the shoulder. "Didn't think you had it in ya. You get a kiss out of her?"

Daniel's face turned redder than a cooked beet. "I told ya, I ain't sweet on no one, and I certainly didn't kiss Abigail Ashton."

"Then what'd the two of you do?" Wes's eyes still hadn't left Daniel.

"They're kissing!" The words filled the small crevice of the canyon that they'd tucked themselves into, and Cain looked up at Sam, who'd folded as soon as the hand had been dealt.

Sam was peeking around the rocky wall that separated the little crevice from the rest of the canyon.

"Who's kissing?" Harrison dropped his cards and scrambled up, probably because he still hadn't decided whether or not to fold, the lout.

"The preacher. Don't he know he ain't allowed to do that?"

"The preacher's kissing someone?"

As soon as the words left Harrison's mouth, Daniel and Wes scrambled up and went to the side of the rock face that acted like a wall to conceal them.

"Who's he kissing?" Daniel whispered from where he fought for a position to see around the wall. "Oh, that's Miss Emmaline. He's been sweet on her ever since she showed up in town."

Cain sighed, then put down his cards and stood. He didn't know what was so all-fired special about kissing. His ma did it all the time, multiple times a day, with different men. It had never been anything he'd cared to watch, not even when she didn't realize he was in the small two-room house where they lived.

He came up behind where his friends had crowded around the small opening. Even though he was the youngest, he was a half head taller than everyone else, which made it rather easy for him to peer around the wall of rock. Sure enough, the preacher stood smack in the entrance of the canyon, sunlight slanting down around him and the woman he was holding.

Wes elbowed him. "Reckon they'll get married?"

"Never can tell." Cain glared at the couple, though they seemed too caught up with each other to notice anyone was watching.

That wasn't something that ever happened to his ma. Whenever she was "entertaining" a man—as she liked to call it—he swore she had only a tiny sliver of her mind on the man in her bed. The rest of her brain was occupied with convincing him to open his wallet a little wider and hand her a few extra bills after he was finished.

Either that or she was thinking about the next "gentleman caller" scheduled to visit her.

"Sometimes men just like to kiss women for no other reason but to kiss them." Cain's words came out low and rough, and he narrowed his eyes as Preacher Russell tilted Miss Emmaline's chin to the side and wrapped a second arm around her.

He had to admit, Preacher Russell was making a pretty good

show of kissing Miss Emmaline. If such a thing as love existed, then the preacher probably really did love their teacher.

At least for now.

Cain might not understand a lot about love and marriage, but one thing was certain, the love a man said he felt for a woman didn't last more than a day or two at most.

Otherwise, his pa would have stayed when he'd ridden into town last month. Because he'd heard his pa tell that to his ma clear as day as he'd sat outside the open window of her bedroom listening to his pa and ma do all kinds of things the preacher said a man shouldn't do with a woman unless they were married.

"A man kisses a lady like that, and they've got to get hitched. It's in the Bible," Sam pronounced, his gaze still fixed on the preacher and teacher.

Cain scratched the back of his head. "I don't never remember reading no Bible verse like that. My ma says..."

"Don't reckon your ma counts," Daniel quipped.

Cain's jaw clenched, and he stalked to the back of the crevice and picked up his cards. Daniel just had to be the one to say that. He walked around town thinking he was high and mighty, better than everyone else because he still had both his parents, and they even seemed like they'd figure out how to love each other for more than a few days at a time.

"Y'all best get your hides back here unless you want to forfeit." Cain sat down on the hard slab of rock that made up the section of canyon floor.

"I don't know." Wes trailed him to the back of the crevice and picked up his cards. "I still don't think it's right for the preacher to be kissing a woman like that."

"It's fine iffin' he's going to marry her, you mule." Harrison pushed away from the entrance and sauntered back to their poker game.

"But they ain't married yet, and that ain't no quick kind of kiss like Ma gives me before bed." Daniel sank to the ground and took up his cards.

"Still don't think he should be doing it." Sam sat next to Daniel and crossed his legs in front of him, completing their circle even though Sam had already folded. "Should we tell Deacon Sutherland come Sunday?"

Cain coughed. Deacon Sutherland? The man had visited Ma last night. Had a standing appointment to visit her every Sunday night—after he spent all day at church dressed up in his spiffy suit and escorting his wife and daughters around town as though they were more precious than gold nuggets.

Cain raised his eyes to realize everyone was looking at him. Had it been how he'd coughed, or did they just expect him to be the one to answer? "Don't look like Miss Emmaline minded the kiss too much. Probably best to keep your mouth shut."

"Pa used to kiss Ma like that, and no one ever said there was nothing wrong with it." A tear streaked down Wes's dusty face.

Oh, hang it all. He hadn't meant to go and make Wes start blubbering. Especially not considering his ma hadn't even been buried for a full month yet.

In fact, this afternoon was the first time the five of them all managed to sneak off since Wes's ma and baby brother died in that blamed carriage accident. They were supposed to be having an afternoon of poker and fun, like cowhands on Wes's pa's ranch.

But nothing felt fun when Daniel up and said mean things about his ma.

It didn't feel fun with Wes crying neither.

"Don't cry." Sam reached for Wes's shoulder.

"I'm not." Wes shrugged away from him, then swiped at the wet streak on his face and grabbed his cards.

"All I know is, I'm never going to get tangled up with some stupid woman like Preacher is. All they do is ruin things." Cain jutted out his chin and gave a firm nod. "Now let's play. Harrison, are you folding or not?"

"Maybe your ma ruins things, but mine didn't." Wes tossed his cards onto the sandy dirt. "My ma was one of the finest women to ever walk Texas soil."

"Then how come you're crying over her? My pa says crying makes a man weak. Don't reckon he ever cries over my ma neither." In fact, he knew for a fact his pa had never shed a single tear over his ma, because he'd told him so before he'd left, riding off to East Texas, where he'd get his next Ranger assignment. *Boy, you listen here. You don't let yourself get all soft over a woman, not ever. All that does is hold you back.*

That had been the answer he'd gotten after he asked his pa if he loved his ma.

That and the words, *And don't call me Pa, neither. I may have sired ya, but I sure ain't your pa.*

"Reckon your ma's cried a whole river full of tears over your pa." Daniel's voice cut into the memory, deep and hard. "Especially seeing how he's only ever around for a few days before he up and leaves you."

Cain glared at Daniel. He had little other choice, really—unless he wanted to tear up like Wes and start blubbering about how it wasn't fair Daniel got such a nice family when no one else did.

And there wasn't any way he was going to admit that Daniel had something better than him. "Blubbering just proves kissing and love and marriage only make you stupid."

Wes shot to his feet, his hands clenched into fists. "My ma wasn't stupid, and neither is my pa."

Cain sighed. Why did Wes have to go and get all riled up? He'd been talking to Daniel.

But now Daniel was standing next to Wes, glaring down at him. "My parents aren't stupid either."

Sam pushed himself to his feet and took a stand beside

them, the three of them forming a wall that blocked him and Harrison into the crevice. "I don't think getting hitched is stupid. I think the stupid people are the ones who spend their lives all alone."

Oh, so Sam, of all people, was siding with Daniel? Wasn't that just dandy. And here he'd thought he liked Sam.

Cain tossed his cards on the ground and rose to stare straight back at Sam. "As if you know anything about it. You're an orphan."

"Anyone's got to be better than Mrs. Codwittle at the orphanage," Sam shot back. "Besides, if Wes and Daniel say mas are worth having around, then I believe them."

"I plan to get myself hitched just as soon as I have a place of my own. Then we'll see which one of us is happy." Wes's hands clenched into fists at his side. "You'll be the stupid one, all alone."

"I ain't stupid neither." Cain dug his heel into the ground and swiped away a stray strand of hair. "You're stupid for wanting to get yourself married to some woman who's going to yell at you when you track dirt into the house, complain when you get your clothes dirty, and cry every time you leave."

"My ma didn't do that." Wes's fists tightened until his knuckles turned white. "And I'll find me a woman who'll take care of my house without complaining."

"So will I." Daniel leaned in. "'*Two are better than one.*' Means a man is better off getting married than being alone. That's in the Bible."

"It is not," Cain spat.

"Is so. In the book of Ecclesiastes." Daniel scratched his head. "Or maybe it's Lamentations. Or Song of Solomon. Anyway, it's in there. And if God says it's so, then I'm going to get married just as soon as I get me a house. Or you can... can... can shave my head."

If the Bible had a verse somewhere that said two people

were better than one, then it was a lie. Because nothing good ever came from his ma and pa being together. All ma did was cry for two months after pa left.

But Cain was smart enough not to cry anymore when his pa walked out, just like he was smart enough not to ever get himself hitched.

Cain took a knife from the sheath strapped to his belt and shoved it at Wes. "Blood swear?"

"Wes, no." Sam shifted in front of Wes. "Think about..."

But Wes met Cain's gaze, then reached around Sam, grabbed the knife, and slit his hand. "If I had any money, I'd wager you end up getting hitched too."

Cain spit. "I ain't never gonna get hitched."

"Yeah?" Daniel sneered. "Then maybe you should swear it too. Unless you're too yellow-bellied to stand by your word. I'm going to swear here and now that I'll get myself a wife one day." Daniel took the blade from Wes and gave it a quick slice down the center of his palm, then thrust the knife back toward Cain. "Your turn to swear. And if you do get married, we get to shave your head."

"Fine." Cain's eyes were hot as they met Daniel's. He hardened his jaw and sliced the blade of the knife against his palm, not even wincing at the fiery pain.

"Well, what about you two?" Wes jutted his chin toward where Harrison and Sam stood. "You both gotta swear. Are you going to get yourself a wife one day or not?"

"By the time you're thirty," Cain growled. "You don't get to live as no bachelor all your life and then find a wife right before you die. And if you're not married by the time you're thirty, then you better believe I'll tie you down and shave your head."

"Harrison?" Sam turned to Harrison, their eyes seeming to share some kind of message, but Cain would be hanged if he could figure out what it was.

Harrison reached out and took the knife. "My pa's gotten along just fine without a wife. Guess I'll do the same."

The edge of the knife bit into his hand, and he winced, just like Daniel and Wes had.

Sam took the knife last and stared down at it, long and hard, but Cain already knew what he was going to do. There was no question about it, really. All Daniel's and Wes's ramblings about their parents and families had gotten to Sam over the years, and there was no question that the scrawny redheaded orphan wanted a family more than he wanted anything else.

In fact, the smartest wager any of them could make was on Sam having a family one day, probably before the rest of them even thought about getting hitched.

Sam just might make a good family man too.

But Cain never would. He raked a hand through his hair. Not in a thousand, million years.

"Sam?" Wes asked, his voice raspy, since Sam was still staring at the blamed knife. "Are you with Daniel and me or with them?"

"I'll get me a wife before I'm thirty. And Cain and Harrison can't get married until after they're thirty."

"I won't need no wife after I'm thirty." Cain's lips twisted into a scowl. "I won't need no wife ever."

"I'm keeping the thirty part," Harrison answered a little too fast.

Cain glared at him, but Harrison only shrugged.

"What? Could be I find a nice woman and want to change my mind."

"Chicken liver," he muttered.

"Before I'm thirty." Sam looked away, then drew the knife down his palm. A thin slice of red appeared against his pale skin. "Reckon it's settled now."

"Sure is." Cain grabbed his knife and wiped the blood from

the edge of the blade on his thigh before shoving it back in its sheath.

He couldn't say whether any of his friends would end up regretting their oath—and he'd be the first to shave their heads if they did—but the one thing he knew for certain?

He didn't have to worry about having his head shaved.

Because he'd never be stupid enough to get himself hitched.

28

Alive. Cain was alive! Anna Mae raced down the road, then skidded around the corner onto O'Reilly Street, pumping her legs as fast as they would carry her.

She hadn't even lingered a full second when Ellie's siblings had burst into the dining room, returning from where they'd been fishing down at the river and shouting over each other about Cain riding into Twin Rivers and being at the camp.

Thank You for protecting him, Father. Thank You so much.

She'd tried not to worry overmuch, had tried to trust God and thank Him for the time He'd given her with Cain, even if it had been only a few hours of marriage before he'd had to leave.

But that didn't mean she hadn't worried. It was as Daniel had told her: Cain was waylaid for either very good reasons or very bad ones.

But now she'd be able to find out what those reasons were.

She was just going to make a quick stop to let Daniel know the news, seeing how his office was right on the way to the camp. If he wasn't there, then she wasn't about to go searching for him. She'd already had to wait far longer than any newlywed should to feel her husband's arms around her.

"Did you hear?" she called as she clambered up the stairs to the sheriff's office, then flung open the door. "Cain's... back."

The last word came out on a rasp, and the excitement drained from her body.

Her husband wasn't down at the camp. Instead, he was sitting in the middle of her brother's office, tied to a chair while Daniel held a razor to his head.

"What are you doing?" She charged at her brother.

Daniel jerked the razor away from Cain's scalp half a second before she barreled into him.

"I'm going to thrash you!" She tried to grab the razor, but Daniel held it above his head and dug his boots into the floor, creating a firm, unyielding wall of man that she didn't have the power to move.

"Calm down, sweetheart," Cain drawled, sounding entirely too relaxed about the fact that he was tied down and at her brother's mercy. "They're getting their revenge. A few more minutes and they'll be done."

She whirled around to face her husband, only to find a mountain of rich golden-blond hair on the floor. "Their revenge?"

She went to Cain, then framed his face in her hands. His skin was warm and scruffy beneath her palms, and it caused a tingling sensation to travel up her arms clear to her heart. "What do they need revenge for?"

"The marriage pact." Harrison was sitting on the front of the empty deputy's desk, legs dangling and mouth grinning as he took a sip of coffee, then nodded at Cain. "When we were twelve, Cain here swore up and down and six ways to Sunday he wouldn't marry until he turned thirty."

"No, Cain swore six ways to Sunday he wouldn't marry. *Ever*." Sam stuffed his mouth with one of the apple dumplings she'd dropped off earlier, then spoke around it. "But the pact said that if he married before thirty, we could shave his head. And we've got long memories."

She thought back, trying to remember something about a marriage pact. If Cain had been twelve, she would have been only five. Still, she seemed to remember the boys ribbing each other about it when she was younger.

"Is that true?" she asked Cain. "You swore you'd never marry?"

He scowled. "Never thought I'd find myself wanting a wife."

"You don't need to look so miserable about it." Wes stepped up behind him and smacked his head, then started untying his hands. "Reckon Anna Mae here's spent the past week imagining all sorts of cruel ways you could have died in the desert."

Heat climbed into her cheeks. "It's true, I'm afraid."

She placed a kiss on the top of Cain's head, then jerked her gaze to her brother. "Pact or not, you still have no right to cut Cain's hair. How would you like it if I tied you down and shaved your head?"

Daniel ran his hand over his head, almost as though checking to make sure his hair was still there. "I was on the side of the pact that swore I'd be married before I was thirty; otherwise I would have been the one to lose my hair on my birthday last November."

"And you better believe I would have held him to it." Cain sent her a smile, and it was just soft enough that a bit of the tension drained from her shoulders. "Relax, love. I ain't one to go back on my word. My hair will grow back."

"But it will take years for it to grow that long again. And I liked it."

Wes made a coughing sound as he finished loosening the rope from around Cain's wrists. "You liked it? You realize your husband had the hair of a woman? We're just doing you a favor, making him a bit more manly."

"Some men need extra help with that." Sam sent her a wink. "Don't know how to be a man."

She planted her hands on her hips and glared at the lot of them. "Cain is the most manly of y'all. Besides, none of this is fair! The rest of you could all grow your hair back in a few months if it gets shaved. Cain can't."

"Anna Mae, darlin,' come here." Cain looked utterly ridiculous as he stood from the chair.

Daniel must have decided to work only on one side of Cain's head at a time, because his left side was still cloaked in a shiny waterfall of gold that cascaded clear down to his elbow, and the right half and back were shaved balder than a peach.

But that didn't make his arms any less comforting as he wrapped them around her.

She sank into the feel of him, hard and strong, yet somehow gentle and caring. "I missed you so much."

He rested his chin on top of her head, and there'd never been another place she belonged quite so much.

"I missed you too." His words rumbled from his chest, low and deep.

"And here I figured you'd be so busy being a lawman that you might forget you were married."

He chuckled, and a warm sensation swirled through her belly. "It was about the hardest thing I ever did, keeping you out of my mind long enough to go on scouting missions. The second I laid my head on my pillow each night, I dreamed of you until dawn."

Heat pricked the backs of her eyes. "You said you were hoping to be back by sundown the next day, yet you were gone seven. I was really starting to think that..." Her voice broke, and she buried herself deeper into her husband's arms.

"I'm sorry, love."

"Did you get what you were looking for?"

He pushed her back just far enough for their eyes to meet.

"I got more. I didn't just find a weakness that I could exploit; I got everything I need to see Velez and his son buried six feet under."

She knew she should probably smile at him and say he'd done a good job, but the mention of Velez only made her wrap her arms around him all over again. "I have a fancy dinner planned for tonight. It's already half made."

"Do you now?" He stroked a strand of hair back from her face, but his fingers stayed behind her ears, on that soft spot of skin that caused her entire body to feel warm. "And just how did you know I was coming today of all days?"

"Um, I may have made a fancy dinner every day, just in case you showed up."

"We've enjoyed the leftovers." Daniel patted his belly.

"Of course you did." The fingers that had been touching the soft spot behind her ear moved into her hair, where he spread them apart, then smoothed them all the way down to where her hair ended at the middle of her back. Then he dropped a kiss on her forehead in a way that made her want to melt into him.

All of a sudden, he sighed and dropped his arms from around her. "Let me finish getting my head shaved, then we'll go home and you can finish fixing that dinner."

Part of her still wanted to protest the head shaving, but there was little point, seeing as how over half of Cain's hair was already gone. "All right."

Cain sat back in the chair and tilted his head to the side, giving Daniel easy access with the scissors.

Wes came up to stand behind her and draped a hand on her shoulder. "Part of me wants to apologize. I swear none of us had any idea you liked his hair. But at the same time—"

"A pact is a pact." Sam gave a firm nod.

"And Cain's harassed the rest of us about it mercilessly over the years." Harrison took a sip of coffee from his perch on the desk. "If he'd been a gentleman about it, maybe we could have let..."

The door opened, and Harrison's words trailed off as a tall, middle-aged man in a cowboy hat stepped inside.

Anna Mae blinked. He didn't just fill the doorway; he seemed to take up the entire room. There was something about him that commanded attention, and not just the gold star pinned to his chest. He was covered in trail dust from head to toe, and sandy blond hair with a touch of gray peeked out from beneath the worn brim of his hat as he scanned the office with serious, narrowed eyes.

Something seemed strangely familiar about him, even though she was quite sure she'd never seen him before in her life.

"I'm looking for..." The tall man's words cut off when his eyes fell on Cain. "Boy, what happened to your hair?"

Cain sent a cocky grin toward the man, then arched his neck to give Daniel better access to the left side of his head. "What does it look like? I lost a bet, and now I'm getting my head shaved, Pa."

∽

THE MOMENT CAIN said the word *Pa*, chaos erupted, and not because his Marshal friend, Jonas Redding, slipped inside behind his father. In fact, no one else even seemed to notice the appearance of the second lawman—and that appearance was more than just a little unusual, since his father and Jonas worked for different agencies.

But instead of greeting Jonas, his friends were all busy guessing why the legendary Frank Whitelaw had appeared when he clearly hadn't been summoned.

But no one looked as upset as his father, whose eyes had narrowed into a furious glare.

"I told you never to call me Pa."

"Why?" Cain drawled. "You think I've forgotten who sired me?"

The exchange quieted his friends and Anna Mae, who were now all looking between the two men as though they'd up and grown horns on the front of their foreheads.

Probably because all of them were wondering what kind of man would refuse to let his son call him Pa.

"You'll look ridiculous with your head shaved," Frank spat.

"Reckon that was the point of the bet." Cain gestured to Daniel. "Well, are you going to finish, or do I need to do it myself?"

"Right. Sorry." Daniel made a few more snips with the scissors, sending even more hair to the pile on the floor. Then he picked up the razor and shaving cream.

"What brings the both of you to Twin Rivers?" Cain moved his gaze back to his father.

"You," Frank snapped.

"Why?" Cain let his shoulders rise and fall in a careless shrug. "I'm not a Ranger anymore."

Frank scanned the room, his flat eyes not revealing a single one of his thoughts. "Not something to discuss in front of strangers."

"These aren't strangers. They're my... friends." The last word stuck in his throat, but he managed to get it out. He didn't remember the last time he'd made such a declaration. There may have been a time or two when he was younger that he'd dared to call Harrison his friend, but he didn't think he'd ever said the word aloud when referring to anyone else, and certainly not in front of so many people.

But Sam, Wes, Harrison, and Daniel didn't seem to think anything of his statement, as though their friendship had never once been in question.

His father looked disinterested in anyone but him.

"They're also volunteer deputies," he added. "Each one of them has been sworn in."

His father's gaze traveled straight to Anna Mae. "Ain't the kind of thing to discuss in front of a woman, then."

"I can leave." Anna Mae jumped up from where she'd been leaning on her brother's desk. Cain had been more focused on his father than her, but something told him she'd been watching the exchange between them more intently than anyone else in the room.

"She's not just any woman." He met his father's gaze, moderating his voice so it sounded almost bored. "She's my wife."

"Your wife?" Heat ignited in his father's eyes. "What kind of half-brained, idiotic thing did you up and do?"

"Wasn't nothing half-brained or idiotic about it." He kept his voice calm, but he couldn't stop the way his muscles tightened.

Daniel must have been able to sense his ire, because he lifted the razor from his head, even though there was only a small patch left to shave.

"I told you before," his father drawled. "You can pay for a woman anytime."

Cain was out of his chair in a flash, bringing himself to his full height as he stalked toward his father. "I'm not interested in paying for a woman in my bed."

Frank didn't even look sorry for the statement. If anything, his lips curled into a faint sneer. "Easier that way."

"Maybe I married her for more reasons than just having her in my bed."

His father dragged his gaze down Anna Mae. "Sure ya did. And I'm the Queen of England."

Cain curled his hands into a fist.

"Wait." Anna Mae rushed to his side, gripping the arm he was ready to let fly. "Don't hit him."

"Wouldn't be the first time," they both muttered.

But rather than shake Anna Mae off and swing his fist, he uncurled his hand and drew her to his side. "He's insulting you. He deserves a couple punches to the jaw."

She sighed. "Probably, but I'd rather just forgive him and invite him back to the house for dinner. I'll put on some tea, and we can visit while I whip up the biscuits and glaze for the pork roast."

"Tea?" His father's eyebrows winged up. "You're offering me tea?"

Cain couldn't stop himself from chuckling, and his father's lips even turned up into a half smile.

Anna Mae, on the other hand, was frowning at both of them. "What's wrong with tea?"

"Can't remember the last time anyone offered me something other than whiskey." Frank rubbed the back of his neck. "Tea, of all the things. You hear that, Jonas? Cain's wife here offered me tea."

"Bet she's even got one of them fancy little teacups for you to drink out of." A wide grin split Jonas's face. "The kind you can't fit all your fingers in."

Anna Mae looked between the three of them, then planted her hands on her hips. "Of course I have proper tea service. What kind of lady do you think I am?"

His father's shoulders shook with silent laughter. "I'll drink your tea, darlin', but only if you put it in a real mug for me."

And suddenly they all found themselves laughing. Even Daniel, Sam, Wes, and Harrison were chuckling at the idea of Frank Whitelaw drinking tea from one of Anna Mae's dainty little teacups. He didn't know how his wife had taken the frustration that had been boiling in the room and turned it into a joke about tea, but he wasn't going to complain.

Just like he wasn't going to complain that Anna Mae was

there to stand by his side while his father explained what had dragged him and Jonas clear down to Twin Rivers.

Because he'd been a lawman long enough to understand that whatever the reason was, it wouldn't make his task of bringing down Velez any easier.

29

As it turned out, Frank Whitelaw actually liked tea. He'd eyed Anna Mae suspiciously that afternoon when she'd handed him the porcelain cup, but then he'd dunked one of her scones in it, sent her a wink, and downed every last drop.

The memory from earlier still made Anna Mae smile as she tromped down the stairs in search of Cain. It was late, bellies were full, dinner was cleaned up, and plans had been made for how, exactly, to go about killing Javier and Eduardo Velez. Daniel had left for the evening, claiming he needed a good night's sleep for what was planned over the coming days. Jonas had said the same and taken himself off to bed.

Anna Mae had expected Cain would follow Jonas in heading to bed, but she'd been waiting in their room for a full forty-five minutes, and Cain had yet to arrive.

Where had the man gotten to?

A quick glance across the courtyard told her the kitchen was dark, so she turned to her left, passing the room that she'd made into their family's private dining room. Scents of pork roast and sweet potatoes still lingered from dinner, and the smells brought another smile to her face. It had been nice having her husband at the table for a meal she'd cooked just for him. The look on his face when he'd taken that first bite of pork had made all the hours of work in the kitchen worth it.

Even Frank had complimented her cooking, though he hadn't smiled at her the way Cain, Daniel, and the Marshal had.

She wasn't sure why Cain's father was so opposed to his son having a wife, but maybe with a few more nights of good cooking, she'd be able to change his mind.

Not that he was planning to stay a few more nights.

Tomorrow evening, Cain, his father, and Jonas would lead another group of men south of the border. If they rode fast and hard, they were hoping they could get to the canyon where Velez hid and surprise the desperadoes before daybreak.

Anna Mae twisted her hands in her skirt. She didn't want to think about what might happen once Cain returned to Mexico, especially considering it involved sneaking into an unfamiliar canyon where he and his men would be outnumbered by at least two to one.

No. She'd save those worries for another time. Because tonight she fully intended to enjoy some time with her husband, just the two of them.

So where was he?

She looked around the courtyard. Every door that opened into it was closed, with darkness visible in the small gap between the bottom of the door and the tile. Except for the door two rooms down. It was cracked open, and soft lamplight filtered into the corridor.

The study. Of course. Why hadn't she thought to check there? Not that Cain's study had much besides a desk and a few maps at the moment, but it still seemed like the place Cain might want to go if he had more details about the attack to work through.

She headed toward the door, only to hear a low conversation filtering into the corridor as she approached. Cain and his father. Even if Jonas hadn't been in bed, she would have been able to tell who it was by the low, rangy timber of voices.

She placed a hand on the knob.

"I still can't believe you were fool enough to up and marry that woman."

Anna Mae stilled. Did everything the man said about her have to be unkind?

"She's a good cook, I'll give you that, but how many times have I told you?" Frank Whitelaw's voice was a bit lower and rougher than Cain's, as though the man had swallowed too much desert dust in his time as a Ranger. "If you need time with a woman, you visit a brothel. Maybe even pay to keep one in a town you frequent if you like her well enough. But you don't go getting yourself tangled up with her. Always ends poorly."

She fisted her hands in her skirt and glared at the door. Why did he think so ill of her? It wasn't as though she'd done anything to offend him.

"It's not gonna end that way for me and Anna Mae."

Anna Mae drew in a relieved breath, the laid-back drawl of her husband's voice both familiar and comforting.

"I can already tell it's gonna end poorly. Your house alone proves that. Just look at it. It's huge and ridiculous. Much bigger than a lawman needs."

Now Frank didn't like her house? What was wrong with him?

Anna Mae leaned forward, peering through the small crack to get a glimpse of the man who seemed to despise her for no reason other than she'd up and married the son he'd never wanted.

"I didn't get the house for me. I got it for Anna Mae, so she can open her restaurant."

Anna Mae nudged the door open a fraction of an inch and could just make out Cain sitting behind the plain wooden desk she'd scrounged up. His father sat on the opposite side of the desk in a chair that looked to have been moved from the restaurant dining room.

"And that's exactly why you're going to have problems." Frank leaned forward in his chair. "Did Jonas tell you what happened to his ma's house?"

Cain straightened, his eyes narrowed at his father. "No."

"Velez's men threw a stick of dynamite inside the window. Nearly started the entire block on fire."

Anna Mae gasped, but Cain's face remained void of every bit of emotion as he absorbed the news. "And Jonas's ma?"

"Killed in the blast," Frank answered. "Along with his fiancée, Harriet."

Anna Mae pressed a hand to her mouth. She'd had no idea. It was true that Jonas had been quiet at dinner and kept to himself a bit, but she'd met him only a couple times before, so she had no way of knowing if that was how he usually behaved.

"How's he holding up?" Cain raked a hand through his hair.

"About how you'd expect. Says he's only here long enough to bring down Velez, then he's heading to Alaska, the Juneau Gold Belt, he called it."

Again, if Cain was surprised by the news, he gave no indication, just stared at his father with flat eyes. "He was a good lawman. It'll be a shame to lose him."

"It's his own fault, and it's the perfect example of why a lawman doesn't get married." His father leaned forward and slapped a hand on the desk. "I used to think you understood the sacrifices it took to be a good lawman. Then I come here to find you took one look at a pretty woman and lost your ever-lovin' mind."

Anna Mae drew back. She was not going to end up dead

simply because Cain was a lawman, and Cain wasn't going to end up dead because he'd married her.

She watched Cain through the crack, waiting for him to tell his father those very things, then add that he loved her for more than just her looks. Or her cooking. That he loved her because...

She blinked. Why did Cain love her? Had he ever said?

Sure, she was pretty—at least men always seemed to think so. But a good marriage, the kind her parents had, was built on more than just attraction.

"I didn't lose my ever-lovin' mind, as you say." Cain leaned forward over the desk, his voice quiet. "Quite the contrary. I knew I was about to lose my ever-lovin' life, and that if I was going to die, I wanted to spend at least a few days with the woman I love and make sure she'll be cared for after I'm gone."

There. He'd said he loved her. He hadn't exactly said why, but at least he wasn't shying away from his feelings for her.

"But what happens if you don't die?" Frank shot back. "Then you're saddled with a wife for the rest of your life."

Again, Anna Mae watched Cain through the crack, waiting for him to tell his father that she wasn't saddling him, that he wanted to be with her and would never, ever consider her a burden.

But all he said was, "I could still die just as easily as you or Jonas. None of this will end until both Velez and Eduardo are dead."

"But we got surprise on our side," Frank answered. "You got a map of the canyon. And you got the support of the Mexican villagers. You'll come out of this alive, and when you do, I want you to come back to Austin and serve with me there."

The breath stalled in Anna Mae's chest. She waited for Cain to tell him they weren't moving, that they were staying right here in Twin Rivers. That he'd promised her he'd stay if he ended up surviving.

But once again the words didn't come. "And just what do you expect me to do in Austin? I'm not a Ranger anymore." Instead, he leaned back in his chair and steepled his fingers beneath his chin.

"You will be once we bring down Velez and I offer proof to the attorney general that Weldon and Moore were on his payroll, and that Velez was being paid by the railroad to send men up north to work. The human smuggling scheme hasn't been uncovered yet, but when it comes to light, it's going to be huge."

A sickening sensation twisted in Anna Mae's gut, and only half because her husband wasn't refusing to move to Austin. She'd had no idea that Javier Velez was smuggling Mexicans over the border to supply the railroad with workers.

"Texans might be able to ignore what happens south of the border, but once that crime comes here? You ain't never seen a news story as big as this." Frank planted his hands on the desk and leaned forward. "Weldon and Moore will both be fired, and they're going to want me in Austin. In fact, Weldon wouldn't even be there now had I taken the job at headquarters when it was offered to me a couple years back. But now he's using his position as the assistant director to strip you of your position and take money from Velez. All while looking the other direction as men are brought over the border and treated little better than slaves."

Cain leaned back in his chair. "You have to admit, it's a well-devised plot. Makes me wonder just how much Velez has gotten away with in the past."

"That's why we're going to stop him, and then you're coming back to Austin with me. We'll make sure something like this never happens again."

"Just what would my position in Austin be?"

Cain's words floated through the doorway. They weren't

loud, more thoughtful than anything, and yet they caused a sickening ball to form in her stomach.

Why wasn't Cain telling his father that he'd promised her he would stay in Twin Rivers? After all, that was the entire reason they'd married, so that she could stay in the town she loved even with the terrible rumors swirling around.

Both Cain and his father settled deeper into their chairs as they talked, going back and forth about how Velez had been able to infiltrate both the Ranger and Marshals' offices. Then they speculated about what would happen after Velez was captured and Frank handed over his evidence against the Rangers and Marshals' offices over to the attorney general of Texas.

But the one thing Cain never said in all this back-and-forth was that he wasn't moving. That he'd promised her he'd stay in Twin Rivers.

And the longer she listened, the more she understood why.

Because while he might claim that he loved her, and was even willing to say so in front of his father and others, he loved the Rangers more.

∼

CAIN SAT BACK in his chair, studying his father. "I can't believe Weldon was on Velez's payroll. Or Moore over at the Marshals' office. His criminal network is much bigger than I thought."

His father's mouth flattened into a hard line. "No one in Austin knew he was behind the cattle rustling. If they had, they never would have sent Rangers down here to deal with it for fear that Velez might end up getting caught."

"I see that now. That's why Weldon moved me up to Alpine the second the rustling cases were prosecuted. That's why he got upset when I went into Mexico after Anna Mae and demoted me. It had nothing to do with how I was doing my job and everything to do with him being paid to protect Velez."

"Exactly." His father leaned back in his chair and stretched his arms behind his head. "As far as I can tell, the attorney general isn't on Velez's payroll, and neither are the directors of either the Marshals or the Rangers. Velez very specifically targeted the assistant directors in both agencies. They assign cases and have a closer working relationship with the opposite offices."

"If only Javier Velez had used his skills for good rather than to break the law and exploit the people surrounding him. Think of all the good he could have done for the people of northern Mexico had he put his mind to being a fair and just governor."

"It's as I said. Once it comes out just how corrupt Weldon is, headquarters will offer me the assistant directorship." His father grabbed a cup of coffee that would have gone cold a half hour ago from the corner of the desk, then reached for one of the leftover scones sitting beside it. "And that's why I want you to come back to Austin and assist me. Will you?"

Cain blew out a breath and looked around the office. It was sparsely furnished with a plain desk Anna Mae had dug up from somewhere and an empty bookshelf behind him.

She'd evidently found his sketchbook in his tent at the camp and had taken a couple of the landscapes he'd drawn and framed them to hang on the walls. The room wasn't fully furnished yet, and both Wes and Harrison, with their fancy office furniture and brimming bookshelves, would probably scoff at the notion of him entertaining anyone in such a blandly appointed room.

But the room felt like home. Like his own space. Like somewhere he belonged.

With his wife.

"I can't up and leave as easy as all that."

His father's lips pressed into a firm line. "I know she's pretty, and I know she's a good cook, but if you're smart, you'll get an annulment."

Cain narrowed his eyes. "I promised to cherish her until death. That's not the kind of thing a man takes back."

His father took another bite of scone, then spoke around it. "Even if you don't come back to Austin with me, the Rangers will still rehire you once they see what you've done to stop Velez and uncover the corruption in Austin. Good grief, the attorney general might even appoint you to some special position in his office instead of with the Rangers. Are you going to walk away from all that because you're married?"

"Anna Mae and I talked about our future, and going back to the Rangers was never part of it."

"You'd really turn your back on the Rangers over a woman?" His father dropped the rest of the scone onto the desk, scattering crumbs across the surface. "You realize that I couldn't bring down Velez by myself, right? Neither could Jonas, even though we're both darn good lawmen. We might have been able to uncover what was going on in Austin without you, but as far as scrounging up information on Velez, knowing which canyon he's hiding in and how best to attack him, all that comes from you."

Cain leveled a glare at his father. "That doesn't change the fact that I'm committed to Anna Mae now. And as you've said, a lawman has no business being married. So yes, maybe the answer is that I should turn my back on the Rangers rather than my wife."

"But what if last year, when you first got here, you went all moony over that wife of yours and decided to turn in your badge and get married? Where would that leave us now?"

He shrugged. "Another Ranger would have been sent to replace me."

"And would he have done as good of a job?"

"Maybe. Reckon it's impossible to know for certain one way or the other."

"Stop lying to yourself." Frank shoved a hand in his direction. "Look at the sheriff. He's a decent lawman, isn't he? Bet he's been helpful to you. No one has any complaints about him as far as I can tell. But if he were a Ranger captain and you'd been the sheriff for the past year, would he have gotten as close as you to bringing down Velez?"

Cain stilled, the wooden chair beneath him seeming suddenly hard. His father was right. As honorable as Daniel was, he wouldn't have gotten this close to stopping Velez. Maybe there was a chance his old lieutenant Pearce would have brought Velez to justice, but the man had been riding with him for seven years, learning from him the way he'd learned from his father.

The spot between Cain's shoulder blades suddenly started to itch. Could he really say no to the Rangers if they offered him his old job back?

Or if they offered him a better one?

Because after serving the Rangers for thirteen years, it wasn't as though just anyone could replace him.

"I'm not going to ask Anna Mae for an annulment," he rasped. "That's not happening."

"Then you're a fool."

Cain slammed his hands down on the desk. "You disparage my wife one more time, and I'll put a fist in your jaw."

His father only glared at him. "This is exactly what I was talking about. She makes you weak, and a man like you can't afford to have a weakness like her. It ends in death. Every single time. And I don't necessarily mean your death. Ask Jonas if you don't believe me."

Cain stood. "I've had enough of this conversation for one night. Now if you'll excuse me, I'm going to spend some time with the wife I don't regret marrying."

Cain strode toward the door. His father stayed seated, his face hard and unyielding.

Cain didn't care. The entire time he'd been in Mexico, he'd told himself the second he got back to Twin Rivers, he was going to take Anna Mae into his arms and kiss her until she couldn't walk straight. Then he was going to heft her into his arms, carry her up the stairs to their room, and show her just how much he'd missed her while he was gone.

Instead, the only words they'd spoken to each other had been over the dinner table, because every other minute of his afternoon and evening had revolved around planning an attack on Velez.

But even as Cain headed up the stairs toward his room, his father's questions swirled in his mind. If he was offered his job as a Ranger back, would he walk away from it because of Anna Mae?

He didn't know. When he'd proposed, he hadn't imagined living long enough that he'd need to figure out how to be a husband—let alone have his old job offered to him again.

And there was no question that he made a good Ranger.

It was more than a job to him; it was a calling. Something he'd spent over a decade of his life doing. Could he leave it all behind because of Anna Mae?

Cain shook his head, then drew in a breath, his hand resting on the doorknob to his room. Maybe once he held Anna Mae in his arms, the thought of not being a lawman anymore wouldn't cause his chest to ache quite so much.

He turned the knob, then stopped. The room was empty. The lamp beside the bed had been lit, casting the room in a warm glow, but the spot in the bed where he'd expected to find his wife lay undisturbed.

He frowned, then crossed the room and stepped out onto the balcony, just to make sure she wasn't stargazing. That was empty too.

Was she still in the kitchen?

He walked back into the corridor and clomped down the stairs, then crossed the courtyard to the kitchen, even though he could tell there was no light coming from the room. Next he checked the parlor, the restaurant dining room, his study, and any other room he could think of.

She wasn't anywhere.

She hadn't left the house, had she? Surely she would have interrupted his conversation if there had been some kind of emergency. He scanned the second-floor corridor, where the bedrooms were. Only two of the four guest rooms were being used. Had she decided to sleep in a different room for some reason?

He pressed his lips together and headed back up the stairs, not sure whether he hoped that she was in a different room or that an emergency had called her away and she'd forgotten to tell him.

After all, there was no reason for her to decide to sleep separate from him...

Was there?

He opened the door to one of the two unoccupied rooms, only to find it empty. He continued to the next room, pausing at the door for a fraction of a second before opening it.

And there she was, lying on the bed with her dark hair fanning out around the pillow.

She rolled over and looked at him, then rolled back the other direction, giving him her back.

"Leave me alone." Tears clogged her voice.

"What happened?" He closed the door behind him, leaving only the faint moonlight from the window to illuminate the room. "Did you get some kind of bad news? Or was it my father? Just tell me what he said to you, and I'll deal with it."

"If I was upset about your father or Jonas, I wouldn't have

gone through the effort to sleep in another room, now would I?"

He blinked. Was that true? Oh, hang it all. Harrison or Sam or Wes would probably be able to tell him the reasons why a woman might not want to sleep in the same room as her husband, but he hadn't realized he'd need to know that going into a marriage.

"Just leave. Please."

He looked at the door, then back at Anna Mae. She couldn't mean it. This was the only full night he had to spend with her since their wedding, and even if they weren't going to make love, he still didn't cotton to the idea of her being so upset she'd sleep somewhere other than their bed.

Besides, didn't the Bible say something about not letting the sun go down on a person's anger?

He walked to the bed, sat down on the side of it, and rested a hand on her shoulder. "Please tell me what's wrong."

She jerked away from him, her face still turned toward the wall. "I heard you downstairs with your father. I know you don't love me."

He didn't love her? Where had she come up with such an all-fired foolish notion? "I'm not sure what you think you heard downstairs, but it certainly wasn't me telling my father I don't love you. I said the opposite."

"Sure, you did." She rolled back his direction and propped herself up on the bed, her dark hair falling in a riot about her shoulders. "Right before you said you'd move back to Austin and help him run the Rangers."

He scowled. "I never agreed to anything with the Rangers. I said I'd think about it, that's all. There's nothing wrong with that."

"You said we'd stay in Twin Rivers when you proposed to me!"

"No, I didn't."

"Yes, you did."

"Those words never once left my mouth."

Her eyes flashed in the darkness, and she crossed her arms over her chest. "Fine, maybe you didn't phrase it in those exact terms, but that's certainly the impression I remember having after we talked about how you'd resigned from the Rangers."

He threw up his hands. "I had no idea Velez was paying men off at the Rangers and the Marshals' office to stop me from bringing him to justice. Had I known that—"

"What? You wouldn't have proposed to me?" Her lip curled into a snarl. "Go on, say it."

"That's not what I meant." He rubbed the back of his neck. Why did his wife have to be so stubborn?

"Fine, what did you mean?"

"That had I known Velez was paying men off, I would have gone to Austin and figured out who was preventing the Rangers from fighting Velez. And once that was done, I would have gotten my men and come back down here to put an end to the criminal and his empire once and for all."

"And you wouldn't have proposed."

He clamped his jaw shut. How did he even answer that? "I don't see why any of this matters. We're married, remember? The rest is all conjecture."

"It matters because I pledged the rest of my life to you!" She threw up her hands, her eyes shooting daggers at him in the darkness. "And ever since we spoke vows, I've begged God daily to let you live, to let you survive this fight so that we could have a family together, a home here in the desert. But now that it looks like you might actually live, you want to up and leave me. That was the entire reason I said no when you first proposed. I don't want to be married to a husband I never see."

"If I go to work with my father, I wouldn't be leaving you. I'd be leaving Twin Rivers. We'd sell this house, and you'd come with me."

"Oh, so now you want to sell the house you bought me? How is that better? I'm opening a restaurant next week!" She looked at him as though he was the strange one, as though he couldn't stop himself from crying or being completely irrational, when she'd been the one to cry through their entire conversation.

"Surely you don't expect to stay here if I go back to the Rangers. It takes over a week to travel to Austin. You're right that I thought you'd be able to open a restaurant here, and that was part of the reason I bought his house, but things change, Anna Mae. You can't be upset at me for not seeing the future. What would happen if after all this is done, I turned my back on the Rangers? You don't really expect me to be a cowpoke if there's a Ranger job waiting for me, do you?"

"I thought I was supposed to be enough to keep you happy. That's what you said when you proposed, that all you wanted was for the two of us to be together, no matter how long you had left. Was that another lie?"

"*Another* lie?" Blood raced in his veins. "I never lied in the first place!"

Confound it. The woman made him want to pull out his hair if he had any. Why was she being so all-fired obstinate? "You said it yourself after I brought you back to Twin Rivers. I have to be a Ranger. It's in my blood. If the Rangers want me back, and I don't go, who will take my place? Who will rescue the next woman who's been abducted or bring down the next criminal terrorizing the countryside?"

"That doesn't mean it's okay to go back on your promises. Do you understand what this proves? That you love being a Ranger more than you love me. Otherwise you wouldn't ask me to give up my dream of opening a restaurant so that you can go back to the Ranger job you've had for the past thirteen years."

That job gave him purpose. And he'd thought she understood that. But sitting there in the dark, watching as tears streaked her cheeks and hurt welled in her eyes, it felt as though she'd never understood a single thing about him.

Calm. He needed to find a way to calm this situation down, just like he did when he was working and two people got into an argument. He didn't want to fight with her, didn't want anything to do with the distance that grew between them each time they traded words.

He reached out and rested a hand on her shoulder. She didn't jerk away from him this time, and the warmth of her skin soon radiated through the thin fabric of her nightdress into his palm. "You can open a restaurant in Austin, I promise. In fact, it will probably be easier to start a restaurant there, seeing as how there's more people. I'll buy you another house you love, too, with a kitchen that's even bigger than the one we have here, and a building for your restaurant on a busy street where people can't help but stop by."

"It won't be the same," She sniffled.

"No, but we'd have each other, and we'd both have part of our dreams."

"No, you'd have your dream. But we both know you'd never be home. And I'd be in a strange city, away from all my friends and surrounded by houses and shops crammed together so tightly that I'll forget what a breath of clean air feels like."

Cain sat back. "My father was right, wasn't he? Nothing good ever comes of a lawman being married." He said the words out of frustration more than anything, because they were the first thing that came to his mind. But once they were out, he could do nothing but stare into the fresh bout of pain filling his wife's eyes. "Anna Mae, I'm sorry. I shouldn't have—"

"No. Don't apologize. At least you're being honest now—unlike when you proposed."

He shook his head. That wasn't what he meant either. Oh, how was he making such a mess of this?

"It's me, isn't it?" he whispered into the darkness. "Is this whole thing between us just impossible? I feel like no matter how much I try, no matter what I do, nothing will ever change the fact that I'm the son of a reckless lawman and a cantina girl." Maybe he'd never have what it took to be a family man, no matter what he did.

"Oh no you don't." Anna Mae raised herself onto her knees, her eyes flashing in the darkness. "You're right that your childhood was terrible. I mean, even now it's clear that your father only wants you for what he can get out of you, but I'm not going to sit here and let you use how you grew up as an excuse to justify all your actions today. Because your childhood doesn't mean I feel any less betrayed by the fact you expect me to leave Twin Rivers, and all so that you can abandon me in a strange city while you go chase down the newest outlaw of the month."

She leaned forward, her dark hair fanning over her shoulders while the anger in her eyes faded into tears that refused to crest. "You made me promises, about staying here, about having a restaurant, all of it. But the moment someone dangles the possibility of going back to the Rangers in front of you, you're willing to forget every last one of the things you promised me. I might be able to understand if you'd actually been offered a job. But all this business about the Rangers taking you back? It's pure conjecture.

"Yet my dreams are the first thing you want to give up." She threw her hands up. "It's selfishness, Cain. Pure and simple. And it's got nothing to do with how you grew up and everything to do with the fact that you don't want to try to be a family with me right now, today. And all this makes me think that maybe… maybe…" The tears building in her eyes finally crested, sending a cascade of moisture down her face as she whispered her next words. "I never should have married you."

He felt as though a boulder had just settled itself atop his chest, large and heavy and making it impossible to drag the tiniest bit of air into his lungs.

He tried to swallow the burning sensation in his throat, too, but it sprang right back up, a giant, hot ball of guilt. "If that's really how you feel, then maybe... we should talk to Harrison about getting us an annulment."

"An annulment?" She straightened. "I didn't say that."

"If you don't want to be married to me anymore, then what other choice is there?" He met Anna Mae's gaze in the moonlight, staring into those beautiful, dark eyes that had haunted his dreams for the past year. "I can't just give up my work as a lawman. It's part of who I am. But our marriage is barely a week old, and if we can't find a way to be happy together, then I'm sure Harrison can push an annulment through the legal system."

"So you're willing to give me up before you give up your job?"

He ran his hands over his head. That's not what he was trying to say. He didn't want to give her up, not ever. But he didn't have the first clue how he could keep her happy, and he couldn't, in good conscience, turn his back on being a lawman. "It's just... I'm not sure if I can give you what you want, or even the kind of future you deserve to have with a husband. So where does that leave us?"

His last words came out as a whisper, raw and open, then he pushed himself off the bed. "Look, none of this needs to be decided now. Tomorrow night I'm leaving for Mexico. If God's good enough to let me live through what's coming with Velez, then we'll settle this after I get back."

"But what if—?"

"We've both said our piece. Now it's time to think things through a bit. Give ourselves both a chance to calm down, maybe even to pray. And if Velez kills me, then this entire conversation is for naught, and we can go back to our original plan of you living here and opening a restaurant and having enough money to live however you want."

"I don't want you to die."

He stopped and turned back to her. It was a mistake. Tangled hair shrouded her shoulders, redness rimmed her eyes, and tears streaked her pale face. And hang it all, but he wanted to return to the bed. To reach out and comfort her, to draw her body against his and stroke his hands through her hair. To kiss the tears from her cheeks.

"I know. But there's little point in making plans for the future until we know I'll live. So for now, for tonight, this is the best I can offer." Then he turned and left the room, closing the door on the woman he loved but wasn't sure he'd ever be able to satisfy in the ways that mattered most.

30

Jonas stared up at the ceiling. He didn't know how long he'd lain there, watching the shadows dance across the white paint and wooden beams of Cain's guest room, only that sleep eluded him as he lay in a comfortable bed. Much the same as it had eluded him each night he'd lain in his bedroll on the trip here, staring up at the stars until pink tinged the sky in the east.

He sighed and turned, rolling onto the side that gave him a view out the window of the mountains on the opposite side of the border. He didn't know what they would face when they rode into Mexico that night. Whether he would live through it was any man's guess.

His gaze fell to the hook on the wall beside his window, where his gun belt hung. Just the sight of the two pistols strapped into their holsters made his stomach turn. He wanted to touch his guns the way a doctor wanted to touch a leg turned foul with sepsis.

If only he could go back in time and tell Frank no when the Ranger had shown up in his office, asking him to pull reports from towns along the border.

If only he'd figured out that Moore was corrupt and thought nothing of sacrificing innocent lives to cover his actions.

If only he hadn't gone back to his office the night the dynamite had been thrown into his mother's house...

Then what?

He'd be dead right along with Harriet and his mother? Was that really what he wanted?

He dragged a breath into his lungs. Dying that day sure would have made things easier. But now he was left here alive, staring at the guns hanging on the wall and knowing what he had to do—or at least had to try doing—before he up and disappeared into the great wilds of Alaska.

Because whether he liked it or not, God had left him alive, and he had too much justice in his veins to let his mother's and Harriet's deaths go unanswered.

∼

DANIEL STARED up at the ceiling of his bedroom, the gray light of early dawn trickling through the crack in the curtains. This morning he was in his bed with Charlotte curled into his side, but where would he be at this time tomorrow?

Still atop his horse, most likely, riding to an undisclosed location in Mexico and hoping that none of Velez's informants spotted the posse from Twin Rivers as it traversed the narrow, winding trails of the Mexican backcountry.

Would they be able to surprise Javier and Eduardo Velez and their men? And if so, would they have enough lawmen to do them harm?

Cain's plan was to sneak into the canyon where the outlaws were hiding first with Jonas and try to kill Velez straightaway, but what if one of Velez's men spotted him?

What if the posse found itself surrounded?

Daniel's heart hammered against his chest, and he turned on his side, reaching for where Charlotte's warm body lay beside his own. He wrapped his arms around her, pulling her flush against himself, then squeezed.

Dear God...

But what did he say? He could hardly ask for his own life to be spared when Cain and Jonas would be in far more danger.

When Jonas had already lost his mother and his fiancée because of Velez.

Could he really ask for God to allow everyone to return from Mexico unscathed? It seemed like too big of a request when there had already been so much death.

And yet he couldn't pray for anything less, because he knew what was going to happen the moment he put out word for volunteers today. Sam, Harrison, and Wes would all insist on riding with him and Cain. But this time they wouldn't be chasing down rustled cattle or searching for someone who was missing in the desert.

No, this time they were walking straight into a situation that would leave every last one of them outnumbered and in incredible danger.

And he didn't want to go.

Nor did he want any of his friends to go.

"Daniel, honey?" Charlotte shifted in his arms. "Are you asleep?"

"I'm sorry. I didn't mean to wake you."

"It's your trip into Mexico, isn't it? You can never sleep before something like this."

He sighed. "You know me too well, I'm afraid."

She turned to face him, her hair tickling his chin. "I don't suppose you could just... not go into Mexico with everyone else?"

He leaned over and pressed his forehead against hers. If only she knew how badly he wanted to stay. "Cain needs as many skilled lawmen as he can get. I might not be as good in a gunfight as him, but I'm not going to send Abe or Bryce in my stead."

She sighed. "I understand."

"Do you?"

"Of course. This is your job. You have to do it."

Right. He did. Because he was the sheriff. But the thing was... "What if I'm not sure I want to be sheriff any longer?"

She raised herself on her elbow to look at him, her hair cascading against his chest. "What? Daniel, no. You make a wonderful sheriff. Of course you want to still be sheriff. Your father was sheriff before you, and everyone in this town loves you and—"

"And I have a family now. A wife who cooks me dinner each night and waits for me to come home. A little baby girl who will need a pa as she grows older." He drew in a breath, searching out his wife's eyes in the darkness. "And maybe I just don't have it in me to leave you and Lucy here at night anymore while I go out on patrols, or know that you're sitting back here worrying about me while I leave for yet another trip into Mexico that will keep me away for days at a time. I just don't think I can do it anymore."

He wasn't sure when the thoughts had started. Maybe it had been when Cain and Anna Mae had disappeared for so long he'd thought they were both dead. Or maybe it had been before that, when he'd arrested Alejandra not realizing she'd been framed by the rustlers, and it became apparent just how powerful the Mexican criminal was that they'd spent the past year fighting. But none of that changed the fact he wanted this trip into Mexico to be the last thing he ever did as a lawman.

"What will you do?" Charlotte asked softly. "If you're not sheriff, will you work for Wes at the A Bar W?"

"No." He smoothed a strand of hair back from her face. "I

can't imagine being happy eating trail dust all day. I want to run for judge."

"You do?"

"I do. Harrison's already on the ballot in November for prosecuting attorney, but we need a judge too. We haven't had one since Mattherson was arrested, and I want our town to be safe. It's ridiculous I need to keep criminals locked up for weeks in the jailhouse awaiting trial when most of them can be tried and shipped off to the state penitentiary in a few days. But here we are, always needing to wait for a traveling judge to come around."

"Oh, I... That's the best idea you've had in years." She reached out and framed his face with her warm hands. "Here I was, trying to imagine how you'd be anything other than a sheriff, but I can see you being a judge. In fact, I love it."

He smiled. "Do you?"

She pressed a quick kiss to his lips. "It's still law and order and justice, but it's also less dangerous. It's perfect."

"I think Bryce would make a good sheriff. Maybe I can talk him into running in November."

Charlotte rolled onto her back and laced her fingers behind her head, staring up at the ceiling much the same as he was. "I suppose that could work."

"You don't like the idea?" Something about her voice was a bit too hesitant.

"I like Bryce, but I'm not sure he'd do as good of a job as you or your father. Now Cain, on the other hand..."

"Cain?" Just the thought of his brother-in-law made his heart feel as though a hole had been carved into it. "We don't know if he'll even live through this trip to Mexico. And honestly, love, I'm not expecting him to stay in Twin Rivers if he survives."

"What?" Charlotte propped herself onto an elbow, her brow furrowed. "But he bought Anna Mae that beautiful house."

"I know." He reached out and clasped his wife's hand in his own, then drew it to his mouth for a soft kiss. "But this situation with Velez is bigger than any of us realized, and if Cain brings down a criminal as powerful as that, the Rangers will want him back. And it's likely they'll want him in Austin. His father already told me as much last night."

"But what about the house? And Anna Mae's restaurant? Surely he wouldn't put the house back up for sale, would he?"

Daniel shrugged. "I can't really answer that. All I can say is that if Cain survives, important people in Austin will take notice of what he did down here."

"Anna Mae will be devastated if she has to leave."

He sighed, the breath rushing out of him in a long gust. There was a time when he'd been able to solve his sister's problems. A skinned knee, a bully at school, a mess in the kitchen that was too big for her to clean up on her own. But her current situation, the fact that she was married to a man who was either going to die or leave—that wasn't the kind of thing he could fix. "I think Anna Mae will come to like Austin, in time."

Charlotte quirked an eyebrow. "You clearly don't know your sister all that well."

He heaved in a breath. "I know her plenty well, but this is the kind of thing she and Cain are going to have to work out for themselves. I'm not sure there's much either of us can do to help. Now this, on the other hand..." He reached up and smoothed the furrows away from his wife's brow with his thumb. "This is something I can fix."

He pressed his lips to the spot where his thumb had been, then pressed them to the tip of her nose, then her cheek.

She grinned. "That was lovely, husband, but I'm not sure it will make up for your sister moving away."

"It won't?" He leaned closer. "Then how about this?"

He kissed her mouth this time, skimming his fingers up her

side before they settled in her hair, where he tilted her head at just the right angle.

She sighed against his mouth, wrapping her arms around his back and drawing herself closer as he trailed his lips across her jaw to the ticklish place where her neck met her shoulder.

She gasped and squirmed. "Daniel. We can't. It's too soon after the baby. The doc said—"

"I know full well what the doc said, but that doesn't mean I can't kiss on you for a bit, or hold you tight."

He pulled his lips away from the softness of her skin, because she was right. If the two of them kept this up, they were going to get themselves into trouble.

As soon as he rolled onto his back, Charlotte settled her head on his chest. "I love you."

He stroked his fingers through her hair in the dim light. "I love you too." And he did, more than he could describe or explain. "Thank you for being such a wonderful wife."

"Mm-hmm," she mumbled against his chest, her body going lax with sleep while her breathing evened out.

And so he held her there, memorizing the feel of her body in his arms and the softness of her hair, the way her breath rose and fell in an even rhythm.

Because while he might plan to resign as sheriff as soon as he returned from Mexico, there was still a chance he wouldn't return at all.

31

How long had he slept? Cain blinked as he stared up at the ceiling, gray with the dim light of early dawn. Not long, if the gritty feeling in his eyes was any indication. But at least he had fallen asleep... eventually.

If he could call the little bit of time he'd tossed and turned with his eyes closed "sleep."

He sighed and rolled over onto his shoulder. It was a mistake, because he found himself looking out the long, wide window at the mountains across the river.

The view alone had been the reason he'd purchased the house. Because he'd known Anna Mae would love it, and he wanted to know what it felt like to lie in bed with her and watch dawn rise over the craggy peaks.

Instead, he was alone, staring at the mountains inside the house he'd purchased for his wife. In the bed he'd purchased to share with his wife. Lying on the special bedding he'd bought just because he'd known it would make his wife smile when she saw it.

And here he'd spent half the night wondering why Anna Mae didn't want to leave everything behind and go to Austin.

He groaned and stood to his feet, then tromped to the dresser and jerked on a pair of trousers and a shirt. Was he the one being a fool? Or was it Anna Mae? Because to his way of thinking, it seemed perfectly reasonable for her to follow him across the state. Women did it all the time.

But probably not after their husbands bought them beautiful houses and told them they could open restaurants.

He sighed as he buttoned his shirt. *God, am I doing something wrong by asking her to come with me to Austin? Is Anna Mae right about me going back on my promises to her if I go back to the Rangers?*

He waited for a moment, pausing to see if God would issue some sort of answer or maybe bring a verse to his mind.

He got nothing, so he opened the door and stepped out into the corridor, then paused when his eyes inadvertently traveled to Anna Mae's door.

Should he go to her now and try to resolve things before he left? Or should they wait and talk after he returned from Mexico like he'd said last night?

When it came to being a Ranger, he never second-guessed himself. But all he felt when it came to being Anna Mae's husband was confusion.

What if she decided she really did want an annulment while he was gone?

His stomach cramped, and a sour taste filled his mouth. He wouldn't let things go that far. In the end, he wouldn't rejoin the Rangers, even if that meant he'd spend the rest of his days as a cowpoke on Wes's ranch. He'd spoken vows to Anna Mae, and he intended to keep them.

But he hadn't counted on feeling like he'd be torn in two, pulled in opposite directions because of his duty to his wife and his skill as a lawman.

Should he tell her that? Go and wake her up and apologize?

Confess that he really would stay in Twin Rivers if going to Austin meant losing her?

He took a step toward her room, but the sound of another door opening stopped him. He looked over to see Jonas emerging into the corridor, fully dressed for the day.

Cain turned and headed in Jonas's direction. The last thing he was going to do was have his friend watch as he went to wake up his wife, who'd slept in a different room. "You're up early."

"Couldn't sleep," Jonas muttered, his voice gritty.

"Me either."

Jonas smirked. "I'll bet you couldn't."

If only his sleeplessness was for the reason Jonas thought. Cain scrubbed a hand over his face. "Let's head to camp. I need to let the men know our plans for Velez and his son."

"Sounds good." Jonas covered his mouth to stifle a yawn, then followed him down the stairs and out into the early morning.

The long shadows of early morning still draped the town, and the two of them looked to be the only ones about. The crushed gravel from the road crunched under their feet as they walked toward the main road.

"Your pa tell you what happened to my ma and Harriet?" Jonas asked softly as they turned onto O'Reilly Street.

Cain swallowed. "He did, and I'm awful sorry. I know my saying so won't bring them back, but I still hate that you lost them, and all because of Velez."

Jonas shook his head. "At least you didn't go off and start lecturing me about how I should have never had a fiancée in the first place."

Cain's eyes snapped to his friend's. "He didn't."

Jonas kept his head down, his ruddy scruff of a beard hiding any emotion that might otherwise play across his face. "He did.

They hadn't even been dead for a full twelve hours when he started in on the lecture."

"I'm sorry," Cain apologized again, though just like last time, the words felt useless.

Jonas blew out a breath, his shoulders slumping. "I won't say I don't feel any guilt over what happened. I do. If I hadn't been snooping around the records at the office and figured out that Velez was moving men across the border, my mother and fiancée would both still be alive. That's something I've got to live with for the rest of my life. But what your father says about women, his attitude toward your marriage, it's not normal. I don't know where it came from, but just because the worst happened to Harriet and my ma, it doesn't mean you and Anna Mae are doomed. I want you to know that."

Cain lifted his head to the sky, which was quickly filling with pink and orange. "My father's been that way for as long as I can remember. I don't know why. All I can say is that his opinion has changed little over the past decade."

Jonas scrubbed a hand over his face. "Makes me wonder if something happened in his past. Maybe before you were born."

Cain stopped walking. Could something have happened to his father once? Or more to the point, could something have happened to a woman his father had once cared for?

He blinked at his friend. If so, that would explain why Frank was so dead set against a lawman ever developing feelings for a woman. "I really don't know. He never mentioned anything along those lines. But it makes sense."

Jonas's shoulders rose and fell in a listless shrug. "It was just a thought. Could be I'm wrong." He started walking, slowly ambling in the direction of the camp.

Cain watched his friend for a moment. He'd never seen a lawman so sluggish. Oh sure, Jonas had agreed to go with them into Mexico, but even while they were planning the attack, he'd just sat back and listened, offering no ideas of his own.

In fact, everything about the man seemed listless, the way he slowly sauntered down the street rather than walked with a purpose, the way he'd eaten only a few bites at dinner last night, the way he kept answering questions with lifeless shrugs.

Cain lengthened his stride, catching up to Jonas just as he turned down the grassy trail that led to the camp beside the river. "If there's anything I can do, about Harriet or your ma, let me know. I'm sure nothing about this is easy."

"There's not. Not anything you can do, not anything I can do, not anything that anyone on this entire planet can do." Jonas's throat worked, the faint lines around his mouth creased with an unspoken pain. "I don't suppose you can know how it feels until it happens. Maybe you could stand there and imagine losing Anna Mae, but I guarantee you, once it happens, it feels a whole lot worse."

"Jonas."

"My days as a lawman are done. I told your pa I'd help you catch Velez and his son, but only because I want justice for Ma and Harriet. Then I'm off to Alaska."

Cain planted his hands on both of his friend's shoulders, then waited for Jonas to bring his gaze up. When he did, Cain found himself swallowing. There was so much pain in his friend's eyes, it was almost as though the will to live had been sapped from them, leaving only hurt behind.

"You can't do this to yourself. Listen to me." He gripped Jonas's shoulders harder, then gave him a little shake. "What happened wasn't your fault. It was the fault of criminals. That's who you should be blaming. You can't let the guilt haunt you like this."

He loosed a bitter laugh. "Can't I?"

"Jonas."

He shrugged off Cain's hands and resumed walking. "Don't. Just leave me be. Like I said, you don't know how it feels, and until you do, I won't be taking advice from you."

Cain sighed as they approached the edge of the camp. "I'm sure once this business with Velez is settled, once it comes out just how corrupt Moore was, the Marshals will want you back in Austin."

"I don't want anything to do with being a lawman."

"But you're good at your job, and Texas is a wild land in need of men who can enforce law and order."

"I already told you, I'm going to Alaska, not back to the Marshals."

"What will you do there?"

Jonas shrugged, the gesture weak and halfhearted. "Work in one of the mines or stake a claim of my own. Or maybe I'll just walk off into the mountains one day and disappear. I suppose I'll do anything, really, as long as it doesn't involve the law."

Cain paused outside his tent. It was a downright shame. A waste of a lawman if he'd ever seen one. "There'll always be a place for you here if you change your mind."

"I won't."

He couldn't say precisely why the words hurt so bad. After all, he and Jonas didn't even work for the same agency. But he couldn't help hoping that something on their trip to Mexico would change his mind. That maybe if they killed Javier and Eduardo Velez, Jonas would see how truly valuable he was as a lawman.

Dear God, please let it be so. Please take this burden Jonas is carrying from him and give him peace again.

A quick glance at his friend told him that if God intended to answer his prayer, it wasn't going to be immediately, because everything about Jonas looked as sullen and listless as it had a few minutes ago.

Cain sighed, then turned and lifted the flap to his tent...

And grew still.

There, in the shadows, he could just make out a small

wooden crate sitting inside, right in the middle of the ground between his bed and table.

His stomach dropped and his heart kicked against his chest. He couldn't say how he knew the package was from Velez, only that it was a feeling that settled in his gut, as sure and certain as the fact the sun would crest the mountains in another twenty minutes.

He strode forward, grabbed the envelope resting on the top of the crate, then pulled off the lid...

And gasped at the sight that greeted him, and the stench.

32

"I'm going." The words wrenched from Cain's chest as he stood in the middle of Daniel's office, surrounded by Jonas, his father, and Daniel. "I don't have a choice."

"No, you're not." His father didn't even look at him as he stood at the table at the back of the room and poured himself a cup of coffee. "Don't be a fool."

He stalked forward. "A fool? You think I'm a fool for not wanting innocent villagers to die?"

How could the man act so calm when Velez was ready to kill dozens of Mexicans, and all because of him?

His father slammed his cup down on the table, causing dark liquid to slosh over the sides. "I think you're a fool for walking headlong into a trap you know you've got no hope of escaping alive."

"You saw the note. If I'm not in El Rebote at noon in two days, they'll start killing a villager an hour. And seeing how Velez has already stripped the town of all its able-bodied men, that pretty much leaves women, children, and the elderly for him to murder."

Frank's eyes flashed, even though everything about his face

stayed calm. "I never said you shouldn't go. I said you can't go walking into a trap."

"I don't see how I have a choice."

"I'm sure we can come up with some sort of plan. Some way to outsmart Velez," Jonas said, his voice even.

"There isn't time to plan anything." Cain thrust a hand toward the note. "Did you read the part that says if anyone is spotted leaving the town with me, Velez will start his killing spree early?"

"But how would he know if anyone leaves the town with you?" Jonas scratched the back of his head. "Seems to me it would take whoever's watching the town two days to get to this village and let Velez know that you're not alone."

His jaw clenched. "Testing whether Velez's informants are watching to see if I leave Twin Rivers by myself is not something I'm willing to risk. Velez sent me a scalp." He still couldn't get the image out of his head. The mess of black hair with dried blood, the sickening stench of rotting flesh—and the sight of the note saying what he was supposed to do next.

He'd known Velez was capable of cruel things, but so far his machinations had been directed at lawmen and young Mexican men who could fight and work.

Terrorizing a farming village was a new level of evil.

"Why do you think Velez decided to draw you down into Mexico?" Daniel leaned against the front of his desk, his arms crossed over his chest.

Cain went to shove his hand into his hair, only to find prickly stubs where his long blond hair had been. "How should I know? Nothing that man does makes a lick of sense."

"Seems like figuring it out might give us some clue about how to outsmart him," Daniel drawled.

"You said that two of the men you captured in the canyon during your scouting trip turned on Velez, right?" Jonas walked to the back of the room and grabbed one of the muffins on the table. "You sent them back to Velez with a story about how a farmer and his daughter had surprised Emilio and killed him with a gun, and that his other men had killed each other in an argument?"

"That's right."

Jonas took a bite of the muffin. "What if Velez saw through their story and figured out they were working with you?"

A heavy weight settled on Cain's chest. Was that what had happened? Had he been wrong to send Hugo and Alfonso back to Velez?

"I agree with Jonas," Daniel said. "The timing is perfect. This crate arrived last night, presumably about ten to twelve hours after you returned to town. Let's say that when you sent those men back—"

"Hugo and Alfonso. They have names. And families. Wives and children, the both of them." Cain pressed his eyes shut, a sickening sensation roiling through his gut. Were they really dead? He'd done many things in his years as a lawman that he wasn't particularly proud of, but he could never once think of a time when his actions resulted in the deaths of two innocent people.

Especially when those people had begged him to keep them and their families safe.

"All right," Daniel continued. "Let's say you sent Hugo and Alfonso back to Velez, then Velez figured out what happened, killed them, and sent one of their scalps to you in that crate. It would have taken two days for that scalp and the note to get here, the same amount of time it took you to travel north, meaning the scalp and note would arrive shortly after you."

Cain scrubbed a hand over his face. "So what you're saying is two innocent men might already be dead because of me, but I'm somehow wrong for wanting to go into Mexico to stop more innocent people from dying?"

"No." His father straightened. "We're saying the stupidest

thing you can do right now is ride off, half-cocked, to your own death."

"That's the problem. It's either my death or everyone else's." His chest burned as he said the words, but that didn't make them any less true. Had he truly thought he could best Velez? What a fool he'd been, sitting down with his father and Jonas and Daniel, making plans as though they actually had a chance to bring down the former governor of a Mexican state.

His argument with Anna Mae last night had been for nothing, because he wasn't going to get out of this alive, and now he wasn't even sure that he'd be able to kill Velez before he died. After all, there was only one reason Velez was going through all this trouble to draw Cain down to Mexico alone.

"Honestly, even if you did what that letter said and left Twin Rivers by yourself, I'm not sure it would do much good." Jonas shoved another bite of muffin into his mouth. "None of the desperadoes Velez is probably paying to watch the trail will recognize you without your long hair."

"He's right." Daniel narrowed his eyes, studying him. "Your hair has always given you away whenever you ride into town. It's how I knew it was you and not an outlaw when you returned with Anna Mae a couple weeks ago. People recognize you and your hair at a distance."

"There's no question Velez is watching the town." Frank scratched his chin. "What we don't know is how good his informants are. Are they regular townsfolk he's paying for every last detail, or are they men on the other side of the border who use a spyglass to figure out who's at the camp?"

Cain frowned. "Does it matter? Whatever those informants have to say, it's still going to take two days to reach Velez."

"It matters if they can tell whether you're the one who rides out of camp in a couple hours, or whether it's someone else posing as you." Frank took a slurp of coffee. "Don't you have a

Ranger with long blond hair? Bet Velez's men would mistake him for you."

Jonas snapped his fingers. "Frank's right. If this village is out in the open, on some kind of plain like everyone says, Velez's men won't be able to get a good look at you. They'll see from a distance that the rider doesn't have any hair, and they'll probably shoot you dead at the first canyon you come to, then figure out too late it was you they killed."

Cain blinked. Was that true? Had a silly pact with his friends jeopardized his ability to save the town of El Rebote? "There's so much about this I never would have guessed. I mean, the reason they're demanding I come to a town two days away is because they want to make sure I'm isolated, and here I'd been expecting Velez and his men to launch an attack on Twin Rivers."

"They still might come here," Daniel said. "They probably just want you gone first."

"Bet they don't know your father is here to help defend the town." Jonas polished off his last bite of muffin, then followed it with a swig of coffee. "Or me."

Cain sighed. "If only having you here would do any good."

"I'm serious about you sending another man in your place," his father drawled. "Now tell me, is there a man with long blond hair riding with you or not?"

"Ridley?"

"Is that his name?"

"Yeah." Cain reached for his own coffee cup, which was sitting on Daniel's desk. "The man could be my brother."

"Let's say we send him to El Rebote, and then we leave some of your Rangers here to keep things looking busy around the camp, like you're the only one who left." Frank scratched his chin, a sure sign he was thinking. "But a small group of us waits until tonight and then sneaks over the border. We don't follow the same path as Ridley. We approach from a different direction, and we have one of your sharpshooters kill Velez just before noon on Thursday, as he's waiting for Ridley to approach. If we can kill Velez straight off, I bet the villagers and some of Velez's men would leave him and fight with us."

It wasn't a bad plan, but there was one major glaring problem. "There's nowhere to hide a sharpshooter around El Rebote."

"Northern Mexico is nothing but mountains and canyons." Daniel crossed his office to the map hanging on the wall. "There has to be a place for a sharpshooter to hide."

"Not around El Rebote." Cain sauntered over to the map. Never mind that he'd been into northern Mexico enough times over the past year to have the thing memorized. "That's probably the reason Velez chose that town. It's on a plain in the middle of a wide valley. There might be a few boulders to hide behind, but there's no cover getting to them, and there's nothing large enough to conceal a group of men."

"So we sneak a few men into the village early, and the rest of us hide on the nearest mountain, and we wait for the sharpshooter to take out Velez." His father joined them at the map. "One bullet might be all it takes to end this."

Cain squinted at the little dot marking the tiny farming village. On the map, the mountains surrounding the town looked close, but the valley was almost two miles wide and over five miles long. Sneaking in there to talk to Cristobal hadn't been easy. The small river winding through the town made it perfect for farming and ranching, but it had to be the worst place in northern Mexico to stage an ambush.

"You'd be looking at a twelve-hundred-yard shot," Cain said. "It's too far for me or any of my men to be on target. In fact, the only person I know who has any chance of making a shot like that is—"

"Anna Mae," Daniel piped up. "Maybe we should take her with us."

Cain whirled around, his heart hammering against his chest. "No. Absolutely not. I will not risk her life on the slim chance she might be able to kill Velez."

"It's more than just a slim chance. You've seen her shoot before. Every Independence Day she puts on a shooting show for us. Last year she hit the target at twelve hundred and seventy-two yards using Pa's Sharps Big Fifty rifle. And that was after she outshot everyone else with her .45-70."

Cain narrowed his gaze on Daniel. "I still won't do it. And I can't believe you'd suggest such a thing. Your sister could die."

"From a hiding place in the mountains twelve hundred yards away? She'd be in more danger here with the town left unprotected." Daniel stepped closer, a determined glint in his eyes. "And seeing as how you've got a mind to take a two-day trip into Mexico on your own that will almost certainly result in your death, I think it's only fair you ask your wife if she wants to go."

Cain's chest felt suddenly tight, as though an iron band had been clamped around it.

"Is that true?" his father asked. "Can that pretty little wife of yours outshoot a buffalo hunter?"

"She's the best shooter I've ever seen."

"Might even be able to outshoot Annie Oakley," Daniel muttered. "If she ever had a mind to up and join a Wild West show."

Frank clapped a hand on his shoulder. "Then you best go talk to your wife. Sounds like she's the best chance we got to get you out of this alive."

"Right," he rasped, his throat raw. He'd just go ask the woman who wasn't sure why she'd married him to risk her life on the slim chance she might be able to save his.

Something told him this wasn't going to be the funnest conversation he'd ever had.

33

Of all the arguments to have with her husband.

Anna Mae sniffled as she plunged her hand into a bucket of hot, soapy water. She quickly found the brush and curled her hand around it, then pulled it out and started scrubbing the floor.

But all the scrubbing in the world still wouldn't erase the fact her husband didn't have any desire to stay in the desert with her. She sniffled again. Was it something about her? Was she somehow not as lovable as Charlotte or Ellie? Alejandra or Keely? Because all of her friends had husbands who would move mountains to keep promises they made to their wives, and here she had a husband who couldn't even stick to the promise he'd made when he proposed to her almost ten days ago.

She'd known he was something of a vagrant, that he preferred wandering around the state to putting down roots. But when he'd looked at her and said he wanted to wake up next to her every morning and run his hands through her hair whenever he pleased, she'd believed him.

And that probably made her the biggest fool in all of Texas.

After all, he was the son of a vagabond Ranger and a cantina girl. His father hadn't wanted anything to do with him—hadn't even allowed him to use his last name—until Cain had been old enough to join the Rangers and ride with him.

Or more accurately, until Cain had been old enough to lie about his age and claim he was eighteen when he was really sixteen so he could join the Rangers.

But that still didn't change the fact he'd grown up with the town prostitute for a mother, or that his mother saw him only as a way to manipulate his father into sending them money and returning to Twin Rivers every year or so.

And just like his father had always left his mother and returned to eastern Texas, Cain seemed intent on doing the same thing to her.

She sniffled again, a tear choosing that moment to trickle down her cheek and plop onto the floor.

So here she was, little more than a week after her wedding, and it seemed like she'd made the biggest mistake of her life.

At least she still had her restaurant, and the dining-room floor needed a good cleaning. She dragged her bucket of water under one of the tables Ellie's brothers had built for her, dunked the brush in the water again, and started scrubbing. She'd set an opening date for later this week, and she wasn't going to let an argument with Cain stop her from having the thing she'd always dreamed of.

Well, after having a husband and family, of course. But it seemed less and less likely that she'd have one of those, so she'd settle for having the best restaurant on the border.

And being a good aunt to Lucy and whatever other children Charlotte and Daniel might have.

The trouble was, when she imagined a future like that, she couldn't even smile. All she wanted to do was curl into a ball and cry.

Instead, she scrubbed harder.

The door opened behind her, and she paused, her hands stilling on the brush. Was it Cain? Maybe he'd come to apologize. Come to tell her that he loved her enough to stay in the desert and be her husband.

"Anna Mae?" Charlotte's voice echoed through the room.

The hope building in her chest drained away. "Over here."

Footsteps clacked against the tile, and then shoes and the bottom of a green skirt appeared beneath the table. "Oh, goodness. You realize you're just supposed to get the dirt up from the floor, right? Not scrub so hard you gouge the tiles."

"I'm not gouging anything."

Charlotte's silence told her that maybe she had, in fact, gouged a few of the tiles with her vengeful cleaning.

"There's an extra brush in the bucket if you want to help. Otherwise, I don't have time to visit. The restaurant opens in four days."

She went right back to scrubbing, her head down so that her hair fell about her face, blocking her from view. The last thing she needed was for Charlotte to start needling her about her argument with Cain.

But Charlotte didn't reach for the second brush. Instead, she kneeled down in front of the table, right on the dirty floor, with Lucy clasped to her chest.

Anna Mae glared at her. "You'd better move. I need to scrub where you're sitting." "What happened?"

Another tear chose that moment to streak down her face and plop on the floor. "Nothing."

"Is it Cain? Are you worried about him, because Daniel thinks—"

"Worried? Why would I be worried about that liar? He's the last person who deserves any worry. I haven't thought of him once all day."

Charlotte's eyebrow shot up. "And you think he's the one lying?"

"Yes! You should have heard him talking to his father last night. He wants to become a Ranger again, which means he's moving back to Austin. But when he proposed, he made it sound like we would stay here. He said that if he somehow defeated Velez, we could live in the desert and have a family and grow old together. But now that his father wants Cain to join him in Austin and take on some fancy position at headquarters, he's forgotten all about the promises he made and is asking me to leave. And I just can't."

"Can't what? Go to Austin?" Charlotte's brows drew down into a furrow. "Why ever not?"

"Because I don't want to leave Twin Rivers!" She threw up her hands, brush and all, causing droplets of dirty water to splatter across both of them as well as Lucy. "That was the entire reason I married Cain. So I wouldn't have to leave."

"Is it?"

"Yes! Don't you remember? I was going to have to move to Houston with my parents because of the rumors, but then he proposed and he made it sound like he meant it. Made it sound like he loved me enough to want a life with me."

"And you don't think he loves you anymore? After giving you this house?" Charlotte looked around the dining room that was all but ready to start receiving customers. "You're right. I don't understand."

"If he wants a life with me, he'll stay here, not move to Austin. I'd be important enough to him that he would choose me over rejoining the Rangers."

"Oh, Anna Mae." Charlotte dragged in a breath and reached for her hand. "I don't know precisely what the two of you agreed to before you said you'd marry him. But I do know this—marriage isn't an agreement. It's a promise, a pledge that lasts the rest of your life. It involves standing by your spouse in sickness and health, in good times and bad, and sometimes, even when unforeseen circumstances arise."

"I know that." She wiped another tear from her cheek, never mind that she smeared dirty mop water across her face in the process. "But I feel like if he truly loved me, he'd be willing to compromise, not just insist I have to go with him."

"Perhaps, but what does compromise look like here? Because while it's nice to think that we can always compromise in a marriage, sometimes there's no middle ground. I mean, there was no way for your parents to compromise when your father wanted to attend seminary. Either they both went or neither of them did. There was no way for Harrison to keep his law practice in Austin and stay here and run Fort Ashton. It was either one or the other." Charlotte stretched her legs out on the floor and patted Lucy's back. "I know it's nice to think a husband and wife can always meet in the middle on a disagreement, but sometimes that simply isn't possible."

"So you think I should be the one to give up my dream of living in Twin Rivers and opening a restaurant here?"

"I didn't say that."

Anna Mae sniffled. "See? This is why I didn't want to marry him."

Charlotte straightened. "You didn't want to marry him?"

She gave her head a small shake. "Not at first, not until I realized that he'd left the Rangers. That was the one thing I never wanted, to be married to a man I never saw but constantly had to worry about. I was prepared to let him go because of it. But then when he said he'd left the Rangers and it looked like Velez was going to kill him..."

"Velez still might kill him."

"I know. But he's got a chance of surviving now, whereas before he went into Mexico and figured out where Velez was hiding, living through this seemed completely impossible."

Lucy let out a small cry and started squirming against Charlotte's chest.

"You realize you can't be upset with Cain for not predicting the future, right?" Charlotte absently patted her daughter's back. "I'm sure when he made you those promises, he fully believed his days as a Ranger were over. No one would have guessed how corrupt the assistant director in Austin was, but now that it's apparent—"

"He wants to go back," she finished. "Because being a Ranger matters more to him than I do."

Charlotte's hand stilled on Lucy's back. "He doesn't think that, Anna Mae. I wish you would—"

"You didn't hear him talking to his father last night. He was so eager to go back to Austin, to become a Ranger again, and I don't want anything to do with him going back to the Rangers."

"Maybe you need to look at this differently."

"How?"

Lucy squirmed against Charlotte's chest even more, her cries growing louder.

"Maybe God wanted the two of you together, and maybe you're stronger together than you are by yourselves." Charlotte patted her daughter's back more firmly, but that did nothing to quell the crying, so she laid the hungry child on her lap, then reached to her neck and began unbuttoning her shirtwaist. "Even though you both have your fears, and even though it seems like your dreams are at cross-purposes, maybe this is all part of God's plan."

"God's plan?"

Charlotte's hands made short work of the buttons, and a moment later she was lifting her daughter to her chest, and satisfied suckling noises filled the air.

The sight caused something warm to unfurl in Anna Mae's heart. How long until she would be nursing her own child?

"Yes, part of God's plan," Charlotte answered, even though Anna Mae had forgotten her question. "If God hadn't wanted the two of you to be alone in the desert, He would have found a way to prevent that. He could have prevented those rumors from spreading, too, or given you deeper feelings for Paul Fordham. He could have brought all this business about corruption in Austin to light before you and Cain married, or done any other number of things to prevent the wedding. But He didn't. And I have to believe it's because God wanted you and Cain together, even if it means you'll end up moving to Austin."

Anna Mae looked down at her hands absently toying with the damp fabric of her skirt. Was Charlotte right? Had how she'd gotten married been God's way of bringing her and Cain together, even though it all seemed like a giant accident?

"The picture God saw when you and Cain married might have been bigger than the picture either of you saw, but that doesn't mean any of this was a mistake." Charlotte sighed, a wistful expression crossing her face. "You complete Cain in a way that no other woman could. It might not be obvious to you, but it's terribly obvious to everyone around you. And what's more, Cain completes you. So even if God's plan seems unbearably dark right now, that doesn't mean any of the promises in God's Word are untrue. '*Whoso findeth a wife findeth a good thing,*' remember? And '*children are an heritage of the* L*ORD*.'"

Anna Mae blew out a breath. Her friend was right. Instead of arguing with Cain over whether they ended up in Austin or Twin Rivers, she needed to trust that God had her best interests in view. Maybe Austin was a bit like Nineveh, and she was something like Jonah. She had no desire to go to Austin, no desire to be married to a Ranger. But if that was the path God was leading her down, then she needed to trust that He would work out the rest.

"I think I need to go freshen up, then find Cain and apologize."

Charlotte reached out her free hand and clasped her friend's wrist. "For what it's worth, I don't want you to leave. I really hope God lets you stay. But if He doesn't..."

Anna Mae swallowed. "If God doesn't let me stay, then

there's a reason for it. Don't forget that Cain's a good Ranger. The best, really. Maybe this is bigger than just me, or me and him. Because if Cain doesn't go back to the Rangers, what will happen to the next criminal like Velez who needs to be brought to justice?"

"I'm sorry, Anna Mae."

"Don't be. This isn't your fault, and it's not anything I can't handle." After all, she'd been ready to leave Twin Rivers for Houston a week and a half ago. If she could do that, then she could go to Austin. She'd do that long before she'd get an annulment. The very idea of it hurt.

She shook off Charlotte's hand, then pushed herself to her feet. "I need to go find him."

A door banged open somewhere in the house. "Anna Mae?"

The sound of Cain's boots echoed down the corridor.

"In here." She started toward the door that led to the courtyard, never mind the filthy water soaking her knees and the hem of her skirt.

Cain appeared in the entrance to the restaurant before she could reach it, his back straight and shoulders taut. Yet even in a snit, he looked so handsome she could barely resist throwing her arms around him.

"Cain, I'm so—"

"There's been a change of plans. Pack a bag and get your buffalo rifle. You're coming to Mexico."

She stiffened. "What? You want me to leave? Today? But I'm opening a restaurant in..." She winced before the rest of the words left her mouth. What was wrong with her? She had no desire to fight with this man, not when she loved him so fiercely.

Fortunately, Cain didn't snap back at her. In fact, his jaw didn't even turn hard. Instead, he reached out, resting two large, warm hands on her shoulders. "Can you postpone the restaurant for a few more days? I wouldn't ask if I had any other choice."

"What's happened?" She took a step closer to him.

"There's been an escalation with Velez, and the safest way to bring him down will be a long-range shot—over a thousand yards. You're the only one I can trust to make it." He swallowed, his eyes searching her face. "I'm not going to lie. I don't like the thought of you going back into Mexico. I'd still be tempted to leave you here if I had any other choice, or if your brother wasn't going to help keep you safe, and Sam and Harrison and Wes."

"I don't need any of the others there to make me feel safe." She laid a hand on his chest, where the steady thump-thump of his heart beat beneath her palm. "Just you."

His throat worked, and he tucked a strand of hair behind her ear. "I fear you trust me a bit too much."

"I don't. You're simply that good of a lawman." She suddenly found herself in his arms, surrounded by his warmth and strength.

"I'm so sorry about last night." The words tumbled out of her in a rush. "I shouldn't have said what I did, been so hard on you. You had no way of knowing Velez had people on his payroll in Austin, and that was why you were forced to leave the Rangers. But when you talked about wanting to go back, I just—"

"I'm sorry too." He smoothed the hair back from her face, tilting her head up until their eyes met. Then he dropped a kiss atop her forehead. "I can't talk about all of this now. There's too much to be done before we leave, but I promise you, we'll talk on the trail. And we'll work through this—together."

She opened her mouth to tell him that she loved him and swear she would never want an annulment, but he'd already dropped his arms from around her and was striding down the corridor with a determined stride in his steps.

Her shoulders fell, and she drew in a breath. But that was the life of a Ranger, wasn't it? When duty called, there was little time for anything other than a hasty good-bye.

And if God wanted Cain to go back to the Rangers, it was something she'd have to get used to.

34

Cain didn't know what was worse, arguing with Anna Mae or setting such a grueling pace through northern Mexico that they didn't have time to talk things through—at least not in a way that they couldn't be overheard by the dozen and a half men with them.

Ridley had ridden out around noon on Tuesday with instructions to the main road that Velez's scouts were sure to watch and take his sweet old time reaching El Rebote. A posse containing three of his men—Lindley, Lenard, and Sims—along with Daniel, Wes, Sam, and Harrison, plus his father and Jonas and several of Wes's cowhands, had left Twin Rivers after dark that same evening, taking a different route and riding at a much faster pace.

Hopefully they would have enough time to reach El Rebote and set their plan into motion before Ridley approached the town around noon on Thursday.

At this point, they had been traveling for nearly twenty-four hours straight, retracing the remote and untraveled path he and Anna Mae had taken out of Mexico several weeks earlier. But this time, instead of traveling only by night, they'd pushed their horses as hard as they could.

He never thought he'd be thankful for getting trapped in Mexico for nearly a month, but now he knew a back way to sneak in and out of the country. And while it was true they may have been spotted at some point during their ride that day, Cain was betting that Velez had moved all of his men to El Rebote for the rendezvous tomorrow.

By the time he brought his men to the very canyon where he and Anna Mae had camped for most of the time they'd been hiding, the posse had been ready to fall off their horses. The canyon was still a two-hour ride from El Rebote, but it was far enough away that they could sleep without worrying Velez's men would find them. Yet it was also close enough that they could ride to El Rebote and be in position before dawn tomorrow.

"Is this the valley and town for tomorrow?" Jonas came up to where Cain stood near one of the boulders on the canyon floor, pemican and hardtack in his hand.

"Yes." He took the stick he'd been using to draw a map of El Rebote and the surrounding mountains in the dirt and then tapped the mountains south of the town. "There's a back way to approach the village. As long as we can manage to silence Velez's scouts without firing a gun, we should be able to move in undetected. I already know the best place for Anna Mae to take the shot."

"Do you think Velez will have many scouts?"

Cain shrugged. "Hard to say, but I'm not expecting it. There's a small canyon in one of the mountains where I'll have us hide, but it's so far away that I doubt Velez will put much effort into watching it. If he's watching anything, it will be the path Ridley's taking, assuming we'll follow that."

But he was still going to be prepared, just in case they were somehow spotted before Anna Mae could shoot Velez.

His father sauntered over and held out a piece of jerky. "You going to eat?"

Cain looked at the meat, his stomach turning at the thought of yet more hardtack and dried meat for dinner. "Not exactly hungry."

It was all they'd eaten since leaving Twin Rivers—jerky, pemican, and hardtack. But building a fire in the canyon meant someone might spot the smoke, so the bland trail fare would have to suffice until tomorrow.

"I taught you better than that." Frank shoved the food at him. "A man in your position needs to keep his strength up."

Cain held up his hand. "I'll eat after I go over the plans for tomorrow with the men."

His father scowled. "You might claim it's plans for tomorrow, but you're really thinking about that wife of yours again, aren't ya? That's what's souring your stomach on food."

Cain rubbed the back of his neck. His father wasn't wrong. He and Anna Mae had spent too much time in this very spot for the memories not to assail him. She had slept over by the wall, near where Daniel and Sam had laid out their bedrolls for the night. And he'd slept right next to the boulder a few feet away, not too far that he couldn't help her if something happened in the night, but not close enough to touch her.

At the moment, Anna Mae was at the front of the canyon acting as lookout. She'd volunteered for the job, and seeing as how she was both a good shot and more familiar with this stretch of desert than anyone else, he'd let her go. That, and he'd hoped having her out of his sight for a few hours would help him better focus on tomorrow.

He'd been wrong. If he hadn't had enough trouble thinking about her before this, knowing that she was alone and the two of them might finally be able to have a conversation made him unable to concentrate on anything else.

"If I'd known how much of a distraction she was going to

be, I'd have told you not to bring her, her shooting skills be hanged." Frank tore off a piece of jerky and chewed.

"Don't start. She's the best sharpshooter we have, and if I'm going to ask Ridley to ride into a trap set for me, the least I can do is bring her along to try to keep him alive."

Thus far, his father had been relatively silent about Anna Mae being with them. Everyone had been, truth be told. No one seemed to mind her presence, and she'd ridden with Daniel, Sam, Wes, and Harrison the entire time, keeping him free to lead the group.

"You best not let her distract you tomorrow." Frank popped another piece of jerky into his mouth, then spoke around it. "There'll be too many lives at stake."

Cain turned to face his father. "For someone who keeps nattering about how I need to up and move my wife to Austin once this is over, you've sure got a lot of disparaging things to say about her."

"She makes you weak. That's reality. I'm not going to sit here and stay silent when marrying that woman was the worst decision you ever could have made."

Cain's hands clenched into fists, and he jerked his head toward where the canyon bent at a sharp angle and narrowed. "Let's take this over there. Now."

He shoved the stick he'd been holding at Jonas, then stalked toward the rock wall that would shield them from the rest of his men. A quick sweep of the new section of canyon told him it was deserted, just as he'd expected.

Boot steps crunched on the rocky ground behind him, and he swung around to face his father, fists ready, but there was something in his father's eyes. Something that wasn't hard and cold but seemed genuinely concerned.

About him?

Was his father really that convinced Anna Mae would lead to his downfall? It didn't begin to make sense.

"What is it?" He uncurled his fists. "What made you so all-fired certain a lawman should never marry? Something must have happened, given how you carry on about it, and I know it's not that you loved my ma and her death devastated you. So what was it? Your parents? A sibling? Someone you cared about must have died."

Frank's body stiffened. "I don't know what you're talking about."

"Stop lying." Their eyes met and held, and just like before, there was something soft in his father's gaze. Something that wasn't entirely hard and uncaring.

He didn't know anything about his father's family. The man had never volunteered any information, and Cain had never cared enough before to ask.

"Fine. It was my wife, if you need to know so badly." Frank's eyes grew hard. "Not your ma. You're right about me never loving her."

Cain drew in a breath. "You were married? When? How?"

Frank's lips pressed into a flat line. "Doesn't matter. It's over and done. The only important part in all of it is that you listen to me and cut that pretty little lady loose before she winds up dead."

"So that's what this is about? You're worried Anna Mae will be targeted because of me. And here you've spent the past several days saying I'm the one who's going to die because of her."

"Happened to Jonas's fiancée and ma, didn't it? Happened to Martha too."

"Was that your wife's name?' His words came out gentle against the hard canyon walls. "Martha?"

"I was in the Panhandle, back before the War between the States, working as a Marshal back then. The Rangers weren't around." His voice emerged coarse and rough, almost as though he'd taken some of the crushed rock beneath his feet and swallowed it before he started talking. "I had myself a nice little wife by the name of Martha. We'd grown up together back East, you see, but when I took a job as a Marshal and got sent to Texas, she up and went with me. Gave me a couple babes too. Sweetest little things you ever did see."

For a moment Frank's lips almost turned up into a smile, but then it disappeared, replaced with the familiar hardness his father always showed. "Did I mention she was good about being married to a man who was gone half the time? And I..."

Frank shook his head, the muscles in his throat working. "There was a bank robbery, and I was sent to chase down the men. Caught half the band, but two escaped. There was a lot about it in the papers. The robbery, how I hunted the men down. Seemed those reporters had something to say about everything. My name got published somehow. And those other two robbers, once they had my name..." Frank's jaw snapped tight. "Bet you can figure out the rest."

"How did you find out?" Cain rasped. "That is, if you were on their trail, how did you...?"

"I followed their trail straight back to the town where we were living. From there, it wasn't too hard to figure out where they'd been headed. They..." Frank rubbed the back of his neck, then shook his head. "They left Martha and my young'uns there for me to find. And they weren't slow or gentle about my wife's death neither."

Cain's chest felt as though an iron band had been clamped around it. "I'm sorry."

Frank drew in a breath. "I decided two things then and there. First, if it took the rest of my life, I was going to track down those two outlaws and kill them the same way they'd killed Martha. And second, I was never going to get tangled up with a woman again."

"How long did it take you to find them?"

"Three days. It was a mistake for the outlaws to come back

to the town where I'd been living. I'd probably have lost them otherwise, but their trail away from my house was easy to follow."

"And when you found them?" He wasn't sure what possessed him to ask the questions, but he couldn't quite stop himself from wanting to know every last detail of the event that had shaped so much of his father's life.

"I disemboweled them and left them to rot in the sun." There was a hard edge to his father's voice. "Some people don't deserve a burial."

Cain drew in a breath. It was Frank's own form of justice, he supposed, even if it wasn't exactly legal. And it explained so very much.

About why his father always left.

About how he'd grown up.

About why he'd never been good enough for the man who sired him.

He stood there for a moment, allowing his father's words to sink in while voices from farther down the canyon trickled to him. Above, a hawk soared through the darkening sky and a gust of desert wind kicked up plumes of dust.

"What happened with your wife—Martha—is why you never let yourself love Ma?" Now it was his turn to speak in a voice that sounded like crushed gravel. "Because she loved you. You know that, right?"

Frank didn't look the least bit repentant. If anything, his eyes only grew harder, his shoulders stiffer. "Love is nothing but a curse for a lawman. It's a weakness that can be exploited at the worst possible time."

"So I'm a weakness? Is that how you see me?"

His father's eyes flicked down him, then came back to meet his gaze, his eyes flat and bored. "When you were younger, yes, that's exactly what you were. Why do you think I left you alone and refused to let you use my last name until you were old enough to ride with me?"

Something hot pricked at the backs of his eyes, but he clenched his jaw and blinked it away. "I don't know."

And he didn't. All he knew was that he had wanted a father, like Wes and Daniel. But his father had thought his son was a curse, and his mother had thought he was little more than a means to get his father to come back and visit.

Whoso findeth a wife findeth a good thing, and obtaineth favour of the Lord.

Anna Mae's verse about a wife came back to him, followed by the verse she was always quoting about children.

Lo, children are an heritage of the Lord*: and the fruit of the womb is his reward.... Happy is the man that hath his quiver full of them.*

This was what Anna Mae had meant with all her talk of wanting a family. It was why having a family—having people to love and be loved by—was such a powerful thing.

"Reckon you made your choice about me and how much I'd mean to you years ago, the same as you did with Ma." A strange calm came over him, and suddenly he knew what he wanted, knew without a doubt what would happen with him and Anna Mae and their fight, knew whether he wanted to be a Ranger. "But I want you to understand this. I'm not going to make the same choice as you. Not about women, not about children, not about any of it.

"I'm not sure I even want to go to Austin with you, but if I do, it will be with Anna Mae by my side, and we will have a family together. I don't care if it makes me weak in your eyes, and I don't care if that's a vulnerability for criminals to exploit. I would rather have Anna Mae in my life for however long God gives her to me and end up losing her than not have her in my life at all."

He blinked away the hot sensation behind his eyes again

and raised his chin, meeting his father's eyes directly. "I suppose you think you're strong, not letting yourself love anyone or grow close to them, but from where I'm standing, my friends are the strong ones. Sam, with a wife who loves him and the eight children he adopted; Daniel, with Charlotte by his side supporting his work as a sheriff. Even Wes and Harrison. They're all better men than you, because they would never, ever turn their backs on their families."

He heaved in a breath, then rubbed a hand over his bald head. The rough prickle of stubby hair only reminded him of the ridiculous pact they'd all made, and how he'd lost, and how his friends had come to remind him of it seventeen years after the fact. And even though he found himself wincing whenever he looked in a mirror and saw his shaved head, he didn't really miss his hair, because his bald head meant his friends cared enough about him to hold him to a ridiculous promise.

While his own father couldn't be bothered to remember a single thing about his childhood.

"Ma's dead because of you. Have you ever thought of that?" The words dropped from his mouth like boulders, heavy and hard. "Had you married her and done right by her, she never would have ended up with syphilis. I wouldn't have had to watch her slowly die while we had no money because she couldn't work. But you were too hard to see any of that, weren't you? Just like you were too hard to see there was a little boy who needed you.

"So, no, I'm not going to make the same choice as you, because while you might not have a wife someone can use against you, you don't have any joy either. You're a hard, lonely man, and you can't be a Ranger forever."

There was nothing about his father's life that he wanted to emulate. "I want the love of a good woman. I want the light she brings into my life and the family we'll have together one day—if I live. So no more about how Anna Mae makes me weak, or how I need an annulment, or how I have to go to Austin with you. Understand?"

His father's jaw clamped shut, but he gave a firm nod. Then he turned without a word.

Cain watched his father walk back around the bend toward where they'd made camp, his chest smarting as though a bandage had been ripped off a festering wound, tearing open the pain, and giving him no choice but to bleed.

The trouble was, he didn't have time to bleed. He needed to follow his father back to camp and go over his plan for tomorrow with the men before it grew too dark to see the map he'd drawn in the dirt.

Instead, he started toward the entrance of the canyon. Anna Mae was down there somewhere keeping watch.

He didn't know what tomorrow would hold for either of them, but he knew that he wasn't going to let the sun set before he apologized the way he'd wanted to for the past two days.

It didn't take him long to wind his way through the familiar stretch of canyon floor. He'd traveled it too many times to count when they'd camped here before. When he neared the opening, he slowed his gait, then peeked into the valley with the winding stream, making sure no one was about.

"Anna Mae," he called softly.

"Up here," she answered from somewhere above him.

He looked up and spotted her on a small ledge about twenty feet above him, crouched behind a pile of rocks.

"What are you doing clear up there?"

She shrugged. "Seemed like the best place to keep an eye on things."

"Or the most likely place to fall from. Come down here."

She hefted her rifle across her shoulders and climbed down, her feet and hands moving quickly despite the heavy gun on her back. "Gotta say, I'm glad to see you. I volunteered to keep watch because I thought it would help give the rest of you time to plan for tomorrow. But this is the most boring thing I've ever done. Not sure it's doing a lick of good either. Nothing's happened."

A smile curved his lips. "It's helping, I promise. Can't risk getting ambushed inside the canyon."

She scowled. "If you say so."

She looked up at him then, their eyes meeting while silence stretched between them, and not the comfortable type where they sat and enjoyed the sunset together.

He drew in a breath. "I don't think I want to go to—"

She spoke at the same time. "Do you want an annulment? I have to know."

He reached for her, drawing her close and setting his head atop her silky hair. "No. An annulment is the last thing I want. I'm sorry for ever suggesting it."

She sniffled into his chest. "Good. Because I'll go to Austin with you. I swear I will. I never should have said that I wouldn't. I should have been supportive and—"

"Do you mean it?" He tipped her head back, staring down into her deep brown eyes. "About going to Austin? Because I'm not sure I want to go anymore. And you were right about when I proposed. I never promised you I wouldn't go back to the Rangers, but we sat under the stars and talked about how our future would look in Twin Rivers. I know everything changed with Velez after that, but the last thing I ever wanted was an annulment. I promise. But you were crying and upset with me. And sometimes I feel so lost when it comes to being a good husband—the kind of man you need. But I'm willing to learn, if you'll be patient with me."

"And apparently I don't know how to be a good wife." She kept her arms wrapped around him, strong and tight. "I was talking to Charlotte before we left, and I realized that I need to be willing to make sacrifices for you, even when they demand a lot of me."

A tear streaked down her cheek, and he reached out to brush it away with his thumb.

"God brought us together," she whispered against his chest. "For better or for worse, for richer or for poorer, in sickness and in health. I can't claim to understand all of it, but I do know that the Bible says, *Perfect love casteth out fear*. But rather than supporting you and loving you when your father asked you to go to Austin, I dug my heels in and insisted on having my own way. It was kind of like Jonah, when God told him to go to Nineveh. I ran the other way instead of saying I'd go with you and support you."

"It's completely reasonable for you to want to stay in the town where we grew up. If we go to Austin, you'll be giving up your dream of living in Twin Rivers and opening a restaurant."

"I want to be with you more, so if your job takes you away from there, I'll follow. You're worth the sacrifice."

He crushed her against him, her words filling up the empty spaces in his life, the places that had been dark for so long, they didn't know what light looked like. The places that had been ruined and damaged since the first time his father came to visit, then walked away from his mother and him. "I don't deserve you, Anna Mae."

"I know." She grinned up at him. "But I don't deserve you either. Yet God gave you to me anyway, so let's make the most of it."

She raised up on her tiptoes and brushed her lips against his, then tried to pull away. But he hauled her back and gave her the kind of kiss that showed her just how sorry he was for their fight.

35

Her husband was going to get himself killed.
Anna Mae steadied her Sharps Big Fifty on the boulder and squinted through the sights. The sun glared down at her from where she crouched near the top of the mountain, and sweat beaded on the back of her neck. It was still twenty minutes or so from when Ridley was due to arrive in El Rebote, but she had a clear shot at a distance of only about eleven hundred yards.

It was obvious by watching the people in the valley below just who Velez and Eduardo were and where they planned to meet Ridley. She couldn't guarantee the bullets would stay on target at such a distance, but Sharps was known for making accurate rifles.

Cain's instructions to her had been clear. Shoot Javier first and Eduardo—if he appeared—second.

But Eduardo was definitely down there with his father, and if she missed one of the shots, she should still have time to get off a third shot—and all before the sound of the first gunshot reached the valley below.

So, no, she wasn't all that worried about the shots.

She was worried about her husband. He, his father, and two of his's men had all snuck into town before dawn. Cain knew the cantina owner, someone named Cristobal. The owner had claimed he would help them, and now they were hiding somewhere in town, perhaps right under the noses of Velez's men.

Oh, why did Cain always have to go and put himself right in the thick of danger?

At the sound of scattering rocks and crunching boots, she looked over to find Jonas Redding sneaking over to her, making sure to stay out of sight in case one of Velez's men might be watching the mountain from the valley below.

"You're sure you have the gun sighted in?"

She rolled her eyes. "The shots won't be a problem."

If anything, the hardest part was being up here all alone, knowing that her husband was hiding somewhere in a town crawling with people who wanted him dead, and her brother and friends' husbands and the rest of the posse were hiding in various places around the mountain, waiting for the assault to begin.

An assault she wouldn't be a part of, even though everyone else she cared about would be risking their lives in under half an hour.

As soon as she killed Velez, the men would spring into action. And if some of Velez's men and the townsfolk sided with Cain in the fight, then they'd probably be able to capture the majority of the desperadoes, putting an end to the iron fist the criminal was using to control northern Mexico.

But if Velez's men didn't turn on him, if the townsfolk didn't side with Cain—

"Everyone's in place. Now all we need to do is wait." Jonas leaned close, peering over the boulder along the barrel of her rifle. "You're sure this is sighted in?"

"I've double-and triple-checked it. There's nothing for me to do now but wait." Which was a lot harder than firing the blasted gun. Why were they waiting for Ridley to show up anyway? It was clear who Velez was down in the valley, and she could have killed him a half dozen times by now.

Jonas checked his pocket watch. "Ridley should be arriving in about twenty minutes."

"I know."

"You'll only be able to get off a few shots before chaos is likely to break out. Once our men are down there, don't take a shot at anyone unless you know it won't hit one of our men."

"I know. Cain went over everything last night."

Jonas looked at her, their eyes meeting for a fraction of a second before he looked back at the gun and swallowed. "Do you really think you can do this?"

"It won't be the most challenging shot I've ever taken."

"Yes, it will. Those are living people down there, and that's always different than shooting a target."

She drew in a breath, then ran her eyes over the man Cain had chosen to command the men hiding on the mountain while he was in El Rebote.

Jonas Redding didn't look like someone spoiling for a gunfight. There was something about the droop in his shoulders, about the pain that seemed to emanate from the depths of his green eyes, even though he sounded every bit like a lawman as he gave her commands.

All in all, he shouldn't be a hard man to look at. He really was quite handsome, with his broad shoulders and red hair and chiseled face.

And yet she found it hard to hold his gaze.

Maybe it was the sadness that draped him like a cloak, or the way he'd only said a few words to anyone during their trip from Twin Rivers to El Rebote. Or how his short red beard was a bit unkempt, as though he didn't quite care enough about his appearance to keep it trimmed.

Anna Mae drew in a breath. "I know shooting people is

different than shooting targets, but this is the man who wants my husband dead. The man responsible for the deaths of your mother and fiancée, right?"

Jonas swallowed. "It is, yes."

She looked back out over the valley, toward the shadowed figure standing in the center of the town, commanding everyone around him. "Then I'm not going to feel bad about killing him."

∽

TEN MINUTES LEFT. Maybe less. Cain kept his body low, crouched beside the swinging doors to Cristobal's cantina with his pistol drawn. Lieutenant Sims was crouched behind him, holding a rifle that would be used once he, his father, and Lenard rushed out into the street and started shooting.

Cain nodded at his father, who hid on the other side of the door with Lenard. All they could do at the moment was wait.

And hope Anna Mae had a clear shot, that she got her target.

Outside, Velez's men had taken over the town. There wasn't a single villager who had stepped onto the street for the past hour. Everywhere was shut up tight except for the two-story hostel that Velez's men had raided at some point the previous night.

Altogether, it didn't seem like Velez had a terrible number of men. But they still outnumbered the eighteen he'd brought with him into Mexico.

Dear God, please help justice to be served. If You need to take my life in the process, I understand. But please help Anna Mae's bullet to hit its mark. Please allow us to end the pain and suffering Velez had caused the people living along the border. Please help—

The clomping of horse hooves sounded on the dusty road, and his eyes sprang open. It was almost time. Would the plan work? Would Velez look at Ridley's long blonde hair and assume the other man was him?

Was Anna Mae ready to take her shot?

He'd instructed Jonas to stay with her until the first several shots were fired, but the rest of his men were under command to flood the town immediately, using the element of surprise to capture and neutralize as many of Velez's men as possible.

His father nodded to him from the opposite side of the doorway as the clomping grew louder. Cain raised himself to a standing position and flattened his back against the wall, then peered out onto the porch.

Cristobal had moved a couple barrels out there earlier, which would give both him and his father something to hide behind as they fired at the men gathered in the street.

Cain pushed onto his toes to see above the door, then craned his neck until he could see Velez standing in the middle of the main road with another man right beside him. Eduardo, perhaps?

Hopefully it was, and hopefully Anna Mae could get off two shots before anyone realized what was happening.

Clomp. Clomp. Clomp.

The air grew still around him as Ridley came into view, his long hair a blazing symbol beneath the hot summer sun.

Cain pinned his eyes on Velez, then waited. If Anna Mae's shot hit the mark, he would fall several seconds before the sound of her rifle made it into the valley.

Cain intended to use that minute to his—

Velez crumpled, a patch of red spreading onto his chest.

Cain darted through the swinging double doors, firing both pistols at the men who had been lining the road.

He dove behind a barrel for cover, and from the corner of his eye, he saw Ridley jump from his horse and dart toward the closest building.

The hostel. *Not that one!* He wanted to cry as one of Velez's men emerged from the door with a gun.

But his father was already sprinting through the cantina doors. He spotted the man with a gun leveled at Ridley and fired at the same moment a loud blast ricocheted through the town.

The sound of Anna Mae's gunshot that had killed Velez was finally reaching the valley.

The man in the doorway crumpled from his father's shot, followed immediately by the man who had been standing by Velez in the middle of the town.

Dear God, please let that be Eduardo.

Cain fired more shots at the men who had been lining the streets waiting for whatever spectacle Velez had meant to make of Ridley.

They reached for their guns at different intervals and scrambled for cover.

More shots sounded from the opposite side of town, likely Daniel and Sam approaching from where they'd been hiding.

Cain fired his gun again while Sims unloaded his rifle from the doorway. Then the booming sound of Anna Mae's second gunshot ricocheted down the mountain.

Everything was going as planned.

Except when one of Velez's men turned and darted for cover. It was almost as though the man paused for a moment and looked straight at him. Cain stared into a pair of hard brown eyes. Eyes he had seen before—at *La Colina*.

And they were attached to a face with cruel, thin lips, and portly body below.

Velez. He wasn't dead.

But no. That was impossible. He'd seen the man standing in the center of the town fall to the ground.

Could that man have been someone else? Not Velez?

Cain cocked his pistol, slid his finger over the trigger, and squeezed.

The man grinned at him, then lunged behind a building just as Cain's bullet splintered the wooden beam holding up the porch roof.

His heart hammered against his chest as he looked around the town. Several bodies lay on the street, each and every one of them Velez's men. Even Ridley had successfully taken cover.

But he couldn't stop the growing sensation in his gut that something was very, very wrong.

∽

ANNA MAE LINED up the sights on her rifle and stared down the barrel, but Jonas was right. It was impossible to tell who was who as men darted back and forth across the street, shooting in what appeared to be every direction. And she wasn't about to blindly take a shot and hope it hit one of Velez's men rather than Cain or Daniel.

If she moved farther down the mountain, she might be able to pick out Velez's men and get off a few shots, but Cain had given her specific instructions not to move after she'd made her shots, and he had enough to worry about without her up and getting into trouble.

So she sat there and watched. It was the hardest thing she'd ever done in her life. Each time a body sprawled on the street below, she had no way of knowing whether it was Sam or Harrison, Daniel or Wes—or Cain.

Nor did she have any way of telling if the townsfolk and some of Velez's men had turned on him and decided to fight with Cain, or if Cain was still vastly outnumbered.

All she could do was sit there and pray.

So she did. Over and over until her brain felt as though it

might overheat from being used too much. And still, the fight raged below.

She narrowed her eyes, straining to see if she could glean any clues whatsoever about who was—

"Don't move," a low voice said from behind her.

She stilled, her hand on the butt of her rifle, but nowhere near the trigger.

Not that she'd be able to swing a twelve-pound, three-foot-long gun around and get a shot off before whoever was behind her shot her dead.

Almost as though the man behind her could sense her thoughts, the metallic clicking of a gun being cocked filled the air. "Put your hands up nice and easy and turn around to face me."

She swallowed, her hand lingering on the stock of her Sharps, but she had little choice but to obey.

She put her hands up and turned.

She didn't know what she expected to find, but it certainly wasn't the man with the slicked-back hair and gold-embroidered vest that was pointing a pistol at her. He looked far too fancy to belong in the middle of a gunfight.

Except there was something familiar about his eyes, about the lines and angles of his face.

She narrowed her gaze. "Do I know you?"

"No." He grinned at her, but there was nothing kind about the expression. "You may have known my brother Raul, though. He's dead because of your husband, and now you're going to pay."

"You're Eduardo." At least that explained why he was dressed so fancy. "But how are you alive?" She glanced at the Sharps lying abandoned on the dusty boulder. "I killed you fifteen minutes ago."

"No. You killed Mateo. He wasn't loyal to my father."

"But..." She licked her lips. "He was standing in the middle of the town, right next to your father, whom I..." She clamped her mouth shut before she admitted to killing Eduardo's father while he had a shiny pistol pointed at her head.

"That's where you're wrong." The man gave her another of his evil grins. "You would have killed us, had we not gotten that lovely little note from one of your husband's men explaining his plans."

The breath whooshed out of her in a sudden rush. A note? From one of Cain's men? "Someone is reporting to your father?"

The man's eyes narrowed. "Do you know how much my family has lost because of your husband? We couldn't risk not knowing what he was doing after he raided *La Colina*."

"Maybe try following the law, and you won't need to worry about lawmen raiding your house." She winced as soon as the words were out. That wasn't the type of thing a hostage should say either.

Something hard flashed in Eduardo's eyes. "We'll conduct our business however we wish. Now down the mountain with you. It's time to pay your husband a visit."

∼

THERE WERE ONLY a few shooters left in the hostel, but getting into the building to deal with them wasn't going to be easy.

From his position crouched beside the blacksmith shop that sat next to the hostel, Cain glanced across the street at where Daniel and Harrison were hiding between two other buildings. Daniel held up two fingers, then pointed at the top floor of the two-story building in the center of the town, where a couple of the shooters had dug themselves in and were firing any time one of his men crossed the street.

Harrison held his hands up and shrugged, as though asking what they should do.

Storming the building was about the only thing he could think of, but there was no chance any of them would get through the front doorway alive, not with how the shooters had positioned themselves. Maybe if there was a window that faced the smithy shop, he could climb through without the shooters noticing. He'd be outnumbered, but at least he'd have surprise on his side.

A bevy of shots sounded from farther up the street, where his father and Jonas were. Cain craned his head around the side of the building but couldn't see where the shots were coming from or if anyone had been hit.

Hopefully it had been Velez. Cain was certain he had seen the man earlier, but then Velez had disappeared, and none of the bodies piling up in the street looked anything like Velez.

Which made him worry that the man had somehow escaped El Rebote, and he would have to wage yet another battle to bring the criminal to justice.

But he couldn't very well go tracking Velez through the desert without first stopping the gunshots coming from the front of the hostel.

He opened the wood shutter on one of the windows to the smithy building and studied the inside of the building. There were a series of windows placed at varying intervals around the building, likely to let in air and thin out all the smoke. But his gaze latched onto the single window facing the hostel. Like the window where he stood, it was shuttered, but as long as it opened near one of the hostel windows, he should be able to get inside the building undetected.

He looked back across the street and held up a finger to Daniel and Harrison, telling them to wait while he climbed inside the building and scouted the far window.

"Cain Whitelaw!" A dark voice echoed through the street. "Come out now or your wife dies."

He stilled, every muscle in his body going taut.

Did someone have Anna Mae? No. It was impossible. His men were the only ones who knew that Anna Mae was with them. It wasn't something Velez's men would guess was a possibility, let alone find where she was hiding near the top of the mountain that sat south of town.

But on the other side of the street, Daniel's face had gone stark white.

Cain left the window and crept toward the side of the building that bordered the street, his heart pounding against his chest.

Dear God, please don't let them have Anna Mae.

But the second he peeked around the building, he realized just how futile his prayer was.

Because there, in the center of the road, right in front of the hostel, a fancily dressed man stood with a gun to Anna Mae's head.

A fresh layer of sweat beaded along the back of his neck, and his stomach cramped. He quickly surveyed the situation. The man holding Anna Mae hostage was too far away for him to risk shooting with his pistol. If he had a rifle, he might be able to make the shot, but the bullet from his pistol was sure to stray from its mark at such a distance, and he couldn't risk it hitting Anna Mae.

And yet, the second he stepped into the street and approached the man holding Anna Mae, he was sure to be shot.

Even if he could somehow get close enough to the desperado to accurately fire his pistol, the two men on the top floor of the hostel would shoot both him and Anna Mae dead before they could so much as take a breath.

"Cain Whitelaw, come out now!" The man's voice rang through the town, strong and confident. "I'm going to count to ten, and if you're not standing in the street with your hands up, I'll put a bullet in your pretty wife's head."

Cain glanced across the road at Daniel, but his friend was frozen, his eyes riveted to Anna Mae as she stood there with the barrel of a pistol pressed against her tumbling hair.

The man holding Anna Mae started counting. *Uno, dos, tres...*

Cain's throat tightened. There was no time left to form another plan or come up with a different method of attack. He'd done everything he possibly could to bring down Velez.

And he still might succeed. After all, it seemed as though far more of Velez's men had died than his own.

But he wasn't going to be alive to see what happened.

The only thing he could do at the moment was step out onto the street and die.

He only hoped Anna Mae didn't lose her life too.

∽

Jonas had to find a way into that hostel.

Each time someone tried to cross the road, they were being shot at, and it was getting old. That was why he'd left his spot inside the stable and had been slowly weaving his way along the backs of the buildings toward where the two-story building sat in the center of town.

He peeked over the top of the barrel he hid behind and watched the back door of the hostel. He needed to cover a distance of only about twenty feet, but he'd be exposed the entire time.

Could he do it?

He squeezed his eyes shut and sucked a burning breath into his lungs. If only he could be somewhere far away. Already in Alaska, perhaps, where no one would know him or expect him to pick up a gun, and no one would put him in charge of other men's lives.

He hadn't realized just how bad holding a gun would be. He

hadn't had a reason to unholster it once since he'd left Austin. But now the weight of it in his hand made him want to retch.

Just this one last thing. You owe it to Harriet. You owe it to Ma.

And if he wanted to make it to Alaska, he had to survive this gunfight.

He forced his gaze back to the hostel, the hand holding his pistol shaking despite how he tried to steady it. Once Velez answered for his crimes, he'd be done, never picking up a gun again for the rest of his life.

He flattened his lips into a firm line, then sprang out from behind the barrel and darted toward the door, his heart hammering in his ears until it drowned out the sound of gunshots farther up the road.

Dear God, please don't let it be locked.

A fresh round of sweat slicked his hands as he reached for the knob. It turned easily, and he jumped through the opening, then reached for his second sidearm. He held both pistols at the ready, eyes scanning the room for any of Velez's men.

It was empty.

A shot sounded from somewhere on the floor above.

Jonas crept through the kitchen that seemed to have been abandoned, then did a quick sweep of the dining room filled with tables where the hostel residents ate.

Again, nothing.

So he turned toward the stairs that led to the second floor—which wasn't going to be empty.

A shout sounded from the street. "Cain Whitelaw, come out now or your wife dies."

Jonas turned cold, his guns growing even heavier in his hands.

Had someone found Anna Mae?

It was impossible. He'd stayed with her until she shot both Javier and Eduardo; then he scrambled down the mountain as quickly as he could to find Cain's forces beating back Velez's men. A couple of Velez's men had surrendered when he'd stormed into the general store, and two more had sworn to fight with Cain, claiming they only fought with Velez because they were being forced to.

All in all, things were going well for them and poorly for Velez.

Except for the two men firing shots from the top of the hostel.

"Cain Whitelaw, come out now!" The voice shouted once more from the street. "I'm going to count to ten, and if you're not standing in the street with your hands up, I'll put a bullet in your pretty wife's head."

Jonas's throat turned dry. It definitely sounded like someone had found Anna Mae.

Dear God, please, not another innocent woman. Enough of those have already died.

But what if the only way to stop Anna Mae from dying was to take out the shooters above him, no matter how much he despised the guns he held in his hands?

He quietly snuck up the stairs, wincing when his boot caused a wooden step to creak. Would the men be shooting from the same room, or different ones?

He reached the top of the stairs to find the first door to his right was open. He peeked around the side. And there he was, a man standing at the window with a rifle pointed down the road.

At Cain? At Anna Mae?

It was impossible to tell from where he stood, and he didn't have the time to find out.

He fired his gun, watched the man crumple, and then darted toward the next room that faced the street.

The door flung open a second before he reached it, and a man stood with a rifle pointed straight at his chest.

Jonas didn't think, didn't breathe, just fired his second

pistol. It was instinct more than anything, years of working as a Marshal coming to him in that single instant.

A splotch of red appeared on the man's chest, and he toppled backward, his finger precariously close to the trigger.

Jonas jumped to the other side of the hall and curled into a ball on the floor.

A gunshot ricocheted through the building, the bullet embedding itself in one of the wooden beams holding up the ceiling above him. A quick glance at the man told him he was dead, and the firing of the gun had been nothing more than a reaction to being shot.

Jonas twisted the rifle from the man's body and dashed into the room.

The scene playing out on the street below chilled him. Cain was standing in the road a building down, both arms raised, while a polished-looking man stood in the street almost directly below the window, holding a gun pressed to Anna Mae's head.

Jonas cocked the rifle, then looked down the sight and lined it up with the man's head. But firing a rifle he'd never shot before at such a precise target made the sickening sensation in his stomach only grow. Would the bullet list to the right or left? Was the gun accurate?

If not, he could end up shooting Anna Mae.

Dear God, I can't. His hands shook as he tried to steady the gun, and a bead of sweat trickled down the side of his face. *I'll never be able to forgive myself if I miss, and I just can't risk it.*

∽

CAIN DREW IN A BREATH, his heart pounding in his ears as he met Anna Mae's gaze and waited for the bullet to strike him.

He tried to convey so many things with his eyes as he stared at her. How much he loved her. How much he needed Velez to be brought to justice. How much he just wanted a life with her in the desert, some fancy job with the Rangers be hanged.

And how sorry he was that he would never be able to experience any of it with her.

He wanted to say he prayed in those last minutes, standing in the street and waiting for the shot that was sure to end his life. And in a way, he did. But his thoughts were something of a tangled mess, asking for justice for Velez, asking for God to spare Anna Mae's life, asking for her to find a man she could grow old with, who would love her better than he ever had.

He only hoped God could make sense of the chaotic words he sent toward heaven.

Then a gunshot sounded, and he froze, waiting for the blunt impact of the bullet against his chest.

But it never came. The desperado holding Anna Mae crumpled instead, not even uttering so much as a cry as he toppled backward, a gaping wound in his head.

Cain sprang forward at the same moment Anna Mae realized what had happened and tried to free herself from the man's grip. She thrust his arm away from her and scrambled forward as his body hit the dusty earth.

A moment later, Cain barreled into her, shielding her from the hostel across the street with his own body.

"No!" A cry rang out from the stable beside the hostel. Then a man stumbled into the street. Cain cocked his pistol and pointed it at the figure running out from a nearby building.

"Don't move or I'll shoot," Cain shouted.

But the man kept moving anyway. Cain cocked his gun, ready to fire, then stilled.

"Velez?"

Sure enough, it was the portly man with the pudgy face, the hard eyes, and the commanding voice. The portly frame and pudgy face, the hard eyes and commanding voice. But there was nothing commanding about the sound of Velez's voice now as he kneeled beside the man lying in the dusty street. Nothing hard about his eyes as he stared down at the body in front of him.

"My son." Velez twisted his hands together, his eyes panicked as they looked up and found Cain's. "What were you thinking? This was never supposed to happen to Eduardo. You have ruined everything. Again!"

Cain took a step closer, his pistol still trained on the criminal. "I ruined nothing. You did this. With your greed. Your selfishness. Your desire to control everything around you."

"You destroyed my house! My sons were born there. I brought my wife there after we wed. I was building a legacy for them, and you came in and destroyed it, then had Raul killed!"

"Raul destroyed your house when he tried to escape one of my men. Had he peacefully come back to Texas for trial, *La Colina* would still be standing."

"No. It is your fault. You were supposed to pay! Oh, how did this happen?" Velez pressed his hands to the sides of his head and looked around, as though seeing the fallen men for the first time. And maybe he was. Maybe he was so blinded by his own greed that he didn't know how to stop and consider the pain he caused others. "I had more men than you. I had a plan. How?"

"Sometimes God's justice is bigger than our plans," Cain drawled.

"I even had an informant," the man wailed. "One of your Rangers!"

One of his men had been snitching to Velez? Cain blinked, then hardened his jaw. "Raise your hands. You're under arrest."

"I will not. I'm not going to Texas with you. Not ever!" He reached for the gun that had fallen beside Eduardo.

The moment Velez's hand clasped around the stock, Cain fired.

Velez jerked backward, blood spreading across his chest.

Behind him, Anna Mae gasped.

She might be the daughter of a sheriff, but he doubted she'd ever seen a person shot at such close range before. He turned to go to her, but Daniel was already at her side, tugging her against his chest with Harrison beside him.

In fact, as Cain looked around, people were filtering into the street, both villagers and his men. Wes and Sam appeared with a couple of Wes's cowhands from a shop up the road. And a family came out of the house on the opposite side of the street. Then Cristobal and his wife stepped through the swinging doors of the cantina, and Lenard and Bryant Lindley emerged from another building with two handcuffed men who wore scowls on their faces.

The entire town seemed to come to life in half a minute, everyone who had been hiding now feeling safe enough to emerge.

Cain glanced around the dusty buildings again, then looked up at the second-story window of the hostel to find Jonas looking down at him, his face grim.

He gave the man a nod. He didn't know how the Marshal had managed to sneak into the hostel, but there was no question that Jonas Redding was the sole reason he was still alive.

"Cain." His father's voice cut through the commotion, and Cain looked up to find his father striding toward him, a serious look on his face. "Got something you need to see."

Cain stepped over Velez's body and started after his father, but Anna Mae appeared at his side, throwing her arms around him.

"I'm so glad you're safe. When you came out from around the side of that building, I thought I'd have to watch you die."

He gathered her against him and burrowed his face in her hair. Was there a way to tell her he'd thought the same thing, or that he'd been worried she would live only a handful of seconds after him?

"Guess God had other plans," he finally managed around the lump in his throat.

"I'm glad," she whispered.

"Cain," his father shouted. "It ain't time to lollygag. You need to see this."

Cain slid his hand into Anna Mae's and started forward. The crowd seemed to open up around him, creating a path for him to follow his father and then pressing in behind him.

Frank climbed up a few sorry-looking steps and stopped on the porch of what looked to be a small store. A body lay there, half hidden by a sack of maize, while another man kneeled beside it.

Cain gripped Anna Mae's hand tighter as he climbed the steps, then gasped. Sims lay there with his eyes shut and a growing pool of blood by his stomach.

"Wake up, Sims," Frank said. "Cain's here."

Cain released Anna Mae's hand, shoved the bag of maize to the side, and knelt on the opposite side of his former lieutenant. "Sims. Are you still alive? Let's get something to stop the blood. There might be a doctor in town."

He turned toward the street, where it seemed every last person in the town of El Rebote had gathered to watch him. "I need a doctor."

One of the men stepped forward. "Our doctor comes from over the pass. Should we send for him?"

"Yes."

"No." Sims croaked, his hand coming up to touch the wound in his side, then wincing as though even a gentle touch caused unbearable pain. "It's too late for a doc."

Cain opened his mouth to argue, but the gray shade of Sims's face and the amount of blood on the porch's floorboards told a different story.

He leaned closer and gripped Sims's other hand. "We'll

staunch the blood, see how long it takes the doc. You never know. I've seen men recover from getting gut shot before."

Only once, and it was very rare. But he wasn't going to give up. *Dear God, You've been so good to me already today, sparing my life, sparing Anna Mae's, but if You could please spare—*

"That's not why I asked for you," Sims rasped. The simple act of speaking seemed to bring him pain.

"What then?" Cain gripped the man's hand harder. "Do you have a letter you want me to deliver or—"

"I want to... apologize."

A hot sensation pricked the backs of his eyes. "There's no need to apologize. You did the best you could today. You were right brave. If not for you, I don't even know—"

"I told Velez you were coming."

Cain stilled. "What?"

"You were the informant?" Anna Mae whispered.

Cain's eyes snapped to hers. "You knew there was an informant?"

"Not until Eduardo found me on the mountain. I asked how he knew where I was. He said one of your men was passing them information, but he never said who."

Cain looked back to his dying lieutenant, the man who had served with him for five years. His throat suddenly felt too tight to speak, but somehow he forced the words out. "Is that true, Sims? Is that what you're trying to tell me?"

The man gave a small nod, then winced. "You know I've always had a bit of a fondness for gambling. Owed men some money around Texas, and one night Velez sent a man to the camp asking for information about where we were headed after Twin Rivers. Velez was already in prison in Mexico, and we were just waiting for his men in Twin Rivers to go to trial. I didn't think it would do any harm, seeing how Velez was locked up and I needed that money."

Sims grimaced again, then sucked in a shallow breath, only

for the air to wheeze right back out of his body. "I thought it would just be that one time, but it wasn't. Every few weeks, when we were in Alpine, Velez would send a man. I didn't want to report anything, but I didn't see much harm in it either. Being in Alpine didn't have anything to do with Velez."

Except it had, but no one had realized at the time that Velez was paying the assistant director in Austin to give the Rangers a trivial assignment to keep them from interfering with the next step of Velez's plan.

"As soon as I learned Velez escaped from prison, I said I was done, that I wouldn't pass on any more information."

"But you clearly told him that Ridley was the one who'd be riding into town today, and that Anna Mae was going to shoot from the mountain."

"He said he'd kill my ma and sister, same as he did to the Marshal's ma and fiancée," Sims gasped, his eyes pressed shut with pain. "I didn't want to, Captain. You have to understand. But I couldn't let what happened..."

"I understand." Cain wrapped his other hand around the hand he was already holding as more blood drained from Sims's body. And this time, when his eyes turned hot, he couldn't quite manage to blink the sensation away. "I wish you would have told him no all those months ago, that very first time you were approached. You know better than to let a criminal start paying you. Once you do that, they'll own you for the rest of your life."

"I know. I'm... I'm sorry. Tell my ma and sister... tell them I love them."

"I will."

But his words were a moment too late, because Sims sucked in one last shallow breath, then his body grew still.

Cain sat there for another minute, holding the hand of the lieutenant who had ultimately failed to fulfill his duties as a lawman.

"I'm sorry, Cain."

Anna Mae's hand landed on his shoulder, slender and warm. Then she wrapped her arms around his head and drew it into her stomach, holding him there.

No words passed between them, but it was almost as though they didn't need to talk, almost as though she understood all she needed to without him speaking.

"Best go on now, boy," his father said. "Looks like you've got some folks waiting to talk to ya. Ridley and I will see to the body."

Cain pulled away from Anna Mae and stood to find the townsfolk still watching him, but one of the men had stepped forward and seemed to be waiting for him to finish.

Cain headed down the steps to meet him.

"*Gracias, Señor Whitelaw. Gracias.*" The man held out an envelope.

Cain took it and muttered, "*De nada.*" Then tore it open only to find an unreasonable amount of pesos inside.

"What is this?" He tried to hand the envelope back, but the man refused to take it.

"This is our mayor." Cristobal stepped forward from the crowd. "We want to pay you for saving our town."

"And pay you to come be our sheriff," the mayor said. "We need someone to protect us and the towns around us so this doesn't happen again."

"You want me to..." He blinked. He couldn't have heard that right, but both men were looking at him expectantly. "...to be your sheriff, meaning you want me to move down here to Mexico?"

"We will pay." The mayor nodded at the envelope. "We are a nice town. You will like it here."

"I... you seem like a very nice town. And I'm sorry your former governor took your men and tried to exploit you. But I need to prevent this type of thing from happening again somewhere else, which means, I should probably go back to..."

He wasn't sure where he wanted to go anymore. Mostly, he just wanted to stay in the desert with Anna Mae. But he couldn't turn his back on the job God had given him or ignore the need for good, honorable lawmen.

"But we want you to prevent it from happening here." The mayor raised his hands to encompass both the crowd standing behind him and the buildings of the town itself. "If you leave, who will maintain order?"

"Cain will." Daniel threaded his way through the group of people and came up to stand beside him. "Because he's going to stay in Twin Rivers and be the sheriff there. So if you need him to come down here and handle a situation, you only need to send a messenger and ask."

Cain looked at Daniel. "I can't be the sheriff. You are."

"Yes, but Twin Rivers is in need of a judge, too, and while I love justice as much as the next man, sheriffing isn't exactly my favorite thing. I'm planning to run for judge in November, and I think you should run for sheriff."

"Wait." Anna Mae came up to Daniel and took his hand. "Are you sure about this?"

Daniel nodded, his eyes serious. "Absolutely. Feels like the best decision I've made in months. And should I resign as sheriff before November. The commissioners will need to find an immediate replacement until the election." Daniel looked back at him, his gaze heavy with meaning. "Because it seems to me like Twin Rivers needs more than just a sheriff. It needs a man who's got a relationship with the Mexican villagers and can maintain law and order on both sides of the border. This stretch of desert, whether it's north or south of the Rio Grande, is desolate and removed from the rest of society. That means we need a sheriff who can hunt down any outlaws who move in and can maintain the peace. For all of us, Mexican and Texan alike. I can't think of any better man for that kind of responsibility than Cain."

"We will still pay you," the mayor said, pushing the envelope closer to Cain's chest. "Help us find a sheriff for El Rebote. Someone you train. And bring your men down and visit every so often to make sure there are no problems. And if someone like Javier Velez ever tries taking our men again, you will lead us and we will follow you. Other towns will do the same. You will keep peace for this part of Mexico. Please."

"I..." He looked from the mayor to Anna Mae to Daniel, then finally to his father, who was still standing on the porch.

He couldn't have asked for a better job, not in all of his dreams. He could stay in Twin Rivers with Anna Mae, but he didn't have to give up being a lawman, and he'd get to protect and defend the people who mattered most to him.

His friends, his family, the townsfolk and villagers who had come to his aid and fought by his side when he needed it most.

"Yes, I accept," he rasped, his throat so rough he could hardly form the words. "I will stay here and run for sheriff in Twin Rivers, and in the meantime, I'll train a man to be sheriff here in El Rebote, and I'll train others to enforce the law in different villages, should they want it."

Anna Mae squealed beside him, and a cheer rose from the villagers. The mayor shook his hand, and then his father came up to him.

"Can't say I'm happy to learn you won't be coming to Austin with me, but..." Frank looked around, then clapped a hand on his son's back. "You did good by the people here today, and that's something to be right proud of, Son."

Son. The word drilled through him, burrowing into a place deep inside, one of the places that had been empty for so long, Cain forgot what it felt like to be full.

Then Anna Mae threw her arms around him, pressed up on

her toes, and kissed his jaw. "We get to stay in Twin Rivers. Did you hear that? We get to stay!"

He chuckled. "That we do, love. That we do."

Then he swooped her into his arms and spun her around, drawing in the familiar scent of her hair and the traces of rosewater that somehow lingered on her skin despite spending two days in the desert.

At the beginning of the summer, he'd ridden away from Twin Rivers, content to never return. But God had other plans. Plans that involved a wife and a house and some terrifying, harrowing days of dealing with a powerful criminal.

Yet through it all, God had been good.

And now he got to go back to Twin Rivers—his home—and have the thing he wanted most...

A family with the woman he loved. It was hard to imagine a better life.

EPILOGUE

Seven Years Later

"Why hasn't someone come out to get me yet?" Wes growled as he paced from one end of the sand pit to the other, his hands shoved into his hair. "Something has to be wrong. Do you think she... Do you think it's...?"

"Fine?" Cain shook his head at his friend. "Yes. I think everything's fine. These things take time."

"It took only five hours when Shannon was born. This has been..." Wes pulled out his pocket watch, and his face turned white. "Five and a quarter hours."

Cain nearly opened his mouth to ask if Wes thought those fifteen extra minutes of Keely being in labor meant the difference between life and death. But this was Wes, so he'd probably say yes.

"Uncle Wes, Uncle Wes!" Hank, Cain's six-year-old son, came running up to Wes with a horseshoe in his hand. "It's your turn to throw the horseshoe."

"Yeah, Pa, it's your turn." Wes's oldest boy, Connor, went

running to his pa and grabbed him by the hand, his small five-year-old body tugging hard on the larger man's fingers.

"My turn," Wes growled, not so much as a smile cracking his face as he looked down at his son. "Right."

"Hank beat me. Now you gotta play him." Connor tugged his father closer to the line that marked the beginning of the horseshoe pit.

"Did you see it, Pa?" Hank pressed up on his tiptoes, his mop of sandy blond hair hanging wildly about his head. "I beat Connor."

Cain smiled down at his oldest son. "I saw. Can tell you've been practicing."

"Do you think I can beat Uncle Wes?"

Cain took one look at his white-faced friend and grinned. "I think you got a really good chance."

As though intent on proving him right, Wes picked up a horseshoe and tossed it a good three feet past the stake.

Cain raised his eyebrow at Hank, then gave the boy a pat on the head. "Go beat him, cowboy."

Cain stood back and watched, a grin on his face as Wes threw every single horseshoe long.

He probably should have a little more sympathy for his friend. After all, Keely was inside the A Bar W giving birth to Wes's third child. But it was better to tease the man than watch his face turn stark with fear as he convinced himself Keely was dying inside the hacienda like Abigail had.

A shout sounded from the closest paddock, and Cain glanced up to see his four-year-old daughter, Mary Kate, sitting proudly atop one of Wes's ponies. Beside her, Harrison helped his own daughter atop a second pony.

As soon as Wes's ranch hand had ridden into town with news of Keely being in labor, the entire lot of them had come out here—Daniel, Harrison, Sam, Cain, and of course their wives and children. Whenever there was a birth, it almost always turned into an unplanned party.

That was why Sam, Harrison, and Daniel were in the paddock with a couple of the ponies, letting the smallest young'uns take turns riding it. Then Sam and Ellie's children—those who were still young enough to be living with Sam and Ellie—were practicing their lassoing skills in another paddock.

All in all, it was a regular celebration—at least for everyone except Wes. He was always irritable at this kind of thing, and it didn't matter whether Keely or someone else was giving birth.

And somehow Cain always seemed to be the one tasked with distracting him.

"I won! I won!" Hank shouted from the horseshoe pit. "Did you see that, Pa? I beat Uncle Wes!"

"That you did. Good work."

"This is ridiculous." Wes stalked away from the pit, the scowl that had been on his face all afternoon only growing deeper. "I never asked to play horseshoes anyway."

"I'm going to go tell Uncle Harrison that I beat Uncle Wes."

"Wait," Wes snapped.

But it was too late. Hank was already taking off pell-mell toward the paddock, with Connor on his heels.

"I let him win. I swear it." Wes dabbed at the sweat along his hairline with his bandana.

"You did no such thing. You were too distracted to bother throwing right."

"Same thing, and none of it means Hank is better at horseshoes than me."

Cain chuckled. "Just tell that to my son."

Wes shook his head, then dragged in a breath and looked toward the house. "It's been another quarter hour, and there's still no news."

"That means things are progressing about as expected. If something worrisome was happening, I'm sure you'd know."

Wes raked a hand through his hair. "I know I shouldn't worry overmuch. I know I need to trust what God has planned for me, but right now, knowing Keely is in there…"

"It's hard. I understand." Truth be told, Cain felt like a bit of a mess every time Anna Mae went into labor too—not that he ever let anyone see it. "But you've already done this twice before with Keely, and you're doing a fine job this time around."

"The baby is three weeks early. It's impossible for me not to worry."

"Hank was four weeks early, and look at how he turned out." Cain jutted his chin toward where Hank and Conner had climbed the paddock fence and were watching their younger siblings take turns on the pony.

When Hank had arrived only eight months after his parents' wedding, it had set a few tongues to wagging in Twin Rivers.

Fortunately, when Doc Mullins saw just how small Hank was and how his lungs seemed to work overly hard to breathe, he had declared the babe had been about four weeks early. That had put most of the rumors to rest.

Little Hank's breathing had gotten better over the next couple weeks, and once his lungs had figured out how to work, he'd grown like a weed and hadn't looked back.

Wes pulled out his pocket watch again. "I'm going inside to check on things."

"You're staying right here. All you'll do inside is drive the womenfolk crazy." Cain rubbed his jaw. "You know, maybe part of the reason you're so antsy is that you're jealous Anna Mae and I will still have more young'uns than you, even after this newest one is born."

Wes rolled his eyes. "I keep telling you, it's not a contest."

"Oh, it's definitely a contest." And he and Anna Mae were winning—at least in terms of biological children. The real question was whether they'd end up with enough young'uns to beat Sam and Ellie, including all of Ellie's siblings. Right now, Sam and Ellie had ten children, eight of Ellie's siblings that they'd adopted, and two of their own.

He and Anna Mae had four children, but Anna Mae was due to have their fifth in another six weeks. So they were halfway to beating Sam and Ellie—as long as Ellie didn't up and have another baby.

Daniel, Harrison, and Wes weren't even close to beating him and Anna Mae, so it was safe to say they were in the lead when it came to children born to a couple.

But pregnancies were always hard on Wes. No one ever announced a baby was on the way without his face growing white and him turning quiet. There was no question Wes did a better job of handling pregnancies now than he had just after he and Keely married, but Cain wasn't sure his friend's fear would ever go away completely, even though Wes tried his hardest to trust God through all of it.

"Wes! Wes!"

Cain looked over to find Anna Mae running toward them, never mind the heavy weight of her round stomach. A huge smile lit her face, telling him the news she brought would be good.

Wes dropped the horseshoe and strode toward her. "How's Keely? Is she all right?"

Anna Mae's grin grew until it engulfed her entire face, then she threw her arms around him. "It was twins. That's why she went into labor early. It was twins!"

Wes took a step back, his mouth falling open, then closing, then opening again. "Twins? And they're both healthy?"

"As healthy as can be. You got two more boys to help around the ranch."

"You're serious?" Cain scowled at his wife. "Twins ain't playing fair. A couple's only supposed to get one young'un per pregnancy."

"Oh, don't be grouchy. I think it's wonderful!" Anna Mae clasped her hands beneath her chin, her smile as bright as the sun above.

Cain surveyed her belly. "Any chance you might be holding twins in there? Then we'd have six and Wes and Keely would only have four."

Wes rolled his eyes. "For the last time, it's not a contest."

Cain smirked. "You only say that because you're losing."

Wes sent him a glare. "I'm going to see my wife and hold my new babies."

Anna Mae started after him, but Cain reached out and caught her by the waist, then pulled her back into his arms. "Is it really twins? Tell me that was just a ruse."

She gave him an exasperated look. "Do you honestly think I'd run all the way out here and tell a man he has the wrong number of children?"

He gave his head a determined nod. "Guess now we'll have to work twice as hard to stay ahead of the others."

"You are ridiculous! Wes is right. This is not a contest, and besides, maybe I don't want a dozen kids."

He dropped a kiss on the side of her neck. "Hush your mouth, woman. We both know you want a dozen young'uns."

She giggled. "All right, maybe I do want a dozen children, but I don't mind having them one at a time."

He slid his hand along his wife's belly, only to feel a kick against her stomach, almost as though the babe inside could hear them and wanted to add its own thoughts. "You're beautiful when you're pregnant, did you know that?"

She turned in his arms, then reached up and framed his face with her hands, smoothing away a strand of hair that had fallen across his cheek. "You tell me that every day, though I can't say I feel beautiful when I'm carrying around a lead ball."

"Well, you are." And he meant it. There was something special about his wife's form as it grew round with child.

He wrapped his arms around her back and held her there with her head tucked under his chin. The sun above blazed hot in the sky, shouts sounded from the horseshoe pit where Hank and Connor had started another game, and cattle ambled through the hills surrounding the ranch.

And to think there'd been a point where he wondered if he could ever be a father, a time when he'd been certain he'd fail simply at being Anna Mae's husband. Now he couldn't imagine living any other life. They could have five children or ten or even fifteen. There was enough space in their house to fit everyone, and enough love between them to fill the house three times over.

~.~.~.~.~

A NOTE from Naomi

Wow! Just wow! Aren't you glad Cain finally found happiness with Anna Mae? And contentment in having a pile of little ones to keep both of them busy?

I have to admit, as I was writing Cain's story, there were times I wondered just how things were going to work out for him. He had such heavy burdens to overcome—and for good reasons. But just as God took Joseph from the Bible and made him into something great despite growing up in a terrible family, I knew God could do the same for Cain. That he eventually found happiness with Anna Mae and a growing family made his story that much sweeter.

One of my favorite parts of this novel is when Cain finally confronts his father and learns why Frank is so hard, and why Cain grew up in such a disaster of a family. I love that scene because in that moment, Cain realizes that he doesn't want to follow in his father's footsteps, that doing so would mean giving up the things that matter most—love, family, and friends.

So now the cattle rustling has been solved, Javier and Eduardo Velez are dead, and everyone in Twin Rivers is feeling happy and blessed!

Except for Jonas. He has a few burdens of his own haunting him. It's safe to say that settling down and becoming a family man like Cain isn't in his future—or at least, that's what he thinks.

Until he ends up in Alaska and finds himself getting a little too attached to a boy with wide eyes and an endless smile.

But even if he can make room in his heart for the boy, the one thing he won't do is fall in love with Ilya's older sister. He's determined not to ever put a woman in jeopardy again like he did with his mother and Harriet...

Until the unthinkable happens, and he finds himself putting his badge back on—and opening up his heart to feelings he thought long dead.

From windswept seas and raging waves to emerald green forests and towering mountains, the Dawn of Alaska Series will sweep you away to a forgotten period of American history—and one family's fight for justice and truth in the midst of a land plagued by corruption and greed. I hope you'll join me for Jonas and Evelina's story, *Written on the Mist*.

Purchase from Amazon

(Or you can turn the page for a peek at the beginning of a brand-new series...)

NEXT BOOK

Buy Written on the Mist on Amazon

The Inside Passage near Juneau, Alaska; October, 1886

Never in his life had he been so cold. Jonas Redding hunkered deeper into his coat and stared out over the railing of the ship. It wasn't just the air, which was cold enough to cause the tip of his nose to ache and the breath from his mouth to puff little plumes of white into the air. It was also the damp. There was a constant sort of moisture that permeated the air at every turn. Even when it wasn't raining, it still felt like it was.

But at the moment, there was no question about whether it was raining. The heavy fog that the ship had been traveling through for most of the morning had turned into a light mist a half hour ago, and now that mist was turning into a steady rain that had driven the handful of other passengers aboard the cargo vessel below deck.

But not him.

There was too much to take in about this new land that he

intended to call home—and too many memories to haunt him in the darkness of the ship's belly.

The wooden vessel chugged past the end of yet another island, with mountains climbing from the shores of the water up into the thick layer of gray clouds above.

At least, he thought they were mountains, but the mist was too thick for him to get more than an occasional glimpse of the dark green trees blanketing the mountains. He had no idea how tall they were, or if their tops were carpeted with trees like their slopes or capped with jagged, rocky peaks.

Or if they were mountains at all, really. They could be... well, he couldn't quite think what they would be if not mountains. But—

"You can go below deck, mister." A boy appeared at his side, rainwater plastering his long black hair against his head. "The rain's only looking to get worse."

Jonas glanced at the boy, who looked like he belonged on the Cherokee reservation near where Jonas's sister lived in Oklahoma. Everything about his features were Native American, from the straight black hair that fell to his shoulders, to his high cheekbones, to his tan skin. Yet he spoke as though English was his first language, wore the clothes of a white man, and seemed completely comfortable standing aboard the deck of the ship.

"And just how do you know the rain is going to get worse?"

The boy shrugged, but his dark eyes took in the surrounding scenery with a keen sense of understanding. "It always rains here. Has to do with the mountains on either side of us. They trap the moisture from the ocean between them, then the clouds form over the valley, and it rains. When the valley widens, less moisture gets trapped and the clouds aren't as heavy. On a lucky day, you might even see the sun."

"On a lucky day?" He almost choked.

"Yes, sir." A smile lit the boy's face. "This is the most beautiful place in the world when it's sunny."

Jonas tilted his gaze up toward the endless mist that didn't allow a man to see much of anything, and the tiny, drizzling drops leaking from the dark clouds above, while the boy yammered on.

He talked about how the trees were the richest green under the bright rays of the sun, and the water the deepest turquoise. How it never got too hot no matter how bright the sun was, and how in the summer, whales congregated offshore near one of the islands.

As the boy spoke, the thick clouds shifted just enough that Jonas could see one of the passing mountains was, in fact, a mountain and not a hill. Though he still couldn't see the top of it. Another layer of gray shrouded that.

To think he'd spent the better part of the year on assignment in the Texan desert, where the sun scorched the earth until the rocky terrain turned yellow and the cacti were as brown as they were green. And now he'd somehow ended up in a place where a glimpse of the sun was considered lucky.

"So I hope the sun comes out a time or two while you're in Juneau," the boy continued, almost as though he didn't know how to stop his tongue from talking. "Like I said, when that happens, this is one of the prettiest places the whole world over."

"Then I hope to see some sun."

And he did, but more because he wasn't sure that his Texan-born body could tolerate being in a place without sun for more than a couple weeks than because he was convinced the murky gloom of his surroundings would somehow morph into the most beautiful place on earth.

His comment made the boy smile nonetheless, his face filling with the optimistic sort of hope.

What was it that made the boy so hopeful? So happy that

something as simple as the idea the sun might shine could brighten his entire day?

The boy had already been on the ship when Jonas had switched vessels in Bellingham, Washington, and nothing about his life seemed fun or optimistic. He'd spent the past two days mopping the deck, running errands for the captain, and fetching items for the other passengers traveling north.

It certainly wasn't the type of job that should inspire bright smiles and an outrageous sort of cheerfulness, especially considering that the Indian boy couldn't seem more out of place, even with all his hard work.

"So are you going to go below deck?" the boy asked. "Your coat is about soaked through."

"No." Though he probably should. The cold and wet only seemed to seep deeper into his bones the longer he stood on deck.

"It's the sea, isn't it? Don't worry, you're not the only one the sea makes sick. Lots of passengers suffer from it. Can't handle the moving of the boat. They say it's best to stand on deck where they can see everything."

If only the sea was what kept him from going below deck, not the memories that haunted him the second he found himself inside the dark, stifling hull.

The boy kept looking at him, as though expecting him to admit to feeling nauseous because of the waves.

Jonas turned toward one of the islands they were passing and settled his arms on the railing of the ship. "How much longer until we dock?"

"Not long. An hour at most, but that's too long for you to be out here. 'Specially without a slicker or hat. You'll catch your death of pneumonia. Leastways, that's what my sister always says."

"Pneumonia?" Even saying the word gave him the sudden desire to cough. The air in this place was so thick and dense it made his lungs feel heavy each time he drew breath. The doctors in Juneau probably kept themselves fed from treating pneumonia patients alone. "And what would this sister of yours say about you, standing there with no hat and your slicker unbuttoned?"

The boy shrugged. "That I'll catch my death, for sure and for certain. But I won't. I'm used to the rain."

He certainly seemed to be. The rain had indeed picked up more since they'd started talking, but the boy didn't seem the least bit bothered by the wet.

"So is Juneau located between mountains, where the clouds will get trapped and the sun never shines?"

"Yes, sir." He gave an earnest nod. "Didn't no one tell ya?"

"No. I don't suppose they did." More to the point, he hadn't bothered to ask. He'd known it would be cold in Alaska, so he'd bought as warm a coat as he could find before boarding the steamship in San Diego that had taken him up the coast to Bellingham.

But considering the temperature in San Diego wasn't much different than that of Texas, the coat he had thought was thick and warm was proving as useless as a shawl.

The other passengers on the ship and the crew had at least known what kind of coat to bring. They all wore oilskin slickers and hats that allowed the rainwater to drip from the brim down their slickers while keeping them perfectly dry beneath.

Then there were the handful of men who didn't even seem to notice the rain. Like the boy beside him, or the tall man headed down the stairs from the upper deck. His slicker was unbuttoned too, and like the boy, he didn't wear a hat.

"Looks like I'll need to buy myself a slicker once we dock," he muttered.

"You'll want to stop by the Sitka Trading Company. It's right on the wharf. They'll have everything you need."

"Will they now?"

"Sure will. Then after that, you'll want to..." The boy's brow scrunched. "Wait. Where are you headed? You never said."

"Ilya." The man from the stairs strode toward them, and the boy's eyes widened. "It's nearly time to dock. Captain White needs you."

"Uh-oh." Ilya's eyes grew wide as he glanced at the man approaching them, then his teeth sank into his bottom lip. "I forgot to bring the map the cap'n wanted from his cabin. Sorry, sir. I've got to go."

And the boy scampered off, his feet racing across the rain-slickened deck as though he hadn't the slightest fear of slipping.

"I'm sorry." The man came up to the railing, claiming the space where the boy had stood only moments before. "He's been instructed not to bother the passengers, but this is only his third voyage. Ilya is still learning."

Ilya. There was that name again. It was smooth and flowing, rolling easily off the tongue, but certainly not the type of name he expected for a native boy. Dark Hawk or Cheerful Owl or Light Foot, he could understand. But Ilya?

"Thanks for indulging him."

Jonas looked over at the man. Just how long had been watching him and Ilya? And where had he been watching from? The upper deck? An unsettling feeling lodged in his stomach. He'd had no idea someone was paying that much attention to him and the boy.

Not that there was anything about the man that seemed menacing. He was serious and tall, with dark hair, a pronounced nose and cheekbones, and prominent eyebrows that slashed in harsh lines above his eyes. But nothing about how he carried himself seemed dishonest or threatening.

On the contrary, he seemed like a man who knew what he wanted and wasn't afraid to get it.

"I didn't mind the chat," Jonas said. If anything, he almost felt like thanking the boy for it. The few minutes of conversation had distracted him from the memories that couldn't seem to leave him alone.

It had been two months, and still they were there, every time he looked into the mist, every time he closed his eyes at night.

Every time he drew breath.

But Alaska was going to fix that. He'd bury himself in a dark mineshaft and...

What?

Would visions of Harriet and his mother haunt him there the way they had in the belly of the ship?

No. He'd work himself hard and fast, until his mind was too tired to form a coherent thought, let alone remember what had happened back in Austin. Then he'd eat a few bites of dinner, stumble into bed, and sleep until his next shift started. Six days a week, twelve-hours a day. That's what the advertisement for workers had said in the paper.

It sounded like the perfect kind of job to purge a man of his memories.

"I'm Alexei Amos."

Jonas blinked, bringing the man beside him back into focus.

Because there was still a man standing beside him. He hadn't walked off while Jonas had gotten lost in his memories, and he was extending his palm toward him for a handshake.

A faint thrumming had started too. It wasn't overly loud, but it was constant, almost as though the crew had fired up a second steam engine below deck, except the noise wasn't loud enough to be caused by anything on the ship.

"Jonas Darrow." Jonas gave Alexei the name he'd decided on somewhere along his journey, then reached out and shook his hand.

"What brings you to Juneau, Jonas?" Alexei asked.

"Gold."

A small smile turned the corners of the man's mouth. "You and every other single man on the Pacific Coast."

He let the comment slide past him. Better to let the man think he came from California or Oregon rather than Texas. "I saw an ad for jobs at the Treadwell Mine, and there was nothing holding me to where I was living. So I figured, why not?"

Alexei raised one of his eyebrows. "You've a mind to work for the Treadwell? Funny. I didn't peg you for that type of a miner."

"Well, I am." Or he would be by this time tomorrow. How hard could it be to haul gold and rock out of the belly of the earth?

"What is that sound?" It was growing louder, and there was a pulsing thrum to it. He scanned the mountains through the rain, but he spotted nothing against the landscape that could possibly make such a sound.

"That, my friend, is the Treadwell Mine. Your new place of employment."

Jonas felt his eyes go wide. "That's the Treadwell? Where is it?" Again, he scanned the surrounding shoreline.

"You hear the Treadwell long before you see it, I'm afraid."

The noise from the mine was already that loud, and they weren't even close enough to see it?

"You smell it too." Alexei sniffed the air, then scrunched his nose.

Jonas could smell it now too, a faint chemical scent that fought its way through the thick, dank air.

"See here, we're traveling up the Gastineau Channel." Alexei gestured toward the front of the ship, then extended his hand to the left. "That's Douglas Island to our left, and the mainland to our right."

"The Treadwell Mine is on Douglas Island." He remembered that from the ad and the few articles he'd been able to scrounge up about the mine before purchasing his passage north.

"It is indeed." Alexei had to raise his voice to be heard over the pulsing noise. "Give it about ninety seconds, and you'll be able to see it."

The thrumming grew even louder as the wooden ship made its way down the narrow strip of water wedged between mountains on either side. And as Ilya said, the closer the mountains were, the thicker the mist became and the heavier the patter of rain.

It took about a minute and a half for a series of buildings to appear along the shore of the island, some made of wood and others of concrete. The chemical stench increased too, clinging to the dampness and rain as though the two were somehow inseparable.

"What's making all the noise?" The pounding of the machinery made it so loud he had to shout lest his words be swallowed.

"That would be the one-hundred-and-twenty-stamp mill," Alexei shouted back.

"Stamp mill?"

"It crushes the rock hauled from the mine so the gold can be extracted. And if you think this is loud, just wait until they finish construction on the other one hundred and twenty stamps they're adding next year. The noise will be twice as loud."

Twice as loud, and he already wanted to cover his ears. "And the smell?" he yelled, nearly gagging on the foul air he dragged into his lungs.

"The chlorination plant. Yet another step in extracting gold from rock." Alexei sent him another one of his faint smiles. "I'm told you get used to both the noise and the stench."

Jonas didn't believe it. He'd handled his share of dead bodies over the years and was all too familiar with the stench of decomposing flesh, but the burning sensation from the chlorination plant was something else entirely.

"What happened to the trees?" He surveyed the mountainside packed with buildings of all shapes and sizes, some clearly houses for the workers and others large and industrial looking. "They appear to be dying."

"You can thank the chlorination plant for that too. Had some kind of fancy scientist out here from the Department of the Interior to figure out why the spruce were losing their needles earlier this year. He determined it was the toxic gases the chlorination plant releases into the air."

Jonas drew a handkerchief out of his pocket, sodden as it was, and pressed it to his nose. "Then why don't they shut it down?"

Alexei quirked an eyebrow at him. "Because gold is more valuable than trees, of course."

"Of course." He surveyed the passing buildings that looked like something one might find in Austin's industrial district or beside the wharves in Houston. It was big and smelly, but even worse, it was almost as though the company that owned the mine had decided to cram as many buildings as possible into one small stretch of beach.

It was one thing to lose himself in the dark quiet of a mine tunnel somewhere, but another entirely to plant himself in the middle of the noisy, stinking hub of activity that was the Treadwell Mine.

When he'd pictured himself coming north to Alaska, he'd imagined a vast expanse of rugged wilderness where a man could lose himself. And he'd been right—even though he hadn't realized just how much rain and gloom would accompany those wilds.

But then there was the Treadwell Mine.

"I won't be working there."

"No?" Alexei gave him another smile, almost as though he

knew a secret of some sort. "Few men start out there, but Treadwell is the only mine that operates year-round. Come November, you'll find yourself working there right along with everyone else."

He wouldn't, but he wasn't about to argue the point with a man he'd just met. Maybe he didn't need to mine at all but could build a cabin, hole up on one of the mountains, and allow himself to be snowed in all winter while he tried his hand at trapping.

Except that seemed like the kind of living that allowed a man's memories to plague him, and he needed something that would erase them.

But it was only September. He still had two months to figure out what he'd do over the winter.

Someone shouted something from the upper deck, and Alexei straightened, then gave him a slap on the back. "I wish you well, Jonas, wherever you end up working. Now if you'll excuse me, we're about ready to dock."

And with that the man was off, calling something to a couple of crew members before stalking to the opposite side of the ship and grabbing one of the thick ropes that was almost as large in diameter as Alexei's forearm.

Jonas couldn't help but watch the other man for a moment. He moved with the utmost confidence, almost as though he owned everything he touched.

But that couldn't be. He'd figured out who the captain was within the first hour of leaving Bellingham, and he was currently on the upper deck in the wheelhouse, slowly guiding the ship toward the wharf that grew ever closer.

They had passed Treadwell completely, and dark green trees now covered the mountains of Douglas Island. But the mountains and trees and island altogether became less visible as the ship edged away from the middle of the channel and toward the mainland.

Just like how he wanted his former life to slip from his memory. Would living in Alaska make his past disappear as easily as the mist did Douglas Island?

Dear God...

But the words wouldn't come. They hadn't been able to come ever since the night of the fire.

So he stood on the deck, watching until the fog and gloom engulfed the mountains on the other side of the channel, and hoping the gloom just might find a way to shroud his heart from the pain ravaging it too.

∽

BY THE TIME the ship docked in Juneau, the chemical scent had dissipated, but there was still a low rumble that could be heard from the stamp mill across the channel, even though the fog was too thick for him to see any part of Douglas Island, let alone a few miles south to Treadwell.

Jonas took his time disembarking the ship. After all, now that he had no intention of working for the Treadwell Mine, it wasn't as though he had any place he needed to be.

He waited until the other passengers had grabbed their things from below deck before he descended into the bowels of the ship, where he grabbed the carpetbag and satchel he'd brought with him. If anything good could be said about a man having his home destroyed in a fire, it was that he didn't have trunks full of possessions to bring on his journey north.

When Jonas arrived back on deck, only the crew and Alexei remained, and they were preparing to haul cargo from the hold.

Jonas hefted his bags onto his shoulders and walked down the plank toward the busy wharf. For a town that could only be reached after days of traveling past uninhabited wilderness, Juneau was teeming with people. Some were already striding along the wharf with handcarts, likely ready to unload the

Alliance. Others had clearly come to watch the ship dock and were gathering across the street. Perhaps they'd ordered goods or knew some of the passengers.

Or perhaps they simply wanted food. Before the ship had left Bellingham, an unusual amount of flour, sugar, potatoes, carrots, and other foodstuffs had been loaded into the cargo hold. It had seemed a bit odd. Certainly someone in Juneau was enterprising enough to open up a flour mill so that flour didn't have to be shipped two days north.

But after what he'd seen, Jonas wasn't sure wheat or corn or any other kind of grain could grow in such a damp and sunless environment, meaning there just might have been a reason so much food had been loaded onto the *Alliance*.

"Excuse me, sir. I need to get up there."

Jonas looked around, only to realize he'd stopped right at the bottom of the gangway, blocking the stevedores' access to the ship.

"Sorry." He moved to the side, letting a group of men pass as his eyes scanned the buildings surrounding him.

Every one of them was made of roughhewn logs, almost as though the people constructing the buildings hadn't had time to sand them smooth or cut the logs into boards or bother with any of the normal things that went into constructing a house or building. It was yet another oddity about Juneau, Alaska.

But now that he was off the ship, his first order of business was to buy clothes that would keep him dry, and that meant finding the Sitka Trading Company.

Hadn't Ilya said it was by the wharf? The row of buildings closest to the wharf all looked to be warehouses, but across the street was a two-story log building that had some type of sign in front of it. He was too far away to read the words, but it certainly looked like could be a trading post.

He started down the walkway as more workers arrived,

wheeling handcarts up the gangway. Perhaps if he got directly across from the building, he could read the sign.

But a group of passengers had gathered at the edge of the walkway, blocking the part of the dock that the stevedores weren't using.

"He stole it, I tell ya," one of the men snarled. "It had to be him."

"Yeah. Weren't anyone else on the ship who looked like a thief."

Jonas pushed himself up on his toes and craned his head, trying to see what was causing the commotion.

"I didn't take anything," a young voice pronounced from the middle of the crowd.

Ilya. Jonas dropped his carpetbag and satchel and shoved his way into the circle only to find a man—Simon, if he recalled from his time aboard ship—holding Ilya by the collar of his shirt.

"You got two seconds to give me my money, or I'll beat the truth outta ya."

"Beat him," one of the men jeered. "That's the only way to teach a dirty In'jun like him."

Jonas quickly scanned the crowd. There were seven men, all of them with bloodshot eyes and the stench of sour liquor on their breaths.

Nearly all of them had their gazes narrowed on Ilya, distrust and hatred radiating from their stances.

But not one of the men. He stood near the back of the crowd, and he was paying far more attention to the men around him than to Ilya.

Jonas studied the man out of the side of his gaze. Long hair, an unshaven face, a red shirt that peeked out from beneath the collar of his slicker. And most importantly, a bulge in the left pocket of his coat. The bulge could be anything. A gun, a stack of letters, money of his own.

But the nervous manner in which the man looked around and kept taking small steps away from the others gave him away.

"Please, Mr. Cutter. I didn't take the money. You know I didn't. Alexei would tan my hide. You're just drunk is all, and you need to let me go."

Simon gripped Ilya's collar tighter and yanked him forward.

"Do you have any evidence Ilya took the money?" Jonas stepped forward.

Bloodshot eyes rose to meet his gaze. "This ain't none of your business, mister. Best just pass on by."

And let a drunkard beat Ilya? "If you're going to search someone, it should be your friend there."

Jonas pointed at the man with the long hair, only to find his finger directed at nothing but air. Sometime in the last half second, the man had disappeared. Jonas pressed up onto his toes and tried to see what direction the man had gone, but there were too many people on the wharf, nearly all of them wearing black slickers and wide-brimmed hats that looked exactly the same from the back.

"Maybe you're the one I should search," Simon snarled.

Jonas drew in a breath and met the man's gaze, trying to insert a certain level of calmness into his stance. "I didn't take your money any more than Ilya. Like I said, it was the friend you brought along with you. The one in the red shirt."

Simon didn't even look around for his friend. Instead, he released Ilya and took a step closer to Jonas, his bloodshot eyes burning with rage and drunkenness. "That was *my* two hundred dollars. *My* grubstake. Do you know how long it took me to save up for it?"

"I... no." Two hundred dollars? If that amount of money was truly missing, then he couldn't blame the man for being angry. That was half a year's wage. "But that still doesn't mean Ilya took it. Like I said, you're much better off—"

A fist connected with the side of his jaw. He hadn't seen it coming. He'd been too busy watching Ilya, who had sidled between the edge of the wharf and the water the second Simon let him go.

"Now look what you did." One of the men pointed to where Ilya was racing up the gangway toward the *Alliance*. "The boy got away."

"You got two hundred dollars on ya?" Simon reached to his belt and pulled a knife out of its sheath.

Jonas swallowed. He had a knife of his own strapped to his belt, but reaching for it when he was already surrounded by six men could only mean trouble.

"Well? Do you got two hundred dollars or not?" One of the men behind Simon drawled, his words slurring together. "Because that's what you owe Simon after letting the thief escape."

He did have two hundred dollars, but that was his savings, all that he had to give himself a fresh start in Alaska. He'd be hanged if he was going to give it to a group of drunkards who would take it down to the nearest saloon and see how much of it they could spend before dusk.

"I keep telling you. Ilya isn't a thief." The lot of them would realize that the second they sobered up. "I'm fairly certain your money was stolen by your other friend who was just here. But no matter who took it, your first order of business should be to visit the sheriff, not take matters into your own hands."

A coarse laugh erupted from the group. "The sheriff. Ya hear that, Simon? He thinks there's a sheriff."

Simon's angry gaze narrowed into two thin slits. "There ain't no sheriff in Juneau, as you're about to find out." He pointed the blade of the knife in Jonas's direction. "Now you give me that two hundred dollars, or I'll knife ya."

Jonas hand involuntarily reached for his gun, only to find nothing but fabric where his holster used to be.

Because he wasn't carrying a gun anymore.

Because the only thing a gun did was escalate situations, and he'd put that part of his life behind him.

And because holding a gun made his hands shake and his stomach roil until he felt like retching.

But at this exact moment, he wasn't sure that he'd retch if he had his gun. Instead he put up his hands, trying to show he only wanted peace and harbored no ill intent. "I didn't take your money any more than Ilya did, and the second you're sober, you'll realize that."

"I vote we search his things." One of the men turned toward where his carpetbag was still sitting on the wharf and kicked it. "Never know. We just might find your two hundred dollars hiding somewhere in there."

"No!" Jonas tried to lunge for the bag, but one of the men caught his arm, which gave Simon a chance to land a second punch to his jaw.

Jonas would have stumbled backward with the blow, but the assailant who was holding him kept him upright just enough for him to glimpse the blade of a knife swinging toward him.

He tried to wrench away, but given how his arm was being held, there was nowhere for him to move.

The blade plunged between two of his ribs, and fire sliced through him. He sucked in a breath, gasping against the pain.

A shout sounded from somewhere in the direction of the ship, and the man who had been holding him let go. Ignoring the pain in his chest, he lunged for the knife, attempting to twist it out of Simon's grip.

No sooner had his palm clasped around the clenched fist of his attacker, he found himself being pushed backward. He scrambled for purchase on the rain-slicked boards of the wharf, then took a step back, only to find nothing under his foot save air.

Another punch landed against his temple, causing his head to scream and the edges of his vision to blur as hands shoved him again.

He felt himself falling backward. Then he hit the cold, deep water of the channel—and his world went black.

∽

"No!" Alexei shouted from the gangway, where he and the first mate, Dobbins, had been threading their way through the workers toward where Simon Cutter and his drunken friends had been loitering on the wharf.

But his shout did no good, and Cutter reared back and punched Darrow while one of his friends held him still and another rummaged through his carpetbag.

Then he saw the glint of a blade in Cutter's hand, and his heartbeat ratcheted up. Surely the fool wasn't going to stab Darrow. Drunk or not—and Simon Cutter was always drunk—that would land him in a jail cell for more than a night.

The moment they'd docked, Ilya had begged to get off the ship and go visit Peter at the trading post. Even though most cabin boys would be expected to stay on the ship until it was unloaded and then take leave with the rest of the crew, Alexei hadn't been able to resist the excitement in his brother's eyes as he'd asked to leave.

But Ilya had returned to the ship only a few minutes later, racing back aboard with words tumbling from his mouth about Mr. Cutter accusing him of stealing money and Mr. Darrow stepping in to protect him.

Ilya hadn't mentioned anything about a knife, but sure enough, that's what Simon Cutter was holding as Alexei rushed down the gangway with Dobbins, and the drunkard drove it straight into Jonas Darrow's ribs.

"Help!" Alexei called, loud enough to stop the activity on the gangway and wharf below. He thrust his finger at Simon Cutter and his friends. "There's been a stabbing. Stop those men."

The dockworkers looked around, as though trying to make sense of his words and figure out who in the throng of people had just been stabbed.

From his position on the elevated gangway, Alexei could see everything unfolding, but he wasn't close enough to stop any of it. A dark patch of red was spreading across Darrow's chest, and Cutter shoved him backward.

Then the largest man of the group lunged forward and slammed a fist into the side of Darrow's temple.

A sickening crack filled the air, and Darrow fell backward into nothing but air, his body limp as he splashed into the water below.

"Man in the channel," Alexei shouted. Then he turned back toward the ship to see Captain White standing at the side with Ilya and a handful of both crew members. "Lower the dinghy."

The water was deep at the edge of the wharf. It had to be for ships to dock there. And the only thing worse than a man being shoved into water that deep was an unconscious man being shoved into it.

"Faster, Alexei!" Ilya called from the ship. "He's going to drown."

Alexei ripped off his slicker, unholstered his pistol, and shoved the gun at the first mate. Then he dove into the murky water of the Gastineau Channel.

If only the sun were shining. Then maybe he had a hope of finding Darrow. But between the salt of the ocean water stinging his eyes and the dark clouds that turned the water a gloomy gray, he could hardly see his hand in front of his face, let alone Darrow's unconscious body.

He surfaced and raked in a breath, turning wildly in the water for any clue showing where Darrow might be.

"Over there, Alexei."

He glanced over his shoulder to find the crew had listened when he'd told them to lower the dinghy. Captain White and one of the sailors, Horace, were rowing toward a series of circular ripples in the water that broke the pattern of lapping waves.

Alexei surged forward, the muscles of his arms straining as he swam through the water with large, determined strokes.

Then a head broke through the surface, Darrow's red hair plastered against his head. Maybe the cold of the water had woken him out of his unconsciousness, but the man obviously didn't know how to swim. He flailed about, splashing the water so wildly, he had little hope of staying afloat.

"Help!"

"I'm coming." Only about twenty feet separated him from Darrow, but the man went down again before clambering back to the surface. Given the thick, sodden coat the man was wearing, he wouldn't be afloat for much longer.

Sure enough, Darrow's head slipped beneath the waves once more, but Alexei had a pretty good idea just how quickly the man would sink beneath the water.

He dove down, forcing his eyes open despite the stinging salt and angling his body at just the right angle to intercept the drowning man.

A moment later, a shadow of black appeared against the murky water, accompanied by the flash of a white, panicked face as Darrow struggled toward the surface.

Alexei gave his legs a finally kick forward, diving through the water with the skill of someone who'd spent all twenty-nine years of his life swimming in the shallows of Alaskan islands. The water nearly parted for him as he surged forward, then wrapped his arms beneath Darrow's own arms and kicked upward.

They broke the surface a second later, Darrow gasping and struggling.

"Don't. Be still or you'll drag us both down. See, the boat's right there." He nodded to where Captain White, Horace, and Ilya rowed the boat toward them.

That seemed to calm him. "Thank you," he rasped as Captain White glided the dinghy to a stop beside them.

Horace and Ilya both reached down and helped pull Darrow aboard. A clapping sound went up from the wharf, where Alexei turned to find a crowd had gathered to watch the rescue.

Alexei hauled himself aboard the dinghy, then frowned when he saw how quickly blood was seeping into Darrow's shirt. "Get us to the wharf, then go for the doctor at Treadwell."

White and Horace looked at each other. "You want us to go clear over to Treadwell for the doc?"

"Yes. Darrow needs more than just a nurse. He's got to have an actual doctor if he's going to survive that knife wound."

"We know." The captain dug the oar into the water, propelling them right alongside the wharf, where hands reached down to haul Jonas up. "But what's wrong with your sister?"

Alexei had clasped one of the men's hands from the wharf above and had been about to climb out of the boat, but he stopped and turned back to Captain White. "My sister? She's in Sitka."

"No, she ain't." The familiar voice of Grover Hanover said from the wharf above him. "Kate's here."

Alexei felt his entire body go cold. "She is?"

He scrambled onto the wharf that stood a good three feet above where the small dinghy sat in the water, then stood to face Grover, the grocer that the *Alliance* delivered supplies to twice a month.

"Sure is. Been here for the better part of two months,

patching up the town." Grover scratched behind his ear. "Don't say you didn't know?"

He didn't have a clue. He left Sitka for California exactly two months ago. What had Kate done? Up and left for Juneau the day after him?

He was going to throttle her.

Alexei stalked forward, trailing the men who were rushing the litter with an unconscious Darrow toward the trading post, which was the mostly likely place for Kate to have set up shop.

Grover rushed up beside him, struggling to keep pace. "I'm sorry. I thought you knew."

"Who's with her?" Alexei pinched the bridge of his nose. "Please tell me she hasn't been in Juneau by herself for all this time."

"'Course not. She brought her sisters with her."

Alexei waited to hear which one of his brothers had come too. Maybe Mikhail had returned from his expedition and had business in Juneau, or Sacha had returned early from his voyage to Japan, or Yuri had come for no better reason than to stay with his sisters—at least one of whom had to have the common sense not to move to a town that amounted to little more than a glorified mining camp, completely unprotected.

But Grover kept right on walking, leaving his words hanging in the air between them. As though…

As though only his sisters had come to Juneau, and no one else.

"Which of my brothers is here with them?" he rasped, a headache starting to form at his temples.

Grover looked back over at him and blinked. "None of them. It's just your sisters, like I said. All three of them. Sorry, Alexei. I figured someone would have written ya."

"No one wrote me anything." Except that wasn't true. All three of his sisters had written to him while he'd been in San Francisco. Each of their letters had been painfully boring, filled with normal, everyday things like what they'd eaten for dinner or what other letters they'd penned that day. Evelina had talked about how Inessa's schooling was going, and Kate might have mentioned treating a patient or two.

But none of them had said a lick about moving to Juneau.

This had Kate written all over it. She was the only one who was headstrong enough to up and move to another town and convince her sisters not to send him word.

Alexei burst through the door of the trading post. Forget throttling her. He was going to lock his oldest sister in a tower and throw away the key.

Right after she saved Jonas Darrow's life, that is.

OTHER NOVELS BY NAOMI RAWLINGS

Dawn of Alaska Series
    Book 1—*Written on the Mist* (Jonas and Evelina)
    Book 2—*Whispers on the Tide* (Sacha and Maggie)
    Book 3—*Above all Dreams* (Nathan and Kate)
    Book 4—*Echoes of Twilight* (Mikhail and Bryony)
    Book 5—*Against the Rain* (Yuri and Rosalind)
    Book 6—*Beyond the Dawn* (Alexei and Clarice)

Texas Promise Series
    Book 1—*Tomorrow's First Light* (Sam and Ellie)
    Book 2—*Tomorrow's Shining Dream* (Daniel and Charlotte)
    Book 3—*Tomorrow's Constant Hope* (Wes and Keely)
    Book 4—*Tomorrow's Steadfast Prayer* (Harrison and Alejandra)
    Book 5—*Tomorrow's Lasting Joy* (Cain and Anna Mae)

Eagle Harbor Series
    Book 1—*Love's Unfading Light* (Mac and Tressa)
    Book 2—*Love's Every Whisper* (Elijah and Victoria)
    Book 3—*Love's Sure Dawn* (Gilbert and Rebekah)

Book 4—*Love's Eternal Breath* (Seth and Lindy)
Book 5—*Love's Christmas Hope* (Thomas and Jessalyn)
Book 6—*Love's Bright Tomorrow* (Isaac and Aileen)
Short Story—*Love's Beginning* (Elijah, Gilbert, Mac, Victoria, Rebekah)
Prequel—*Love's Violet Sunrise* (Hiram and Mabel)

Belanger Family Saga
Book 1—*The Lady's Refuge* (Michel and Isabelle)
Book 2—*The Widow's Secret* (Jean Paul and Brigitte)
Book 3—*The Reluctant Enemy* (Gregory and Danielle)

AUTHOR'S NOTE

In 1867, after the close of the Civil War, ranchers in southern Texas returned to find their herds had been decimated by cattle rustlers who were crossing the Rio Grande and driving cattle into Mexico by the thousands. From there, a good number of the cattle were shipped to Cuba, to the point that some historians estimate the entirety of the Cuban beef market was comprised of rustled cattle. One of the most prominent figures behind this rustling was a former general in the Mexican Army, who used his resources to destroy the beef industry of southern Texas.

Because of the extreme rustling going on along the border, the State of Texas commissioned what is now the first state police force to ever exist—the Texas Rangers. They started with the sole purpose of protecting Texas livestock, but their role soon grew.

Cain's father, Frank, is based on the real-life person of Leander Harvey McNelly, who was something of a legend among the Rangers. He was known for bringing order to the Nueces Strip, but many thought his tactics too aggressive, particularly when he took his men into Mexico and engaged in gunfights with bandits to recover stolen livestock.

When I happened upon the reason the Texas Rangers had been started and McNelly's role stopping the cross-border rustling activity, I knew I had to include it in my Texas Promise Series, and so the plot for the entire five-book series was born. There would be a powerful Mexican who was responsible for stealing cattle and moving it over the border, and there would be a rough, rugged Ranger who was sent to stop him.

Historically, the bulk of the rustling took place in the Nueces Strip (closer to the Gulf of Mexico than where these books are set), and most of the rustling took place about fifteen years earlier, between 1867-1877. But after moving Ellie from Eagle Harbor at the beginning of this series, I was locked into a certain timeframe, so I moved a few things around, as one does when writing fiction.

I hope you enjoyed the grand conclusion to the Texas Promise Series, and I hope you'll follow Jonas to Alaska, where countless new adventures await in a land more undeveloped and rugged than either Twin Rivers or Eagle Harbor.

ACKNOWLEDGMENTS

Thank you first and foremost to my Lord and Savior, Jesus Christ, for giving me both the ability and opportunity to write novels for His glory.

As with any novel, an author might come up with a story idea and sit at his or her computer to type the initial words, but it takes an army of people to bring you the book you have today. I'd especially like to thank my editors, Erin Healy, who started editing for me partway through the Texas Promise Series. Her keen insight and ability to understand my characters and their worlds have made my novels shine in ways that I had never thought possible before meeting her. And thank you to Roseanna White, for answering my random emails, brainstorming, and pointing out ways to make this book stronger.

Many thanks to my family for working with my writing schedule and giving me a chance to do two things I love: be a mom and a writer.

Also, many thanks to the hospitable people of Terlingua, Texas, and the staff at Fort Leaton for answering my numerous questions and helping me make the Texas landscape come alive. Thank you to Janelle at Lajitas and Big Bend Stables (https://www.lajitasstables.com/) both for the tour on horseback and for answering my many questions. Thank you to James at Big Bend River Tours (http://bigbendrivertours.com/) for a memorable trip down the Rio Grande. My only complaint was that the trip was too short. Thank you to the wonderful park ranger at Fort Leaton who answered my numerous questions on two separate occasions. I'm so sorry I don't remember your name.

And finally, thank you to Curt Swafford of Tarantula Ranch for hosting me and my traveling companions in your guest cabins. Your stories and detailed explanations brought my Texas experience to life and gave me a deeper understanding of the Big Bend.

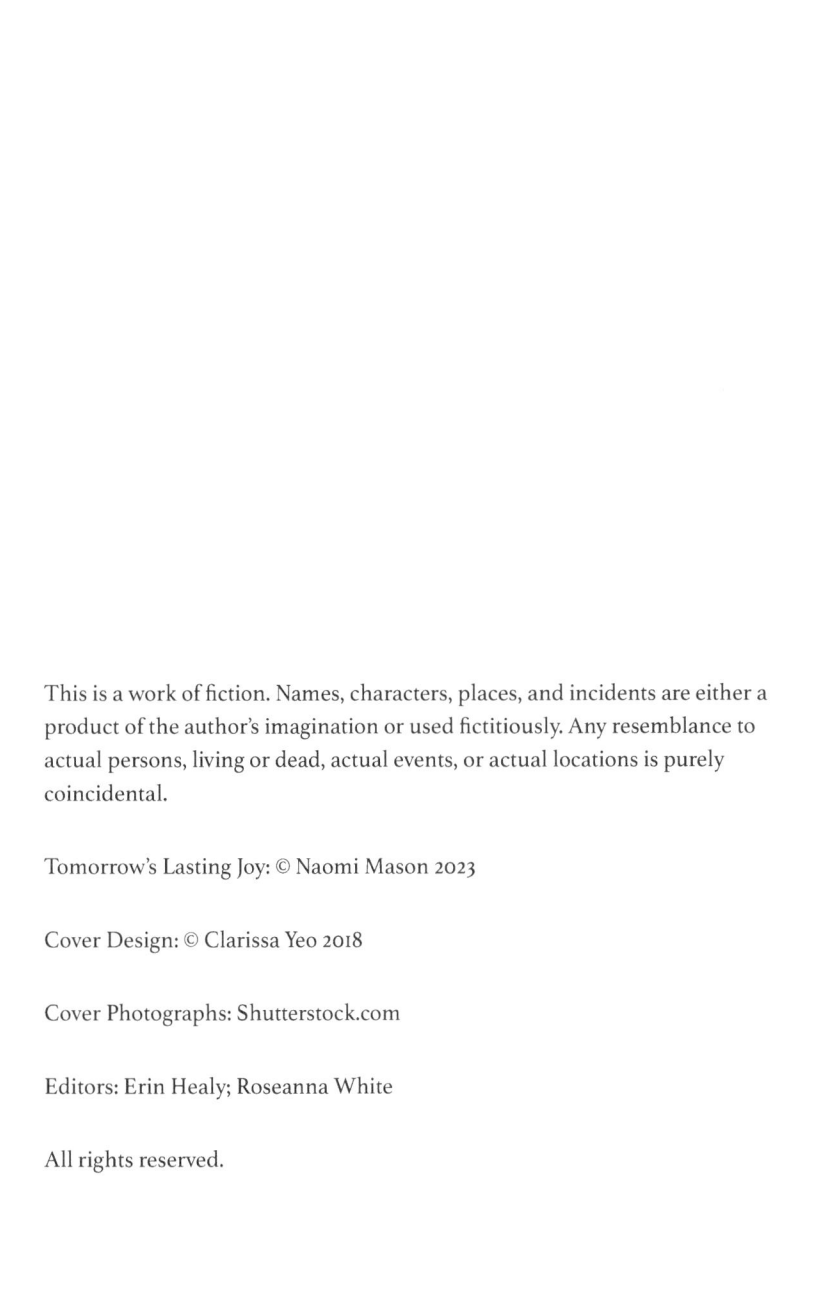

This is a work of fiction. Names, characters, places, and incidents are either a product of the author's imagination or used fictitiously. Any resemblance to actual persons, living or dead, actual events, or actual locations is purely coincidental.

Tomorrow's Lasting Joy: © Naomi Mason 2023

Cover Design: © Clarissa Yeo 2018

Cover Photographs: Shutterstock.com

Editors: Erin Healy; Roseanna White

All rights reserved.

ABOUT THE AUTHOR

Naomi Rawlings is a *USA Today* bestselling author of over a dozen historical novels, including the Eagle Harbor Series, which has sold more than 450,000 copies. She lives with her husband and three children in Michigan's rugged Upper Peninsula, along the southern shore of Lake Superior, where they get two hundred inches of snow every year, and where people still grow their own vegetables and cut down their own firewood—just like in the historical novels she writes.

For more information about Naomi, please visit her at www.naomirawlings.com or find her on Facebook at www.facebook.com/author.naomirawlings. If you'd like a free novella, sign up for her author newsletter.

Made in United States
Troutdale, OR
02/28/2024

18047625R00278